LOIS McMASTER BUJOLD

LOIS McMASTER BUJOLD

Edward James

UNIVERSITY OF ILLINOIS PRESS
Urbana, Chicago, and Springfield

© 2015 by the Board of Trustees
of the University of Illinois
All rights reserved
Manufactured in the United States of America
1 2 3 4 5 C P 5 4 3 2 1
∞ This book is printed on acid-free paper.

Library of Congress Cataloging-in-Publication Data
James, Edward, 1947-
Lois McMaster Bujold / by Edward James.
pages   cm. — (Modern masters of science fiction)
Includes bibliographical references and index.
ISBN 978-0-252-03932-4 (hardback : acid-free paper) —
ISBN 978-0-252-08085-2 (paper : acid-free paper) —
ISBN 978-0-252-09737-9 (e-book)
1. Bujold, Lois McMaster—Criticism and interpretation. I. Title.
PS3552.U397Z68   2015
813'.54—dc23   2014048356

To Farah

contents

Acknowledgments

Thanks are due, first, to Bill Regier of the University of Illinois Press: for inviting me out of the blue to contribute a book on a major British writer to his new series; for being enthusiastic when I noted that this writer already had several books written about him and that I would like to be the first to write a monograph on Lois McMaster Bujold instead; and for being very tolerant when the book was finished much later than I expected.

Second, I owe a very great deal to Farah Mendlesohn, with whom I have written or edited several books on science fiction and fantasy. She made me read Bujold's books back in the mid-1990s, when I had only read what Bujold had published in *Analog*, and since then I have read every new Bujold book as it has been published. Over the years we have talked about the books and reread them, particularly the Vorkosigan books, and she has offered constant encouragement during the writing of this book. At this stage, I have no idea how many of the ideas in this book are mine, or whether they have been suggested to me by Farah. For this, and for everything else, I dedicate this book to her.

Third, I would like to thank Lois herself. I had not met her at the time I contracted to write this book, although we began to communicate by email not long afterward, having been introduced by Lillian Stewart Carl (whom I had met at the Montreal Worldcon in 2009). I finally met Lois when she was a guest of honor at the Finnish National SF Convention (Finncon) in Tampere, July 2012; the convention chair, Marianna Leikomaa, asked me to conduct Lois's guest of honor interview, and I was able to spend some time with her. Both then and through email, she has always replied to my questions graciously and promptly.

I have not met, but owe a great debt to, the British sf fan Michael Bernardi, who created and sustains *The Bujold Nexus*, Bujold's official website, at www.dendarii.com. This is an invaluable resource, as is *The Vorkosigan Companion*, a book edited by Lillian Stewart Carl and John Helfers. When I started writing this book, there were a few published critical essays on Bujold, and one slim volume of essays partially devoted to her, by Sylvia Kelso; halfway through writing this book, the collection of essays on Bujold edited by Janet Brennan Croft was published, and my own book was able to proceed in dialogue with this. A word of thanks is due as well to Grover Gardner, whose excellent readings of Bujold's Vorkosigan books on Blackstone Audiobooks kept me entertained over many months as I walked to and fro between home and university in Dublin.

Finally, I would like to thank the following friends and fellow Bujold fans for kindly looking over this book in draft, correcting many mistakes, and offering many valuable comments: in alphabetical order, Lillian Stewart Carl, Julie Hofmann, Sylvia Kelso, Kari Maund, Una McCormack, Farah Mendlesohn, Cheryl Morgan, and Hallie O'Donovan. Thanks to the two readers for Illinois University Press for comments; and thanks again to Lois McMaster Bujold, who read through the whole text with great care, correcting numerous errors and making many valuable suggestions. In what follows, if there is mention of a comment by Bujold that is not referenced in any way, then this is a comment made on the electronic draft version of this book during August 2013. Thank you for all your help, and for making the scary experience of writing about a live author less traumatic than it might have been. The subject of my next book died in A.D. 594.

ABBReViaTiOnS

ACC   *A Civil Campaign* (1999)
Bar   *Barrayar* (1991), usually cited in CH version.
BA   *Brothers in Arms* (1989)
BI   *Borders of Infinity* (1987)
Bord   "The Borders of Infinity" in *Borders of Infinity* (1987)
CC   *The Curse of Chalion* (2001)
CH   *Cordelia's Honor* (1996 omnibus of *Shards of Honor* [1986] and *Barrayar* [1991])
Cry   *CryoBurn* (2010)
CVA   *Captain Vorpatril's Alliance* (2012)
Cet   *Cetaganda* (1995)
DD   *Dreamweaver's Dilemma* (1996)
DI   *Diplomatic Immunity* (2002)
EA   *Ethan of Athos* (1986)
FF   *Falling Free* (1988)
HH   *The Hallowed Hunt* (2005)
Kom   *Komarr* (1998)
Lab   "Labyrinth" in *Borders of Infinity* (1989)
LMB   *Lois McMaster Bujold*, ed. Janet Brennan Croft (2013)
MD   *Mirror Dance* (1994)
Mem   *Memory* (1996)
MM   "The Mountains of Mourning" in *Borders of Infinity* (1989)
PS   *Paladin of Souls* (2003)
SH   *Shards of Honor* (1986), usually cited in CH version.
SK1   *The Sharing Knife, Volume One: Beguilement* (2006)
SK2   *The Sharing Knife, Volume Two: Legacy* (2007)
SK3   *The Sharing Knife, Volume Three: Passage* (2008)
SK4   *The Sharing Knife, Volume Four: Horizon* (2009)
SR   *The Spirit Ring* (1992)
VC   *The Vorkosigan Companion*, ed. Lillian Stewart Carl and John Helfers
VG   *The Vor Game* (1990)
WA   *The Warrior's Apprentice* (1986)
WG   "Winterfair Gifts" (2004)

Full publication details and a list of the Vorkosigan stories in internal chronological order are to be found toward the end of this book. All quotations are from the first editions listed in the bibliography unless otherwise specified.

LOIS McMASTER BUJOLD

CHAPTER 1

AN INTRODUCTION TO LOIS McMASTER BUJOLD

In 2012, when she turned sixty-three years old, Lois McMaster Bujold remarked that her life had been strangely balanced—she had been single for twenty-one years, married for twenty-one years, and divorced for twenty-one years. She noted, however, that "the thirds don't all seem to have the same weight."[1] In terms of her writing career, however, each third has equal, but different, importance. In the first third she built the foundations of a writing career; in the second third she established herself as a professional writer; and since then she has consolidated her position as one of the most popular writers of science fiction and fantasy in the United States and beyond.

Lois McMaster was born in Columbus, Ohio, on November 2, 1949, the third child and only daughter of Robert Charles McMaster and Laura Gerould McMaster. Her parents had graduated from the same high school in Wilkinsburg, Pennsylvania (in the eastern outskirts of Pittsburgh), in 1930, although they did not start dating until after this. Bob received his first degree, in electrical engineering, from Carnegie Mellon University in Pittsburgh in 1936 and then progressed to graduate work at the California Institute of Technology (Caltech) in Pasadena, getting his master of science in 1938 and his doctorate in 1944. He moved to Ohio in 1945, initially taking a post as supervisor of electrical engineering at Battelle Memorial Institute's laboratories in Columbus. From 1955 until retirement in 1977 he was a professor at Ohio State University, specializing in welding engineering. In his spare time he was a television weatherman, one of the world's first, broadcasting weather bulletins twice a day on WBNS-TV in Columbus, from 1950 to 1964. The family home where Lois and her two elder brothers grew up was in Upper Arlington, a suburban city just to the west of the university campus, whose origins had been a Garden City development in 1913: a safe, middle-class environment.

Bob McMaster's obituary by Robert I. Jaffee, in the National Academy of Engineering's *Memorial Tributes*, remarks that he was a superb teacher, whose neatly printed blackboards and booming voice would never be forgotten by his students. It also notes that he was as meticulous a teacher of English as he was of engineering: if a student submitted a piece of writing with grammatical errors in it, it would be handed back, "with pithy comment," to be corrected before final submission. Lois's brother Jim has also published his own reminiscences of his father, with whom he studied on the five-year Welding Engineering course. "Doc," as he was called around the department, used to have a cartoon of a man collecting an enormous ball of string posted on his office door, with the caption "Whatever you do, do it to the best of your ability."[2]

Lois's father was clearly a crucial figure in her development. Like many engineers at the time, he was a science fiction reader. He subscribed to *Astounding Science-Fiction*, which became the leading science fiction monthly magazine at the end of the 1930s, and he gave Lois her own subscription to it for her thirteenth birthday. At that point it had just been renamed *Analog* by its longtime editor John W. Campbell Jr., and *Analog* would eventually publish a number of Lois's own works, both short stories and novel serializations. Her monthly copy of *Analog* was clearly important to the young Lois, for once or twice her mother took the copy from the mailbox herself and retained it until after Lois had cleaned her room (VC 49). McMaster was a writer himself: he was the editor of the *Nondestructive Testing Handbook*, which became a standard reference book around the world—*McMaster on Materials*. It was a massive work: Jaffee's obituary reports that the typescript stood twenty-six inches high. He did the work on it at home in his upstairs office: "Memories of my dad center around the clack of his IBM Selectric, the scent of professorial pipe smoke, and the constant strains of classical music (WOSU-FM) from his hi-fi" (VC 29). It is no accident that at least two of Lois's protagonists, Miles Vorkosigan and Fiametta, learn (and to some extent suffer) from the experience of growing up as the child of a Great Man.

Lois soon became a voracious reader. She started reading science fiction when she was nine years old. Her favorite writers in the field included Poul Anderson (his Van Rijn stories) and James H. Schmitz (best known probably for his "Federation of the Hub" sequence: space opera notable for featuring three intelligent and adventurous young women, Telzey Amberdon, Trigger Argee, and Nile Etland). Bujold read the juveniles of Robert A. Heinlein (published annually by Scribner's between 1947 and 1958), which long remained the touchstone for science fiction written specifically for adolescents. But in the 1950s there was very little adult science fiction that was not readily accessible to adolescents (one reason, of course, was that the category of Young Adult did not yet exist), and Lois read widely. In a conversation with Lillian Stewart Carl (VC 30–31), Lois mentions most of the big names of the period: Isaac Asimov, Fritz Leiber, L. Sprague de Camp, Mack Reynolds, the British writers Arthur C. Clarke and Eric Frank Russell, and one of the most prolific early women writers, Zenna Henderson. Later on, she adds, she came across Anne McCaffrey (who began publishing novels at the end of the 1960s), Randall Garrett, Roger Zelazny, Cordwainer Smith, and J. R. R. Tolkien. She was mostly dependent on public libraries, which, until she started driving at age sixteen, and apart from a time when she cycled, meant that she was dependent on her mother for taking her the ten or twenty miles to the nearest libraries.

Lois, like many other adolescents in the 1960s (the author of this book included), was enormously impressed by Tolkien's works. She bought the first volume of *The Lord of the Rings* in the pirated Ace paperback edition while on holiday in Italy with her parents in 1965. Six months later "with overwhelming joy" she found the second and third volumes.

I can still remember where I was sitting when I first opened up *The Two Towers* and read, with a pounding heart, "Aragorn sped on up the hill . . ." My father's home office, the air faintly acrid with the scent of his pipe tobacco, in the big black chair under the window, yellow late-afternoon winter light shining in through the shredding silver-gray clouds beyond the chill bare Ohio woods to the west. Now, *that's* imprinting (VC 32–33).

She added that the book "has stitched itself like a thread through my life from that day to this, read variously, with different perceptions at different ages" (VC 33). It may be a flawed book, as all are, but "it is in my heart; it binds time for me, and binds the wounds of time," and after quoting from the chapter "The Field of Cormallen" in *The Return of the King*, where the minstrel sings of the deeds of Frodo and Sam, she comments, "I could crawl on my knees through broken glass for the gift of words that pierce like those." In the light of such a tribute, it is not at all surprising that Bujold would write several fantasy novels; and it should be noted that two of them (*The Curse of Chalion* and *Paladin of Souls*) are among the very best of the many medievalist fantasies of the post-Tolkien era. However, we may perhaps be grateful that the Tolkienesque epic she wrote at age fifteen (in Spenserian verse, the result of reading both *The Lord of the Rings* and *The Faerie Queen* twice that year) has not been published.

In the summer of 1966 Lois spent three weeks hitchhiking with her older brother Jim in Britain, which she has said was the highlight of her high school years.[3] She was fifteen, and he was twenty-one. Luckily, perhaps, her parents did not know that Jim was being so parsimonious that, when they arrived at Oxford, they hopped over the wall into Worcester College (with the help of a friendly policeman) and slept the night in the gardens. For Lois the visit to Stratford-upon-Avon was the highlight: *Love's Labour's Lost* at the Royal Shakespeare Theatre, she writes, "just blew me away" (DD 200).

Like many science fiction readers before and since, Lois did not find it easy to fit in to the conforming demands of school life, which is no doubt how she bonded so closely with Lillian Stewart (now Lillian Stewart Carl) when she first met her, at Hastings Junior High School in Upper Arlington. Lillian's father was a professor of agricultural engineering at OSU. That Lois and Lillian decided to try out for the school talent show by singing Tom

Lehrer's "Poisoning Pigeons in the Park" reveals quite a lot about them. "The silence after we finished could have swallowed a planet," says Lillian (VC 31). They watched television together, being particularly excited by *The Man from U.N.C.L.E.* (originally broadcast between 1964 and 1968). David McCallum, who played the Russian-born secret agent Illya Kuryakin, was one reason Bujold chose Russian culture as the background for Miles Vorkosigan's Barrayar (VC 123), while Illya himself transmuted into one of Bujold's most interesting characters, Simon Illyan, the head of Barrayar's ImpSec. For a season they both watched and loved *The Wackiest Ship in the Army*. Lois introduced Lillian to science fiction and fantasy in general; Lillian introduced Lois to history and mythology. The two of them discovered Arthur Conan Doyle and C. S. Forester together. They both read Heinlein's *Stranger in a Strange Land* when it came out in 1961 and, Lillian recalls, "were unduly impressed by this first exposure to 'adult' content in sf" (VC 122).[4]

Lillian returned one year from vacation to discover Lois enthusing about a new TV series, *Star Trek*, which had begun its initial three-year run in September 1966. They started watching it together and invited other friends in to watch, and they even used Lois's father's reel-to-reel tape recorder to record the soundtracks, which included, in Lillian's words, "half a dozen female squeals as Spock actually (be still, my teenage hormones) *smiled!*" (VC 124). One tape preserved Lois's mother saying, "You girls are going to be so embarrassed when you grow up and remember how you acted over this program." For many people in the 1960s and 1970s, *Star Trek* was actually a route into a lifetime in science fiction, as a fan, a professional, or both; and few were as embarrassed as their parents had anticipated. Lois and Lillian both began to write stories set in the *Star Trek* universe, an activity widely replicated in the Anglophone world and generally taken as being at the origins of contemporary fanfic. They eventually found having to fit in to the *Star Trek* universe stifling, so they moved into compiling a multigenerational future history together. But their love of *Star Trek* continued. Their mothers' words when the girls threatened not to go to their own high school graduation because it was a Thursday—in other words, *Star Trek* night—are not recorded.

Lois did not discover science fiction fandom until a few months later. She was working in the book section of a downtown department store and met a young man from COSFS, the Central Ohio Science Fiction Society. By the time Lillian came back from college Lois was a well-established member of the society, and Lillian saw Kubrick's movie *2001: A Space Odyssey* (it opened in April 1968) with Lois and the whole group. Lois and Lillian were not the only members interested in writing, and some of them used to meet up at the house of Lloyd Kropp, a graduate student in English at Ohio State. Kropp would become a novelist of some repute; his most famous novel was probably *Greencastle* (1987), a coming-of-age story set in New Jersey in the early 1950s, about three boys who love science fiction and who set up a club called The Denizens of the Sacred Crypt. Lois wrote a story at this time about a hermaphrodite, a precursor of her character Bel Thorne (VC 125) and an early indication of her later interest in speculation about gender.

Lois and Lillian announced to the group that they were going to produce a fanzine focused on *Star Trek*, called *StarDate*, and ignored the response: that there was no such thing as an sf fanzine devoted to a TV show, or an all-fiction fanzine (VC 125). In fact *Spockanalia* had come out not long before *StarDate*, and that inspired Lois and Lillian to persevere. They wrote most of it themselves, while some of the illustrations were provided by a student at the Columbus College of Art and Design (graduated 1970), Ron Miller, who is now regarded as one of the world's best space and astronomy artists. The fanzine was produced on the mimeograph machine belonging to COSFS member John Ayotte, who had his own fanzine, and Lois and Lillian saw their own "words in black and white type for the first time. Daring to air our psyches before the world. We were giddy, and not only from the fumes of the corflu" (VC 125–26).[5]

Lois and Lillian carried their copies of *StarDate* to Midwestcon, in Cincinnati, their first sf convention. There was never to be a second issue: Lillian's family moved to Texas, where Lillian has lived ever since.

Lois went to other local conventions during her college years (1968–1972) and to two World Science Fiction Conventions (Worldcons): BayCon (San Francisco, 1968) and St. Louiscon (St. Louis, Missouri, 1969). Initially, she was an English major, but she soon shifted to the sciences, and an interest in both wildlife and close-up photography led her to embark on a six-week field trip to East Africa, from which she returned with eight hundred slides of bugs and a fascination for insects that she was to utilize with great fun in

A Civil Campaign. It was not long after that trip to Africa that she told Lillian, as Lillian's infant son crawled over their feet, of a story she had been thinking about writing, set in the *Star Trek* universe, in which a red-headed female Federation scientist and a Klingon officer are stranded together on a planet that looked very much like East Africa (VC 126). The hypothetical novel was never written: and, as Bujold notes, "the urban legend that *Shards of Honor* began as an ST novel with the serial numbers filed off is both untrue and, apparently, unkillable."

In 1971 Lois married John Bujold, whom she had met at a science fiction convention two years earlier (Marcon IV, in Columbus). (Despite her subsequent divorce, she has preserved her married name, under which she has always published, and henceforth I shall refer to her as Bujold.) On leaving university she worked for several years (from 1972 to 1978) as a drug administration technician in the Ohio State University hospitals. This gave her a staff card to the stacks of the university library, and she started reading everything that looked interesting. Partly as a result of this, she did not do much writing, although her Sherlock Holmes fanfic "The Adventure of the Lady on the Embankment" dates from late in this period. From the point of view of her future career, however, the library may have been the least of it: she has calculated that during her time at the hospital she must have met around fourteen thousand patients, as well as many staff—an invaluable introduction to the variety of human experience.[6] She gave up her job, as her mother had done before her, to look after her two children: Anne, born 1979, and Paul, born 1981. In 1980 the family moved to Marion, Ohio, and lived in straitened circumstances; John's company went under, and he was unemployed for some time.

Meanwhile, Lillian had sold some stories, which inspired Bujold to persevere with writing: "It seemed to me this might be a way to make some money but still get to stay home with my kids" (VC 34). She dates the beginning of her writing career to Thanksgiving Day in 1982, when she tried out her father's new Kaypro II computer, which came bundled with word-processing software. She worked on a fragment that she had tried out for a local writers' group: it became, a month later, a novelette called "Dreamweaver's Dilemma," the starting point of the Vorkosigan Universe. She got feedback from the minister's wife at her parents' church, and she teamed up with Lillian and another fledgling writer, whom Lillian had met at the 1982 Chicago Worldcon, Patricia C. Wrede. "The three of us fell into a sort of writer's workshop by mail, sending chapters of our assorted novels back and forth to each other for critique" (VC 35). One of these was the novel that would become *Shards of Honor*, in which a redheaded female officer, Cordelia Naismith, treks across an alien planet—somewhat resembling East Africa—in the company of her militaristic captor, Aral Vorkosigan. Bujold had the idea that the two characters would have a son, who would be inclined toward the military despite physical disabilities. There were, Lillian writes, many other influences at work: Aral, for instance, she claims is an amalgam of Ignatius Loyola, Winston Churchill, and the Oliver Reed version of Dumas's musketeer Athos (VC 127). There were many other influences in play, including Bujold's readings in Russian and Japanese history, C. S. Forester's Hornblower books, and the numerous World War II books that she had read in her childhood.

Bujold's first professional sale was a short story, "Barter," which was published in *Twilight Zone Magazine* in spring 1985. It was later bought, adapted, and mutilated almost beyond recognition for the TV series *Tales from the Darkside*. It was broadcast, though she counts herself as lucky that she has never seen it (it was not shown in the Marion area); Lillian Carl saw it, in Texas, and could not recognize it as Bujold's work. "Barter" reflects Bujold's constant struggle as a mother of two to get some peace and quiet in which to write. The story tells how an alien rings the doorbell of a housewife, driven to distraction by noisy kids and vomiting cats. He desperately needs ammonia, which is to his metabolism roughly what water is to ours. In exchange he offers her a remote-controlled biostasis field and a focal stimulator; the former brings temporary paralysis, and the second replaces laziness with buzzing activity. Without a second thought she uses the first on her cats and children, and the latter on her husband.

In fall 1984, Bujold finished her second novel, *The Warrior's Apprentice*, and while she was writing the third she sent the first two manuscripts to more than one New York publisher. Eventually she heard back: a rejection of *The Warrior's Apprentice*. Lillian Carl saw Betsy Mitchell (then of Baen Books) at LoneStarCon 1, the North American Science Fiction Convention in Austin, Texas (at the end of August 1985),[7] and Carl said that that Mitchell might like Bujold's work. Within a few weeks Jim Baen had read *The Warrior's Apprentice* and then rang to ask Bujold about the other two books she had completed. He finished by making an offer on all three of them: *Shards of Honor, The Warrior's Apprentice*, and *Ethan of Athos*. Bujold simultaneously tap-danced on the ceiling according to Carl (VC 37)—Bujold remembers lying on the kitchen floor and hyperventilating—while prudently asking Carl to check the credentials of the people involved. Baen Books, founded by Jim Baen in 1983, was still quite young at the time, and no one sensible would sell three books to a company that was going to fold the next week. She was reassured, and the books did indeed appear, in paperback, in 1986, at three-month intervals, in June, August, and December, "leaving the uninitiated to imagine that I wrote a book every three months."[8]

Baen Books has flourished, survived the death of its founder in 2006, and become a leader in the promotion of its writers through electronic forms. All Bujold's Vorkosigan books have been published by Baen; the hardcover publication of the second to last, *CryoBurn*, was bundled with a CD containing the texts of all the previous novels except *Memory*. The association between Baen and Bujold was clearly mutually profitable for them to do this; although to offer *all* the books bar one on the CD was the result of a bureaucratic mistake, for the original idea had been to offer just two or three. Nevertheless, Baen must have had considerable confidence in Bujold's ability to attract new readers by this means—readers who would be enthusiastic enough to buy hard copies of books they already had in electronic form. Toni Weisskopf, who became editor-in-chief at Baen and had edited most of the books in the series, certainly had that enthusiasm herself: "I started with *The Warrior's Apprentice* and never looked back. I got the same sort of feeling reading her novels as I had gotten from classic Heinlein: a renewed faith in humanity and a desire to explore and do good in the universe. Great feeling" (VC 78).

Bujold first met Jim Baen in person while waiting for an elevator in the Atlanta Marriott, at the Worldcon in 1986. Bujold recalls that as he was swept by the crowd into the elevator, he called back "something like, 'If you can write three books a year for seven years, I can put you on the map!' To which my plaintive reply was—and I can't now remember if I voiced it or not—'Can't I write one book a year for twenty-one years?'" (VC 37). Bujold was terrified by Baen's comment, Carl remembers: "[She] spent that whole convention looking like a deer in the headlights" (VC 37). Bujold was afraid of failing to get established; indeed, she did make some elementary mistakes. She had signed contracts for her first seven books before getting an agent: the only advantage, as it transpired, was that waiting that long had enabled her to acquire a top-ranked Eleanor Wood as her representative. Among the first things Wood did was to use new contracts with Baen to "buy back" some of the rights that had been signed away in the earliest agreements.

Publishing three paperback novels, of course, is only the first step to establishing a career. Each of Bujold's first three books each had an initial print run of between thirty-five thousand and forty-five thousand copies. *The Warrior's Apprentice*, for instance, shipped 37,113 copies by the end of December 1989, with 58,764 printed by June 1991. *Falling Free*, published in April 1988, had shipped 43,884 copies by December of that year, and 72,590 by December 1991. "My backlist was starting to show some endurance."[9] Even so, this did not make Bujold wealthy overnight: *Shards of Honor* did not earn out its initial $5,000 advance until the end of 1989 (three years after publication), and her first royalty payment in December 1989 was $106.28. "I probably paid my water bill."

Any publishing house finds it difficult to bring a new writer to the attention of a public faced with such a variety of choices. *Locus* estimated that 294 new science fiction books (and 263 new fantasy novels)—new, that is, not reprints—were published in the United States in 1986.[10] Building up a loyal readership, at which Bujold has been very successful, is a slow and uncertain process. Perhaps the most important development for Bujold's career was being showcased in *Analog*; still one of the top three magazine publications of sf and fantasy fiction in the English-speaking world, in 1987 it had a declared circulation of 97,209 copies per month.[11] In December 1987 *Analog* began publishing *Falling Free* in four parts.[12] With its engineer hero and its engineering problems (how to turn a space station into a spaceship), it is a classic *Analog* story, and Bujold herself had planned it that way, as a marketing exercise. Stanley Schmidt, the editor, had sent her some notes on what lends a novel to serialization, and Bujold "tried to hit all his bullet points and apparently succeeded."[13] *Analog* subscribers would soon meet Miles Vorkosigan, too: "The Mountains of Mourning" was published May 1989, "Labyrinth" in August the same year, and the first part of *The Vor Game*, "Weatherman," in February 1990. *Analog* also serialized *Barrayar* in 1991, and *Cetaganda* in 1995. It is hardly possible to calculate the effect these publications in *Analog* had on the creation of Bujold's fanbase, but it was probably considerable. The three novellas in particular, very different from each other, highlighted Miles Vorkosigan effectively, and alerted *Analog*'s readers to the existence of the six books she had published by the time of the last *Analog* story. Bujold was showcased by *Analog* seven times, by my count: that is, the cover of the magazine featured her name in larger typeface, and the cover artwork illustrated her story. The cover art of her first appearance in the magazine, with the first installment of *Falling Free*, was by Vincent Di Fate and featured a rather generic space station, but subsequent illustrations displayed aspects of the Vorkosigan world much more specifically: a female quaddie apparently floating unprotected in space (by Vincent Di Fate, February 1988); a white uniformed officer, clearly well under five feet tall, standing among green uniformed soldiers (Alan Gutierrez, May 1989); Nicol, a black-haired quaddie playing her dulcimer (Kelly Freas, August 1989); a very short soldier (with M. Vorkosigan on his identity patch) kitted up for severe weather conditions (Dell Harris, February 1990); Cordelia, with gun, next to a soldier (presumably Bothari) (Ron and Val Lakey Lindhan, October 1991); and Miles presenting the Great Key to a woman in her float bubble (Terri Czeczko, October 1995).

One of the great strengths of Bujold's writing was that it could appeal to the readership of *Analog*, perceived as largely male, and (at least in the early years of Miles Vorkosigan's career) to those with an interest in military sf or traditional space adventures (so-called "space opera") while at the same time winning a large female readership. Bujold's most ardent fans, and certainly most of those who write fanfic in the Bujold universe and contribute to online discussions, are probably women, but my own personal observation (totally unsupported by genuine statistics) is that she seems to have retained the loyalty of many of those early readers. Bujold's own impression, judging from the audiences she faces, is that her readers split roughly equally between male and female (whereas the sf readership as a whole is reckoned to be closer to 60 percent male, 40 percent female).

The rest of Bujold's career is a series of triumphs. There are three main awards in the science fiction and fantasy field. Most prestigious is the Hugo Award, voted for by those who are members of the annual World SF Convention and awarded in a ceremony at the convention itself. The Nebula Award may, however, be more highly prized: this is chosen by votes from fellow writers, the members of the SFWA, the Science Fiction and Fantasy Writers of America. And finally there is the Locus Award, which is based on the results of a poll conducted by *Locus: The Magazine of the Science Fiction Field* among its readers (fans, writers, critics, publishers, booksellers). These awards are, of course, not for "excellence," whatever that is: these awards are recognition that a large number of sf readers regard a writer as one of their favorites and as someone likely to write what they regard as their own favorite book of the year. All three of these awards come in various categories: Best Novel is generally regarded as the most prestigious (though *Locus* separates that into Best SF Novel and Best Fantasy Novel), but there are awards for other lengths too: the novella, novelette, and short story. During the 1990s Bujold won each of these awards, more than once, and was short-listed for each of them more than once. It was her fourth novel, *Falling Free*, that won her the first Nebula for Best Novel in 1989, as well as a short-listing for the Hugo in the same category. The following year, her story about Miles Vorkosigan's trip into the Dendarii Mountains, "The Mountains of Mourning," won both the Nebula and the Hugo in the novella category. The year after that, 1991, *The Vor Game* gave her a Hugo for Best Novel; she followed that up with the same award for *Barrayar* in 1992. In 1993 her first fantasy novel, *The Spirit Ring*, came second in the *Locus* poll for best fantasy novel of the year. In 1994 *Mirror Dance* won both the Hugo and *Locus* Awards for Best Novel. *Paladin of Souls* won Best Novel category in both the Hugo and Nebula Awards, and topped the *Locus* poll for the Best Fantasy Novel of 2003. This listing does not count short-listing for these major awards on several occasions, or awards for best novel in Italy or in Japan, let alone the lesser awards in America. Her tally, to date, in the three biggest awards, is a total of nine Best Novel awards, made up four Hugos, two Nebulas and three Locus Awards. The only other writer to win four Hugos in Best Novel category was the man generally regarded as one of the founding fathers of modern science fiction, Robert A. Heinlein himself.[14] Bujold wrote that she was relieved to get the fourth Hugo, for *Paladin of Souls*, "because it finally stopped people driving me crazy by saying brightly, 'Just one more and you'll match Heinlein!' It's not a race, drat it" (VC 54). She added that she had no idea why some of her books won awards and others did not, except that the ones where she was least concerned with other people's response seemed to do best.

The other form of recognition one can measure is invitations to conventions as guest of honor. Bujold's first such invitation to a major convention was in 1993, when she was so honored by Wiscon, the annual feminist sf convention. In 1994 she was guest of honor at Confabulation, that year's Easter convention in London. Thereafter the invitations flowed: she was guest of honor at three U.S. conventions in 1996, and in 1998 she added to her roll of honors an invitation to be guest of honor at the major Western Australian sf convention, Swancon, as well as an invitation to be guest writer at the largest get-together of academics and writers in the science fiction and fantasy fields, the International Conference on the Fantastic in the Arts, which meets each March in Florida. Since then she has been guest of honor at conventions all around the world, including at the most prestigious conventions of all, the World Science Fiction Convention (Denver, 2008). The first convention devoted entirely to her works was in April 2002: it was called VorCon. It was held, interestingly (given the Russian background to her Barrayar novels), in Moscow, Russia, but Bujold was unable to attend.[15] For many busy authors, of course, conventions, while a good opportunity to meet fans, fellow writers, publishers, and agents, are a distraction from writing. Bujold estimates that she loses "one to two weeks of writing time / attention / energy" for each three-day convention.

There are parts of her life that she rarely refers to in print. There was the death of her father in 1986, while she was writing *Falling Free*, a novel she had to abandon for a while. There was the divorce from her husband, which was finalized in December 1992: "more teeth-gritting than acrimonious." She stayed in Marion, Ohio, after the divorce, until 1995, when she and her children moved to Minneapolis, Minnesota, near where her good friend Patricia Wrede lived, and where she has lived ever since. Finally, there was the difficult year on either side of the death of her mother, at age ninety-one, in 2003. At that time she read a huge amount of online fanfic—not Bujold fanfic, of which there is a considerable amount, but the fanfics of various other fandoms. She published no new Vorkosigan books for seven years after that but instead started exploring a very different kind of fantasy from anything she (or anyone else) had done before.

Judging by the online comments by fans, Bujold's success has been largely a result of writing characters that people enjoy reading about. Her success has certainly not been the result of fine packaging by her publishers: indeed, Bujold's books have been cursed with some fairly mediocre covers, which must have put off many potential fans. There was a discussion of this in the online comments following Jo Walton's retrospective review of *Shards of Honor*.[16] Walton herself, an enthusiastic Bujold fan, pointed out that "the whole [Vorkosigan] series has no cover, hardback, softback, British or US, that says to me 'I bet you'd like this, Jo!'" While picking up on another of Walton's points, Bujold commented: "Oh, heavens, you've had that thought about my books *too*? I've often wondered if, somewhere in my writerly apprenticeship and unknown or forgotten by myself, I'd made some sort of deal with the Infernal Powers that my books would stay in print forever, but the covers would always be *dire*." The crucial thing is that most of the books *have* stayed in print, mostly forever, and that they are now having a new lease on life as e-books. She has continued to entertain readers and win fans: one needs no more proof than that her most recent novel, *Captain Vorpatril's Alliance*, was one of the five books shortlisted in 2013 for the Hugo for Best Novel of 2012, and, indeed, was voted into second place (losing out to John Scalzi's *Redshirts*).

In her essay "The Unsung Collaborator" Bujold describes a book as a process, not an object. It depends on an author to produce it and a reader to respond to it. This to some extent defines the way she writes: she is very clear about the need not to exclude potential readers, either by concentrating in a solipsistic fashion on "fine writing" or by using language or scenes that repel the reader—or repel too many readers, at least. In her essay on "Writing Sex" she talks about how she had herself stopped reading a couple of books because of repellent sex scenes; in both cases she decided not to read that author again. She wanted to describe a sex between Fawn and Dag, because it was integral to what she wanted to show about their relationship, and tried hard to produce something that would not cause her readers to respond very negatively. Bujold can monitor this to some extent, because she meets her fans frequently, online and in person at science fiction conventions, and can read what they write. Bujold fandom, like most varieties of fandom, is keen to communicate, and nowadays much of it is done online, which enables Bujold herself to participate, reading posts and reading comments on her blog. Thanks to her willingness to do this, she can keep a finger on the pulse of her readership, to see what parts of her books succeed and what parts fail, in a way that was just impossible to earlier generations of writers.[17]

Readers react not only by direct comment and criticism but also by writing their own fiction set in Bujold's universes. Some authors have a very negative reaction to fanfic, seeing it as a cross between trespassing and plagiarism. Others, like Rowling and Bujold, are much more relaxed and view it as a form of advertising. Bujold was introduced to fanfic through *Star Trek*, and has since read fanfic from various fan communities. In the early 1980s she was lent some slash fiction by a friend, which she read "with rising eyebrows. Until around 6 AM if I recall correctly."[18] Slash fiction is about the emotional and/or sexual relationship between two characters, almost invariably same sex, and generally male: the "slash" is the typographical link joining the two erotic halves of the relationship, such as the classic Kirk/Spock pairing. Sometimes these two characters are real people, such as actors: Bujold is far from alone in finding RPS, Real Person Slash, beyond the pale. But she found that slash fiction was the first pornographic writing that she had been able to read without feeling either threatened or deeply repelled. She has in the past read fanfic about her own universes too, although she reluctantly gave that up on the advice of other writers: the risk of legal action if she found herself even unconsciously drawing on ideas about character and plot that she had read in the fanfic was too great. In a written comment on this text, she added "it's really depressing when some of them write better than I do."

There is a considerable amount of fanfic inspired by Bujold's writing, some of which is slash. Miles/Gregor and Ivan/Byerly are the most common slash pairings.[19] But most of Bujold fanfic is not slash at all: many stories supply scenes missing from the books, or develop characters, or in other ways extend or even critique "the canon." There is fanfic from Chalion and the Wide Green World as well as from the Vorkosiverse. There are even some rather bizarre crossovers, such as "Vorbarra's Terrier," about Captain Vimes (of Ankh-Morpork), working on a case for Ezar Vorbarra and coming into conflict with Captain Negri (as naturally the Municipal Guard will occasionally come into conflict with ImpSec); or Kathryn Anderson's "Testing," in which Miles and Ivan are students at Hogwarts.[20] At its best, the fanfic offers a critical perspective on Bujold's fiction and actively engages in broadening and extending the universes she creates.

Fanfic is, Bujold has written, "a natural reader response laboratory." Given her background, she naturally sees it in biological terms: pieces of fanfic are "little story-petrie-dishes."

> One can *see* the difference between controlled subcreation and the mere use of characters as hand-puppets to act out the writer's own internal psychological concerns—and the interesting border area between the two. One can see *inside readers' heads*, that otherwise inaccessible stage where all this art takes place.[21]

Future research on Bujold fanfic might actually tell us interesting things about Bujold's writing, and about reader-response: about what readers regard as the gaps or mistakes that Bujold has made, and about the scenarios and characters that readers have found particularly interesting.[22] What we cannot doubt is that many readers have found Bujold to be one of the most exciting and entertaining of writers in the science fiction and fantasy genre. Some readers never encounter her, or are put off by the covers or by the space opera overtones; when a reader does enjoy a Bujold book, they very often go on to devour all the others, a sign that Bujold has created something very special.

When I was editor of *Foundation: The International Review of Science Fiction* back in the 1980s and 1990s, I discovered that some bestselling authors in the field get very little critical attention (while others, sometimes not bestsellers at all, get rather too much). Critics frequently ignore bestsellers because the books supposedly do not meet some intangible quality of literary excellence; but bestsellers should always be of interest to scholars because, whatever their "quality," the fact that they have become bestsellers tells us a good deal about the historical context in which they were produced. In Bujold's case the critical neglect may partly be because she has been typecast (wrongly) as a writer of space opera. Space opera is a subgenre dominated by male authors whose fictional worlds seem sometimes to be almost exclusively populated by men. Female critics have not taken it seriously, therefore, while male critics do not take female writers of space opera seriously. Bujold is not the only female writer of space opera who has been neglected by critics; so has Carolyn Cherry, who writes stunning space opera under the pen name C. J. Cherryh. Space opera is close to the core of the whole science-fictional project, however, and anyone interested in science fiction needs to understand it. Bujold's problem, if she has one, is that she has not been a reliable writer of traditional space opera. She plays with its conventions; she subverts them. Moreover, not all her science fiction is space opera, and not all of her output is even science fiction. As I hope will emerge in the course of this book, she has taken fantasy in new and original directions, and indeed won over many of her dyed-in-the-wool Vorkosigan fans. My apologies, however, to those who would have liked more on the fantasy; I thought that would not be wholly appropriate in a series about "Modern Masters of Science Fiction."

The best reason for writing any nonfiction (and perhaps fiction too) is to learn something and to clarify one's own ideas. In undertaking this work I wanted to understand *why* I liked Bujold's books so much (and why so many others do as well). How is it that her books entertain me, but also move me, teach me, and addict me? I hope that this book will be some kind of answer. And I am pleased to report that constant rereading of her books has not caused me to lose my fascination with her work but rather to appreciate her artistry still more.

Bujold's books may stem from the adventure stories of 1950s and 1960s space opera, but they make us think about important issues—disability, the role of women, the morality of genetic experimentation, the significance of warfare in society. All Bujold's books deal intelligently and critically with different kinds of moral and ethical issues that are just as relevant to us as to her fictional characters. However, it also needs to be emphasized that the books are fun. The characters are almost invariably individuals who develop in interesting and at time unexpected ways across the books of the three main sequences (Vorkosigan, Chalion, and the Wide Green World). The writing is deceptively simple and straightforward, but it is clearly extremely carefully crafted so that every word counts. The dialogue, in particular, is tightly written and often very witty; the commentary supplied by the focalizing characters in the narratives is often equally entertaining. It is Bujold's sense of humor, I suspect, that helps to make us so fond of the main characters, not just their sheer humanity.

Bujold has the power to write very movingly, too. What moves (and I mean, often, moves to the point of tears) obviously differs from reader to reader, so I will just list a few of the scenes from the Vorkosigan saga that I find emotionally powerful: the reassignment of Lieutenant Koudelka at the end of *Shards of Honor*; the epilogue, "Aftermaths," to the same book;

the sudden death of Bothari in *The Warrior's Apprentice*; Ethan's proposal to Quinn at the end of *Ethan of Athos*; Bannerji's little revolt against Van Atta at the end of *Falling Free*; the conclusion of "The Mountains of Mourning"; Miles's confrontation with Metzov at the end of the "Weatherman" sequence in *The Vor Game*; Cordelia's delivery of Vordarian's head in *Barrayar*; Mark's walk through the forest with Aral in *Mirror Dance*; Miles's little ride with Pel Navarr in *Cetaganda*; Miles's first confrontation with Haroche as Imperial Auditor in *Memory*; Ekaterin's destruction of the terrorists' apparatus in *Komarr*; Nikki locking himself in his great-uncle's study to contact Gregor in *A Civil Campaign*; the quaddies' ballet in *Diplomatic Immunity*. These are sometimes versions of Tolkien's eucatastrophe: that moment of joy when something happens to divert a threatened tragic ending. Bujold wields this particular trope very skilfully. But sometimes the emotional moment comes simply because Bujold creates characters that are so real, or so sympathetic, that one's own emotions become invested in their successes and failures. It is the very rare writer who can do that.

CHAPTER 2

THE SCIENCE FICTION

Lois McMaster Bujold has to date written fourteen science fiction books and a number of short stories: approximately six thousand pages of text. Almost all of her science fiction stories are set in the same future history, and most concern the Vorkosigan family, who live on the human-colonized planet Barrayar some two thousand years in our future. The Vorkosigan sequence, within which we might place also the hundreds of pieces of fan fiction using Bujold's characters, is a kind of "future history," as pioneered by Robert A. Heinlein from 1939. It might also be described as an "unfolding text" or a "vast narrative," using terms that have been applied to similarly expanding fictions in recent years, such as Doctor Who or the various superhero franchises.[1] But, certainly earlier in Bujold's career, the Vorkosigan stories were usually branded as "space opera," and that label has tended to stick.

"Space opera" was originally used derogatorily (in the early 1940s) to refer to run-of-the-mill adventure stories set in space, some of which only differed from westerns by having "six-shooter" replaced by "blaster," "redskins" by "aliens." But in the course of the 1950s and 1960s some writers began to take pride in the label and to write more and more sophisticated space operas that still fit the definition of "colourful action-adventure stories of interplanetary or interstellar conflict."[2] Bujold began writing during a major flourishing of the subgenre. Space opera was dominant among Hugo-winning novels between 1981 and the mid-1990s. The popularity may stem from the remarkable success of Frank Herbert's *Dune* (Hugo winner in 1966) but probably above all from the television and movie phenomena that were *Star Trek* (initially 1966 to 1968) and *Star Wars* (beginning 1977). C. J. Cherryh won Hugos for *Downbelow Station* (in 1982) and for *Cyteen* (1989); David Brin for *Startide Rising* (1984) and *The Uplift War* (1988); Dan Simmons for *Hyperion* (1990); Vernor Vinge for *A Fire upon the Deep* (1993); and Bujold herself for *The Vor Game* (1991), *Barrayar* (1992) and *Mirror Dance* (1995).

The second great wave of space opera, sometimes called the New Space Opera, began around the same time. This is generally associated with British writers such as Iain M. Banks, Alastair Reynolds, and Ken MacLeod, although also with Canadians (Peter Watts and Karl Schroeder) and Australians (Greg Egan and Sean Williams). The New Space Opera was largely written by men; and the British writer Gwyneth Jones has contrasted their big ideas and wide open spaces with the "baroque political intrigue of former doyennes like C. J. Cherryh and Lois McMaster Bujold,"[3] Gary Westfahl, rather more kindly, described Cherryh and Bujold as providing "blends of classic, Ruritanian and romantic space opera, with wars in space balanced by a nuanced understanding of politics and persuasive attentiveness to personal relationships."[4] The hard fact is that no practitioner of the New Space Opera won a Hugo (although Ken MacLeod was short-listed in 2002); the apogee of space opera, judged solely in Hugo terms, came in the 1980s and early part of the 1990s, just when Bujold was establishing herself as a major writer in the field.

Bujold has described her writing process as channelling her inner 13-year-old. By this, Bujold was primarily referring to the part of her personality that is "fiendishly self-centred," ornery, sometimes "*insufferably* smug"; "she's where Miles comes from, and all the rest of the gaudy crew too."[5] But we also have to think about what the thirteen-year-old Lois was reading around 1962. The true literary antecedents of Miles Vorkosigan are characters from the space opera of that era: the highly entertaining adventures of Nicholas van Rijn and Dominic Flandry, chronicled by Poul Anderson from the 1950s through to the 1970s; the interstellar exploits of Jaime Retief, told by Keith Laumer from the early 1960s through to the 1980s; and the stories of the Federation of the Hub, by James H. Schmitz, many of them published in *Analog* in the 1950s and early 1960s. There were others doing similar work (Murray Leinster and H. Beam Piper, for instance), but the tone of the work of Anderson, Laumer, and Schmitz resonates through Bujold's work. Bujold notes the British writer Eric Frank Russell as another of her influences; the creativity and lack of respect for authority shared by most Russell heroes is clearly part of Miles Vorkosigan's makeup. Finally, she has noted the significance of the classiest of all space-operatic writers, Cordwainer Smith, writing largely between 1955 and his death in 1966. Bujold tells me that she once wanted Miles to be Smith's Lord Jestocost when he grew up, and that she can imagine Miles's universe developing into the biologically diverse far-future universe of Smith's Instrumentality.

Apart from a few short stories written early in her career, all Bujold's science fiction written between 1986 and the present has been set in the universe sometimes known by her fans as the Vorkosiverse after its central character, Miles Vorkosigan. Although her writing as a whole has expanded beyond that universe, with the publication of eight fantasy novels, her science-fictional universe has remained unusually restricted. Indeed, it is not just a question of writing within the same fictional universe: only two of her science fiction novels have no appearance by a member of the Vorkosigan family, and since 1988 her science fiction has been set exclusively within the lifetimes of Aral Vorkosigan and his son Miles. Bujold has varied the tone of her Vorkosigan books, with some being primarily space adventure stories, while others are mysteries, or romances, or comedies of manners, or a mixture of them all, and she has written novels that take Miles Vorkosigan to visit new planets and societies, as happens in *Cetaganda* or *CryoBurn*. Nevertheless she has largely restricted herself to writing about people from one family, coming from one society, Barrayar, over a period of some forty years.

One explanation for Bujold's decision to restrict herself in this way is that Bujold is interested above all in character. While some science fiction writers are interested in developing different "what-if" scenarios and focusing on how that "what-if" changes a society, Bujold has shown herself to be concerned primarily in how her characters and the society they live in develop over time; she has built up a large and devoted body of fans not because they want to see her develop numerous new universes and explore all the boundaries of her genre, but because they share the author's own fascination with her characters and want to see how they change and grow.

Bujold started her Vorkosigan saga thinking that she would write it rather like C. S. Forester's Hornblower books. Forester started in the middle of Horatio Hornblower's career and then filled in the story, jumping both forward and backward as it suited him. Thus, Bujold wrote stories about Miles Vorkosigan's adult achievements long before she wrote about his birth; she wrote about his adventures on Cetaganda as a young man long after she had written stories about his later career. It gave her freedom, but she also discovered the limitations of the approach: "There needs to be some explanation of why events are not causal in the intervening books, why an episode important enough to write a novel about is never subsequently-in-book-time thought about by the point of view character" (VC 10). From the eleventh Vorkosigan Universe book (*Memory*), which signals a major change in Miles's career path, the books are written in the chronological order of Miles's life, except for the most recent book, *Captain Vorpatril's Alliance* (2012), in which the action is set shortly before *CryoBurn* (2010) for reasons that the last pages of *CryoBurn* explain. Bujold tries to avoid any inconsistency that might emerge from writing segments of the arc out of sequence; and she is also very aware that readers may enter the story arc at any point, and she therefore tries hard to make these new readers welcome by giving enough back story to fill in the necessary gaps without actually boring those readers who may well have reread the earlier books several times. Each story, she has said, thus needs to be two books at once: a complete tale in itself, but one that also occupies a "unique place in the growing structure."[6]

Very few of Bujold's books deal with adventure and conflict in space, the traditional subject matter of space opera. Once Miles ceases to be Admiral Naismith, his adventures perforce become largely planetbound: thereafter only *Diplomatic Immunity* takes place solely in space (although mostly on a space station). Nevertheless, the whole Vorkosigan series does share a number of similarities with traditional space opera. The stories are adventure stories, which focus on people (not exclusively Miles) around whom action happens, and whose actions are often historically significant within the fictional universe. The New Space Opera occasionally flirted with the dangerous possibilities of democratic or anarchistic space opera, but Bujold writes within the much more familiar world of traditional space opera—"traditional" in more than one sense: a world of established hierarchies and rituals, of monarchies and aristocracies, in which uniformed military officers (whether in space or on a planet) are important players. The action of space opera is frequently military action, and Bujold's work has sometimes been placed within the subgenre of "military sf," to which belong, for instance, many of the novels by David Weber (whose female space commander Honor Harrington is modeled on Horatio Hornblower far more closely than Miles Vorkosigan was). Bujold has mused that her fiction might better be called "medical sf" than "military sf."[7] Her own work experience, outside writing and mothering, is, after all, medical and not military. There are some similarities between the worlds of military and medical fiction: both feature life-and-death emergencies and require similar order, discipline, structure, and training. Despite the surface similarities that are doubtless attractive to fans of the genre, Bujold does not so much write military science fiction as subvert it. She seldom describes direct military action; the comments of her leading characters frequently complain about loss of life, whether of their own personnel or that of their opponents; her leading characters are mostly peacemakers, using persuasion rather than violence wherever possible. When Bujold was first faced with describing a serious fight, in *The Warrior's Apprentice*, Miles, her point-of-view character, lost consciousness because of his bleeding ulcer, and missed most of it. "In part I was being deliberately ornery, exploding the stereotypes," Bujold wrote, "but in part I was falling back on my strengths."[8] In this, she is reminiscent of James White: the action in his twelve Sector General books, published between 1962 and 1999, focused almost entirely on what the doctors on his multispecies hospital–space station were doing, which often involved trying to save the lives of those damaged in military action by offstage space-operatic action. Older space-operatic examples of "medical sf" were L. Ron Hubbard's Old Doc Methusaleh stories (1947–1950), and the Med Service stories of Murray Leinster (1957–1966).

Bujold's most significant subversive element, however, is surely her choice of hero. As Miles Vorkosigan developed, she has written, he was "in some ways very much a space-opera counter-hero, or critique of the original genre, and indeed, of the whole male-adventure genre." She lists the usual attributes. Tall and handsome? "Nope. Try short, fragile-boned, and odd-looking." Tragic orphan? Nope. If anything, an "anti-orphan" who has his family to fall back on when there are problems (except when his family *are* the problem, Bujold noted to me).[9] Goes through women like tissue paper? Nope. "Unselfconsciously heroic? Not Miles. He's a post-modern hero, and can't help being conscious of just about everything."[10] Miles is, nevertheless, heroic, and indeed rashly so. In the first chapter in which he appears, he jumps off a wall, hoping against experience and common sense that he is not going to break both legs and suffer great pain. He is quite good at suffering great pain; he's had a lot of practice. The fact that he succeeds at most things, despite his physical weakness and impetuosity, is the result of his major asset (apart, of course, from birth, privilege, and wealth): brains. Most readers can identify with that.

Bujold has experimented with genre expectations in other ways, pushing the "space opera" envelope as far as it could go. As she wrote in the afterword to *Miles in Love*, by the end of the 1990s she "had already explored blending several styles of story within the putatively-space-opera series: gothic romance, coming-of-age, military, mystery, suspense, Golden-Age-engineering, and a much less common subject, coming-of-age *again*, because growing up isn't something that you do once and stop."[11] Her subversion and her experimentation are two of the things that make her science fiction so attractive.

The future history that Bujold imagines in the Vorkosigan sequence fits generally within what Donald A. Wollheim has called the "consensus cosmogony," a view of how the future history of mankind might develop over the next few millennia. The consensus cosmogony was developed in the course of the 1930s and 1940s, and by the 1950s this tacitly agreed framework for future history enabled writers, particularly writers of short stories (which still dominated in the 1950s), to cue their readers very easily and concisely into an understanding of the story's context. In its classic form there is the initial exploration and colonization of the solar system; then the first flights to the stars, by generation-ship or by some faster-than-light (ftl) gimmick such as wormholes; the colonization of planets and perhaps the meetings with alien civilizations; then the rise of the Galactic Empire; the Galactic Empire in full bloom, and the exploration of the rest of the galaxy; the decline and fall of the Galactic Empire; the interregnum, with worlds losing contact with other worlds and reverting to primitive conditions; then the return of galactic civilization; and finally (for really ambitious writers) the end of the universe and ultimate apocalypse.[12]

In the Vorkosigan universe, as in Asimov's Foundation universe, there are no intelligent aliens—merely various worlds colonized from Earth, which develop their own structures and societies. There is no general Galactic Empire, as we find in Asimov's series. The title of "Emperor" for the ruler of a Barrayaran hegemony consisting of only three worlds (and two of them recently acquired and relatively thinly populated) seems unnecessarily grandiose; the Cetagandan Empire, its main rival, is much more substantial, but even so is made up of only eight developed and densely populated worlds, with a number of allies, either voluntary or intimidated into dependence. As in the "consensus cosmogony" model, we have the usual historical stages of exploration and expansion (although, Bujold notes, "the *important stages* are the ones marking human speciation by bioengineering"). The exploration of the universe proceeds first by slow means and then by ftl travel through wormholes that link one part of galactic space with another. Control of and access to wormholes (a term coined by theoretical physicist John Archibald Wheeler in 1957) are an important aspect of galactic politics and strategy in the Vorkosigan universe, just as they have been in TV shows such as *Star Trek: Deep Space Nine* (1993–1999) and *Babylon 5* (1994–1998). Some of Bujold's planets, like Barrayar, have easy access to only one wormhole, which gives them some safety from enemy attack but also makes them dependent on having friendly relations with (or control over) the planetary system nearest the other end of their wormhole connection. Systems like Komarr and Marilac, which have access to several wormhole connections, have the opportunity to become rich by imposing tariffs on trade passing through "their" wormholes, but they also provide tempting targets to expanding empires. There was a time when the planet Barrayar lost contact with other colonies and reverted to primitive conditions: Barrayarans refer to this as the Time of Isolation. Then the Komarrans allow a Cetagandan invasion force to conquer Barrayar through its wormhole connection. After the Cetagandans are thrown out following a prolonged war, Barrayar moves swiftly to take control of Komarr and their wormhole link. It is only during the lifetime of Miles's father Aral Vorkosigan (and indeed thanks in large part to his energy) that Barrayar emerges from its isolation and acquires its two other worlds, Komarr and Sergyar.

An early story by Bujold, not published until 1996, gives some of the historical background to the colonization of space. "Dreamweaver's Dilemma," set some six hundred years earlier than the Vorkosigan books, is about an artist, commissioned to record dreams for others to experience, who discovers that her work is going to be used to drive the user to suicide. Some of the action takes place in the house of her friend DuBauer, who had travelled between Earth and Earth's first colony world, Beta Colony, without the benefit of ftl technology. He has spent twenty-five years of his life traveling; as he did so, 160 years passed in the lives of his planetbound contemporaries and descendants. We learn in an aside that Cleveland, Ohio (a city which Bujold never liked), has been destroyed in some kind of nuclear incident and remains radioactive. (One is reminded of the glee with which H. G. Wells had Martians destroy Woking in *The War of the Worlds* [1898].)[13] Bujold has explained that she had envisaged that the first colony established before ftl travel was Alpha Colony, which perished, by analogy with Roanoke Colony (in what would become Virginia). Beta Colony, which is flourishing, is largely settled from the United States of America, before the Cleveland disaster; when, as a consequence of that disaster, the U.S. colonization program collapses, other worlds are colonized through the efforts of other Earth nations (DD 222). Escobar, for instance, is settled largely by Spanish speakers; Barrayar is settled by (in order by population size) Russians, British, French, and Greeks.

John Lennard has suggested that there are two types of imaginative writers: the icebergs and the searchlights. Tolkien was an iceberg, leaving much of his imagined world underneath the surface, his invented languages and the detailed history of Middle-earth staying mostly in his notes and his memory. Most of the world-building had been completed even before he started on *The Hobbit*, which was the first time that he showed his world to readers. In Bujold's science fiction she is a searchlight, "imagining only what necessarily fell within protagonists' experience."[14] The "Vorkosiverse" appeared only gradually, through slow deliberation over several decades; new parts of it were invented when they were needed. In the rest of this chapter, I intend to explore how Bujold developed her universe and at the same time how she developed as a writer, and therefore I shall discuss the books and associated short stories in their published order, attempting to bring out what makes them interesting.

Bujold describes *Shards of Honor* (1986), her first published novel, as a "Gothic romance in SF drag" (VC 5). It is the first Vorkosigan novel proper, as it tells the story of the meeting of two military officers from two opposing planetary systems, Aral Vorkosigan and Cordelia Naismith, and the gradual shift of their relationship from that of captor and prisoner to that of husband and wife. The two main settled planets of Beta Colony and Barrayar are here barely seen: they are discovered for the reader very largely through the interchanges between Aral and Cordelia, who represent their planet's culture to the reader. There is a lot that is sketchy here, which means that there is little or nothing to contradict the world-building that will take place over the next few novels. The novel is episodic and not nearly so well plotted as her later books, but it is a book that still works well as an introduction to the Vorkosigan series, if only because the events that are described resonate with Aral and Cordelia, and therefore with their as-yet-unborn son Miles, for long afterward.

The writing of the first draft of *Shards of Honor* took Bujold from December 1982 until fall 1983 (the revisions took place in late 1984). Initially, she found it difficult to see how Cordelia's story would develop, and at one time she flirted with the idea of inventing an alien invasion in order to force Beta Colony and Barrayar together. The saga would have turned out very differently if her universe had contained alien allies or enemies rather than merely human ones. Instead, she decided on the idea of Barrayar's abortive invasion of Escobar, "thus accidentally discovering my first application of the rule for finding plots for character-centered novels, which is to ask: 'So what is the worst possible thing I can do to *this* guy?' And then do it."[15] She already knew that Aral and Cordelia would have a disabled son, and, "although I was not really aware of it when I was writing Chapter One," having Dubauer severely injured at the very beginning of the novel, she said, would be "the first statement of this theme [of disability]." Having a disabled child was the worst thing that she could do to Cordelia and Aral, given that Barrayarans exalted physical prowess and feared any deviation from the bodily norm. Bujold had originally intended that the birth of Miles would feature in this first book, and Bujold was well into the story of the early days of Aral and Cordelia's marriage before she realized that the novel had become far too long. She wrote an ending to *Shards of Honor* (initially called *Mirrors*), put what would five years later become the opening scenes of *Shardssequel* (later named *Barrayar*) to one side, and began writing *The Warrior's Apprentice*.

Shards of Honor, although flawed, has many of the strengths of later books and introduces some of the themes and motifs that Bujold develops throughout the series. In some ways the book has these characteristics in extreme form. Doing the worst possible thing she can to her protagonists means in this book that the focalizing character, Cordelia, comes very close to being raped—something that one does not expect in space opera. Later on we are shocked to discover that her apparently benevolent Betan government is prepared to go to extreme ends to assure themselves of Cordelia's loyalty. She extricates herself from her problems with the ingenuity, skill, and ruthlessness that readers would later associate with her son Miles, and Bujold—already in this book—plays on the readers' emotions just as skillfully. In many of Bujold's books we encounter that moment that Tolkien called *eucatastrophe*, "the joy of the happy ending" or "the sudden joyous 'turn,'" which he saw as characteristic of fairy stories but which has a much broader application within genre fiction.[16] But even more frequently we encounter the agony of ethical choice, which defines Bujold's characters and frequently acts as a major plot driver. In this book there are several such ethical pivots, such as Sergeant Bothari's decision to assassinate Admiral Vorrutyer rather than let him rape Cordelia. More far-reaching was Vorkosigan's decision to allow himself to be involved in the deaths of tens of thousands of his own comrades in what he knew to be a hopeless attack on the planet of Escobar. Unusually, but very effectively, the book ends with "Aftermaths," a short story featuring none of the characters we have met in the novel but which confronts the personal damage that warfare inflicts on families and individuals. The intense emotions and ethical decisions turn from the level of high politics to the purely domestic, as a woman searches for the corpse of her daughter in the wreckage of the space battle off Escobar. Parenting is a theme that extends throughout the sequence; this novel begins with Cordelia becoming the parent of the disabled Dubauer and ends with a parent seeking closure after her child's death.

The Warrior's Apprentice (1986) introduces Miles Vorkosigan at one of the turning points of his life, when, at age seventeen, he breaks the brittle bones of both his legs and flunks out of the military academy. By a series of accidents, he acquires, in order, sworn armsmen, spaceships, and a military force, the Dendarii Mercenaries. When he returns home, Miles, now known among the mercenaries as Admiral Naismith, is allowed a second chance at a career in the Barrayaran military and is sent off for officer training. Miles's apparently irreversible advance to power and authority is the result of trying to keep one step ahead of his problems: "I've got forward momentum. There's no virtue in it. It's just a balancing act. I don't dare stop" (WA 113). In her retrospective review of the book, called "Forward Momentum," Jo Walton notes:

> What makes this so good is that it has about ninety percent more depth than you'd expect it to have. The plot may be "seventeen-year-old with physical dis- abilities becomes admiral of space mercenaries" but the themes are much deeper and more interesting. This is a story about loyalty, duty, the weight of family expectations, and what it means to serve.[17]

Characteristically for Bujold, the ending is by no means so obviously trium- phant as it appears at first sight. The young admiral goes back to being a cadet officer (attempting to take the path followed by the heroes of Heinlein's *Space Cadet* and *Starman Jones*); not only does he lose a career, though that is tem- porary, but Sergeant Bothari, the man Miles grew up with, has been killed, and Miles has failed to win over Bothari's daughter, with whom he is in love. Moreover, at the end he is rescued from imprisonment or even execution for the crime of controlling a private army by the personal intervention of his childhood friend, the emperor—that is, by the kind of favoritism that Miles dislikes and is embarrassed by. Already, the parameters of Miles's ambiguous success are being sketched out.

Bujold began *The Warrior's Apprentice* in the autumn of 1983, only a few weeks after sending *Shards of Honor* off to a publisher. She wrote the book, she says, from beginning to end, but "it was generated from the inside out."[18] The first image that had come to her was the scene of Bothari's death, and "the rest of the book was written, more or less, to get to that point and explain it satisfactorily to myself" (VC 6). She had originally intended for Bothari to die in defense of Miles; what finally emerged was very different and much more interesting. Bothari is killed by one of Miles's mercenary recruits, a woman whom Bothari had raped during the conflict with Beta Colony in

Shards of Honor and who had given birth to their daughter, Elena. Bothari does not attempt to defend himself; he allows the woman to take her revenge. Miles is left bereft; Elena is devastated to discover that she was the product of a rape. The other change Bujold made, during the editing process, was to remove Miles's younger sister Nile (named after a character in a couple of James Schmitz's stories).[19] Not only did "Nile" occupy "the same ecological niche" as Elena, but the confusion possible between siblings called Miles and Nile was also considerable. The plot, as well as the whole idea of "forward momentum," was in part supplied by the story that inspired the title, "The Sorcerer's Apprentice" (Goethe, via Disney and the music of Dukas), in which a hapless young man (or mouse) makes a mistake and is drawn deeper and deeper into a nightmarish scenario entirely of his own making. But it was also, Bujold has said, a "theological romance," wherein Miles was brought up against the most obvious of his three besetting sins: pride, imprudence, and despair.[20] Miles is someone the reader soon learns to love: but he is far from being perfect (which is, of course, why he continues to be so interesting).

Miles does not figure in the third novel, *Ethan of Athos* (1986), at all: representing his Dendarii mercenaries is Commander Elli Quinn. Indeed, even the word Vorkosigan makes no appearance, although Quinn refers to Admiral Naismith several times. One of Bujold's intentions in this novel was to explore the possible effect of the uterine replicator upon human history. This device, first appearing in *Shards of Honor*, allowed for the development of a fetus outside the mother's body. It would thus, she reasoned, allow for the possibility of a society that could be self-reproducing without the presence of women at all. She realized how interested people might be in such "what-ifs" when she got into a conversation at a New Year's Eve party (at the end of 1984) and found herself talking to a surgeon and a hospital administrator who took opposite ideas on the workability of an all-male society: the macho unmarried surgeon thought men would never be able to cope without women, but the administrator, who had two children of his own, was intrigued. Bujold thought it would be interesting also to reverse the male fantasy, well represented in science fiction, of an all-woman planet; in the process, she created the first mass-market science fiction novel with an all-male planet *and*, therefore, a necessarily homosexual male protagonist, Dr. Ethan Urquhart.

Ethan's planet Athos is named after the peninsula in northern Greece in our world, a territory of 130 square miles, home to twenty monasteries from which all females are banned. In the fictional Athos, also, religion is at the root of the revulsion with which men regard women; women are thought to be the direct cause of evil. Ethan has to leave his planet and encounter women for the first time, including Elli Quinn. Ethan and Elli together find the fresh reproductive material he needs, and they rescue Terrence Cee from the Cetagandans: Terrence has been genetically engineered as a telepath, and the Cetagandans want to use him as a weapon. At the end Ethan and Terrence go to Athos, taking with them the organic remains of Terrence's telepathic sister to start a new life together (and presumably also to begin the creation of a new race of telepaths—a possible plot opening that Bujold has yet to exploit).

The next story to be published was a novella that focused on a rather more adult and experienced Miles. In "The Borders of Infinity" (1987) Miles is one of ten thousand soldiers in a Cetagandan prison camp on the planet of Dagoola IV. Miles solves the problem of planning an organized escape with what readers were beginning to see as his expected ingenuity and imagination. Beatrice, a woman that Miles has fallen for, plunges to her death in the final lift-off, a failure on Miles's part that would frequently return to haunt him. Bujold credits *Escape from Colditz* and other World War II books lent to her by Lillian Carl back in high school days as being an inspiration for this story (VC 13).[21]

Bujold's fourth novel, *Falling Free* (1988), is her only science fiction novel that has no mention of the Vorkosigans or Barrayar: it is set two hundred years before the events of *Shards of Honor*. Leo Graf, an engineer, rescues the "quaddies" (humans who have been genetically adapted to permanent life under zero gravity, in free fall) from the huge company that is treating them as little better than slaves. They are called quaddies because the most visible aspect of their enhancement was the replacement of legs with an extra pair of arms. Bujold's initial impetus had been the desire to write about a group of people bioengineered to work in space; she intended to center the story on Arde Mayhew, a character from *The Warrior's Apprentice*, thus bringing *Falling Free* firmly into the lifetimes of Aral and Miles and making it, perhaps, like

Ethan of Athos, a Vorkosigan novel that does not mention Vorkosigan. She described her idea on the telephone to Jim Baen, who wanted a followup to the three novels he had already received from her. He was enthusiastic about the bioengineered people but not about Arde Mayhew. That inspired Bujold to start planning the quaddies in more detail, which led her to place the story earlier in the days of space colonization. A conversation with Wally Voreck, an engineer friend of her brother Jim's, led her to look at ice-die formation, which gave her an idea for one plot element. Once she had decided on the shape of the novel, which was basically the story of Exodus—an escape from slavery—she thought of a trilogy: forty years in the wilderness for volume two, and the Promised Land in volume three. But she got distracted from that idea by *Brothers in Arms*, and the trilogy was never written.[22]

Falling Free was serialized in *Analog* over four issues in late 1987 and early 1988, and it brought Bujold to the attention of many new readers, a process which was accelerated when the book won the first of her many major awards: the Nebula Award for Best Novel. The novel turned out to be a very different book than it would have been with Arde Mayhew as the protagonist. Leo Graf, the hero (and for once that is an appropriate word), is a welding engineer. The book was dedicated to Bujold's father, a professor of welding engineering, and, as her brother Jim has confirmed, Leo was partially modeled on their father. Dr. McMaster had taught welding just as Leo does in the book; both he and Leo share a disdain for administrators and a dedication to integrity and honesty.[23] There are other ways in which Bujold drew from her father's career: the names of Leo and Graf were just two of the names borrowed from Dr. McMaster's colleagues and students.[24] Bujold's father died in July 1986, when she was just five chapters into the work; she took a break and wrote "The Borders of Infinity" before she was ready to finish *Falling Free*.

The following year saw the appearance of three more episodes in the life of Miles Vorkosigan, although they did not appear in the chronological order of Miles's life. The first, a novel, is a direct sequel to "The Borders of Infinity." During the escape from Dagoola IV, Admiral Naismith's fleet had suffered considerable damage. He goes to Old Earth for the repairs: as a consequence, *Brothers in Arms* (1989) is set almost entirely in London. Miles has a hair-raising adventure, which involves him in several rapid changes between his Lieutenant Vorkosigan and Admiral Naismith personae, threatening the discovery of his double life. Miles discovers that his cover story, devised on the spur of the moment to fool a journalist—that Admiral Miles Naismith is actually Lord Miles Vorkosigan's cloned brother—is far closer to the truth than he imagines. A cloned double of Miles has been created by a Komarran patriot to kill Aral and bring chaos to Barrayar. Miles keeps hearing his mother's voice, "*Miles*—she says—*What have you done with your baby brother?!*" (BA 186). According to Betan law and custom, the clone is Miles's brother, and following Barryaran naming customs he comes readily equipped with a name: Mark. With Mark, Bujold introduced a new complexity to Miles's life, and new possibilities for character development. Initially, it places Miles in an unaccustomed role: Miles has to become a parent to Mark, who may be indistinguishable physically but is much less experienced or mature than Miles himself. A good deal of the novel is about people who are not what they appear—both Miles and Mark, of course, but also Miles's superior officer on Earth, Duv Galeni. Miles is convinced that Galeni, who comes from Komarr, is a traitor. It transpires that Galeni is perfectly loyal to Barrayar; his father is the Komarran patriot who has engineered the cloning of Miles.

The other two stories from 1989 were both published in *Analog*, and later that same year they were brought together with "The Borders of Infinity" in a collection called *Borders of Infinity*. What unites the three stories is that each describes an event that continues to resonate in Miles's life: this is made explicit in the first story itself, "The Mountains of Mourning," and later novels bring out a similar significance in the other two tales. "The Mountains of Mourning" is set after his graduation from the Imperial Academy, and during the period he is waiting for his first assignment (which would be described the following year in *The Vor Game*). He is sent as the Voice of the Count, his father, into the backwoods of the Dendarii Mountains on Barrayar to investigate the murder of a baby with a harelip. Miles experiences the popular hatred of mutants (he himself, with all his disabilities, is usually taken for a mutant); he finds the culprit and begins a self-imposed mission to bring education and work to the rural poor and to turn around the prejudices that are so deeply rooted in Barrayaran society. This novella won Bujold her first Hugo Award (for Best Novella), and a second Nebula. Bujold was able to triumph in the good-humored argument she had had with Jim Baen over whether the books should be named after Miles Naismith or Miles Vorkosigan.[25] One wonders what might have happened to her career had Bujold been less determined: a series named after Admiral Naismith might have stuck her in space-operatic or military sf mode for much longer and could have made it much more difficult for her to develop Miles, and to develop herself, by experimenting with different kinds of writing.

The second story was "Labyrinth," in which Miles helps a genetic scientist to defect from Jackson's Whole, a planet that is the embodiment of cutthroat capitalism. The scientist was engaged in a project to breed the perfect soldier: he wants Miles to destroy the last surviving super-warrior and retrieve the genetic material that he has injected into this being. Miles finds the super-warrior and befriends her, and, indeed, becomes her lover: she is Taura—the minotaur at the center of the labyrinth—eight feet tall, with fangs and claws, but also with intelligence and vulnerability. Miles also manages to rescue a quaddie named Nicol, a talented musician being kept as an exotic pet by one of the corrupt barons of Jackson's Whole. "The Mountains of Mourning" and "Labyrinth" together focus on a theme that Bujold would develop in later stories: the fight against prejudice and exploitation.

The three stories of *Borders of Infinity* were tied together with a brief but implausible narrative (which Jim Baen insisted on, since apparent novels had better sales than collections of stories). Miles is under investigation by Count Vorvolk, of Accounting, over the high cost of his missions; his boss, the security chief Simon Illyan, is trying to find out details of those missions. "The Mountains of Mourning" does not fit into that framework narrative, since it had no cost to the Barrayaran treasury. The missions to Jackson's Whole and Dagoola clearly do, of course, but it is difficult to understand why Illyan at this point needs to hear the full stories, even if Miles's reports had been, as he claimed, "as usual, masterpieces of understatement and misdirection" (BI 2). However, the frame story brings a new insight into the ending of "The Borders of Infinity," which comes to Miles, and the reader, when Miles's mother Cordelia arrives onstage at the end of *Borders of Infinity*. Miles realizes that his dead love Beatrice was a "tall, aggressive redhead," just like his mother. He never gets to the stage of considering that the succession of tall, forceful women he falls in love with are in the image of Cordelia.

At the beginning of 1990 Bujold published another story in *Analog*, "Weatherman," which later that year formed the first part of *The Vor Game* (1990).

Miles's first military assignment, to his enormous disappointment, turns out to be as meteorological officer at the military base on Kyril Island, known familiarly as Camp Permafrost. He takes the side of mutinous soldiers against his brutal and unyielding commander, Stanis Metzov, and is brought back home in disgrace. Later, on a mission to the Hegen Hub, he meets up with the emperor, Gregor (an escapee from the "prison" of his Barrayaran palace), and with Metzov, the Barrayaran officer who had lost his post at Kyril Island thanks to Miles's brave protest. Miles retakes control of the Dendarii, rescues Gregor, routs a major Cetagandan attack, and is reunited with his father. His position as Admiral Naismith is consolidated, and he is promoted to a Barrayaran lieutenancy.

The first part of *The Vor Game* was a mix, Bujold has explained, of reading T. E. Lawrence's account of "the dismal horrors of army basic upon a nervy, intelligent man" and the story of the Forty Martyrs of Sebastiani, where soldiers in the Roman army refuse to abandon their Christianity and were sent to stand naked on a frozen lake until they changed their mind: they didn't, and one of the Roman officers who is impressed enough to join them on the ice dies with them (VC 16). Other inspirations include Bujold's father, who had himself been a part-time television weatherman; a print of an arctic weather station, which hung on her father's wall for years before coming into Bujold's possession; and a reading of B. H. Liddell Hart's book on military strategy, which Jim Baen had lent her. The first section of *The Vor Game*, "Weatherman," makes an effective and rather moving stand-alone story. At its core it—so common with Bujold—is an ethical choice, and the starkest one a soldier could make: whether or not to mutiny. Miles asks his father afterward whether he had done the right thing. "Yes," he is told. "A right thing. Perhaps not the best of all possible right things. Three days from now you may think of a cleverer tactic" (VG 95). Life is never simple for the Bujold hero.

As Bujold has noted, the dark first section of *The Vor Game*, borrowing its tone from T. E. Lawrence's autobiographical *The Mint*, fits somewhat awkwardly with the sunnier sections of the later part of the book, whose plot is influenced by a reading of Captain Liddell Hart (coincidentally a great admirer of Lawrence). Bujold has wondered whether *The Vor Game* should have been two novels rather than one (VC 17), but it won Bujold her first Hugo Award for Best Novel, "and," she said, "I would hardly dare mess with it now."[26] *The Vor Game* and *The Warrior's Apprentice* follow very similar plot arcs: both books begin with a setback in Miles's Barrayaran military ambitions, leading him into space, where he is enormously successful in his mercenary admiral's role, which in turn enables him to advance in his much more humble career in the Barrayaran military. This plot repetition is something that Bujold avoided thereafter.

After these successes, Bujold finally turned to the completion of the story she had begun in her very first novel, the story that was to end in the birth of Miles Vorkosigan. *Barrayar* (1991) begins just one day after the events of *Shards of Honor*: Aral is the target of two assassination attempts, one of which is by a soltoxin grenade lobbed into the Vorkosigan bedroom. The soltoxin damages Cordelia's unborn baby; the fetus has to be transferred to a uterine replicator for treatment. Soon afterward, a full-scale rebellion against Aral's regency is launched by Count Vordarian. Cordelia, Aral's father (Piotr), and Bothari hide the infant emperor, but Vordarian takes the uterine replicator that holds Cordelia's baby. She launches a rescue mission in the capital and recovers the uterine replicator. The end of the novel shows the five-year-old Miles—severely disabled yet totally intrepid and already as manipulative as he is to be as an adult—beginning to forge a relationship with his skeptical grandfather, Piotr.

Shards of Honor and *Barrayar*, originally conceived as one novel but published as two, are now widely available as an omnibus, *Cordelia's Honor* (first published in that form in 1996). The passion of parenthood is a major theme in the book. Bujold has described *Barrayar* as being "about the price of becoming a parent, particularly but not exclusively a mother."[27] Cordelia is the focus, of course, and the climax shows how she is transformed into someone who risks her life and her principles to save her child. Her rescue mission to find the uterine replicator results in the capture of herself and Bothari by the rebels. She is able to give the emperor's mother, who had thrown in her lot with Vordarian, the information that her son is still alive. In response the princess physically assaults Vordarian, but she is killed in the mêlée. Cordelia, who had so often condemned the primitive barbarity of Barrayarans, orders Bothari to behead Vordarian: it comes as much a shock to her (and to Vordarian) as it does to readers (although they ought to recall that in *Shards of Honor* she waterboards a fellow Betan). Cordelia returns to tip the severed head out of its shopping bag onto the table at which Aral and the loyal counts were sitting. "Aral was perfect . . . 'But of course,' breathed Aral, 'Every Vor lady goes to the capital to shop'" (CH 563).

Cordelia is far from the only parent in the book, however. Princess Kareen dies for her little son Gregor; Aral severs his relations with his father for the sake of his son. Other parents in the book include Padma and Alys Vorpatril, whose son Ivan is born very shortly after the father Padma is killed by one of Vordarian's rebels. But among the stories of parenthood, "most strangely and SFnally," as Bujold puts it, is the story of Bothari and the uterine replicator containing his daughter Elena's fetus. Bothari's death, some seventeen years later (in *The Warrior's Apprentice*) reads rather differently depending on whether one encounters the books in publication order or in order of internal chronology. Bothari becomes much more real as a personality in *Barrayar*, and it is his role as a parent that humanizes him, both in the fictional world and in the mind of the reader.

Barrayar won Bujold her second Hugo for Best Novel. It is a much more mature novel than its predecessors. *Shards of Honor, The Warrior's Apprentice,* and *The Vor Game* all suffered from being rather poorly structured, with breaks in the action that disturb the narrative flow, and with the action sequences rather too frenetic and superficial. *Barrayar* and the books that follow all have more carefully constructed plots, and with a much more effective buildup to a satisfying conclusion. Bujold was working hard at her craft. Or, as Walton put it, "*Barrayar* is where the Vorkosigan books stopped being really good and lots of fun and became brilliant."[28] The fact that Bujold took a break from writing science fiction after *Barrayar* in order to write her first fantasy novel (which was her first book to have first publication as a hardcover) may be an indication that she was contemplating the future directions of her writing career.

Mirror Dance was published in spring 1994, two-and-a-half years after *Barrayar*. It is the book that develops the potential created in *Brothers in Arms* with the introduction of Miles's clone brother Mark, and it draws on the glimpse of Jackson's Whole that we had in "Labyrinth." *Mirror Dance*, Bujold notes, is Mark's book. Mark, masquerading as his clone brother Miles, leads a Dendarii raid on a clone crèche on Jackson's Whole, where clones are raised to be new bodies for elderly plutocrats. Mark mismanages the raid, and Miles, attempting to rescue him, is killed. The cryo-chamber into which his body was placed is lost. Mark becomes the point-of-view character for most of the book, and is thus given a chance to develop his own personality. In order to allow Mark to develop, "it was also necessary to ruthlessly suppress Miles, which proved not without its satisfactions, and fruitful consequences" (VC 17). But it is also, as ever, Miles's book. Miles is indeed suppressed: he dies but is then resurrected. It is a turning point in his life, in that he is never able to take up his old life as before and is forced to renew himself. One thinks of Gandalf's death in the Mines of Moria and his subsequent resurrection as the White Wizard, and one does not have to be a medieval biblical exegete to see the deliberate parallels with the life of Christ. *Mirror Dance* is a much bleaker book than its predecessors and provides its readers with a number of visceral shocks. Nothing could be more shocking in a space opera saga about a genius hero than to read about that hero's death; and all the time you are reading it for the first time you are thinking, "Can Bujold do this to her readers? Can she kill off her hero?"—and getting the disturbing answer: "Yes."

A much more joyous and equally emotional element is Mark's discovery of his family. He is fully accepted by Aral and Cordelia, and he forges a new identity for himself: no longer trying to imitate Miles but trying instead to become as different from him as possible. Some of the most moving parts of the book come as Mark learns to accept Aral and Cordelia as parents. While walking with Mark in the forest, Aral has a heart attack; it is a potential crisis, as the other characters know that Mark had been trained as Aral's assassin. Aral survives: thus Bujold, who has described this passage as her rewriting of her own father's last heart attack, can "make it come out right."[29] Mark celebrates his new family and tries to expunge his own shame and guilt by going off to rescue Miles from the medical facility on Jackson's Whole, where Miles has been resuscitated—but only after Mark has been captured and tortured by Baron Ryoval. The torture irrevocably changes Mark's personality, or, one might say in positive terms, expunges his old personality by an overlay of new psychoses. Mark can finally start a new life: the novel ends with Miles saying to him "Welcome to the beginning" (MD 560).

It is perhaps not surprising that after writing this emotional rollercoaster, Bujold turns for light relief back to Miles's youth. Miles is twenty at the time of the events of *The Vor Game* (though, luckily, his medical problems made him look much older, or he could hardly have masqueraded as an admiral). Two years later, he and his cousin Ivan Vorpatril are sent to represent Barrayar at the funeral of the Cetagandan empress Lisbet Degtiar. *Cetaganda* (1996) is couched in the form of a detective story, with Miles, inevitably, as the detective (a role he had already taken up in "The Mountains of Mourning"). What was the strange object brought by a Cetagandan onto their spaceship as it docked? Why does Lord Yenaro twice try to kill Miles? Why is the body of the person who had held that strange object found brutally murdered next to the funeral dais of the late empress? Miles ends by uncovering an internal Cetagandan conspiracy, saving the Cetagandan Empire and winning the gratitude of the Cetagandan emperor—all things viewed with distinct suspicion by those in Barrayar who see Cetagandans as their natural enemy.

By this stage Bujold had clearly recognized the problems of writing the books out of sequence. Miles learns a great deal about Cetaganda on this mission; but this is not knowledge that he uses in any way in books that are later in terms of their internal chronology. She does take the opportunity to retrofit the narrative of *Cetaganda* into her sequence, however. While on Cetaganda, Miles had overheard the empress-designate Lisbet Degtiar giving permission to a certain Ghem-Colonel Millisor to draw on Cetagandan funds to pursue something or someone called Terran-C. Thus is set up the course of action that had been described in *Ethan of Athos*, published ten years earlier. In turn, *Cetaganda* seems to be setting Miles up for a future career that is, in his own lifespan, some eight years in his future, but which Bujold was about to introduce him to in her next novel: a life as an investigator.

Memory (1996) marks changes in the lives of several characters. Gregor gets betrothed to Laisa, a Komarran heiress; Illyan retires and starts going out with Ivan Vorpatril's widowed mother, Alys; Miles proposes to Elli again, and, having been refused, makes her the admiral of the Dendarii fleet; his double life as Lord Vorkosigan and Admiral Naismith is over, but he finds a new career. That summary does not capture the emotional depth of this novel, however. Bujold, as usual, does the worst possible thing she can imagine to both Miles and Illyan: she ends their careers. In both cases it is a result of mental problems, which mirror each other strangely. Miles has been having epileptic seizures since his "death" in *Mirror Dance*; he is dismissed from the service as a consequence of concealing them from his superiors. Illyan, who has a memory chip installed and is noted for his perfect recall, starts losing his memory. Miles turns detective, as he did in *Cetaganda*, believing that Illyan's chip has been tampered with. To get around the fact that Miles has no official status any longer, Gregor makes him an imperial auditor, one of nine such investigators and troubleshooters in the empire with almost unlimited powers of investigation (yet who have not hitherto been mentioned in the books). His problem of what to do after Naismith is solved; and so is the crime.

Bujold has said that at least since *Brothers in Arms* (and the appearance of Mark) she knew that "Miles's eventual destiny was to reassemble himself whole, sometime before age forty" (VC 19). She also says: "The epilepsy is surely a metaphor for something in Miles's life; that his handicap has mutated from something external to something internal as he matures surely has significance, and if I ever figure out what it is, I'll let you know" (VC 19). One element of autobiographical background to this story of Simon Illyan's failing memory is Bujold's own experience with the mother of her sister-in-law Trudie, whose Alzheimer's condition seemed so "boundlessly horrific," in Bujold's words. Some of the passages relating to Illyan's loss of memory are almost unbearably poignant, among the most moving scenes in the Bujold saga. He was a secondary character before, a provider of sarcasm at Miles's expense. Now he becomes someone who seems as close and dear to the reader as he is to Miles. By the end of the novel Illyan is healed, sort of; but not Trudie, who died shortly before the book was published. There is thus a very grim side to this book, and, at the same time, a liberation. Once Illyan is healed, he can live the kind of normal life denied to him for years; once Miles is dismissed from the service, he can get rid of the millstone of Naismith, which has distracted him from finding his own life. In other hands the story might have been written in such a way that Miles's dismissal from ImpSec would be seen as an error made by a disturbed Illyan, and Miles would triumphantly return after his unjust dismissal. (It is a pattern followed in the career of David Weber's Honor Harrington.) But the dismissal is perfectly just, and Miles knows that it is so. Miles's military career is over. The willingness with which Bujold forces Miles to suffer such reverses and hence to change and to develop is at the core of the series' success.

There is a sense, as Jo Walton notes, that *Memory* is the obvious end to the Vorkosigan books. It is the conclusion, "the capstone," to everything that has gone before. "*Memory* is a climax for the whole series so far, and I think if it had ended there, there would have been a feeling of rightness, a satisfaction, about that." More pertinently, perhaps, she adds "It is also my opinion that *Memory* is the point where the series stopped getting better. The other three books, while they're a new direction for the series, while they're never repetitive or just more-of-the-same, are no better than *Memory*."[30] There is certainly nothing (yet) that is as powerful as *Memory*; but the four subsequent books have their strengths, and the case can be made that, in terms of craft and skill, *A Civil Campaign* is a better book. It, too, may be seen as a kind of ending (and the fact that after its publication Bujold began planning and writing her Chalion trilogy may suggest that Bujold had that feeling too). But, as Walton says, the books that follow *Memory* are different books, and some relaxation after the intensity of *Mirror Dance* and *Memory* may be no bad thing.

The two books that immediately follow *Memory* have been described as a pair by Bujold: "*Komarr* is the romantic drama, *A Civil Campaign* the romantic comedy."[31] In *Komarr* (1998) Miles is sent to Komarr as imperial auditor to investigate a case of possible sabotage to the mirror array, which is helping to terraform the inhospitable planet, that is, to engineer its atmosphere and biosphere to make it habitable for humans. He meets Ekaterin Vorsoisson, the niece of a fellow auditor, who is in an unhappy marriage; she has a son called Nikolai (Nikki). Miles uncovers a plot to destroy Barrayar's sole wormhole link, threatening the return of Barrayar's Age of Isolation. Ekaterin, who appears to be channeling Cordelia at her boldest, helps foil the plot, and Miles determines to woo her and marry her.

Komarr alternates focalization between Miles and Ekaterin: as Bujold says, "The romance allowed me to put the two halves of human experience back together, even if not in one person."[32] It also allowed her to get back to some real science-fictional engineering: for research on this book she used Martyn J. Fogg's *Terraforming: Engineering Planetary Environments* (Warrendale, Pa.: Society of Automotive Engineers, 1995). Bujold's late father inspired her with the character of Professor Vorthys, and memories of reading in her father's library, such as on the investigation of engineering accidents and failures, also formed part of the background. The novel was provisionally called *Ekaterin*, but *Komarr* fitted better into the series as a whole, which already had two titles that were planetary names (*Barrayar* and *Cetaganda*).[33] Komarr is one of several planets that are being terraformed, although we have more details of the processes involved in this novel; as the Australian critic Sylvia Kelso has pointed out (thinking no doubt of the sad history of Australian ecology), "terraforming is an unquestioned part of heroic struggles for colonial survival, with no whisper of doubt that the colonists may and can erase an unfriendly ecology for their own benefit."[34] The book is about terraforming; but it is also about terrorism. One wonders if the book would have been different if written after 9/11. The terrorists (or freedom fighters) are not psychotic, as was our previous Komarran terrorist, Ser Galen (in *Brothers in Arms*). They are somewhat amateurish as plotters, but they are scientists, who prepare carefully and who have a plan that, if it had worked, would have had a devastating effect on Barrayar (yet with relatively few fatalities). One of Bujold's sympathetic characters is Dr. Riva, who works out what the terrorists are going to do but is reluctant to tell ImpSec because she is in favor of freeing Komarr from Barrayar. The political and ethical complexities are interesting and, as usual, are wrapped up with much else: the revelation that Ekaterin's son Nikki has inherited a genetic problem from his father, which links the book with all the previous discussion about mutants on Barrayar; the detective work; and, of course, the growing attraction between Miles and Ekaterin.

A Civil Campaign (1999) is the first Vorkosigan story than can in no sensible way be described as "space opera"; all the action takes place on a planet's surface and involves political intrigue and romance rather than military conflict. The book is also the only Bujold novel to bear a subtitle, which helps to distance it from anything space-operatic: *A Comedy of Biology and Manners*. Of *A Civil Campaign* Bujold wrote, "I'd been dying to write a Barrayaran Regency romance ever since I'd realized I'd given Barrayar a regency period."[35] (Ironically, of course, by this stage Aral's regency is long over.) The novels of Georgette Heyer, the queen of regency romance (and supplier of Bujold's favorite comfort reading), were a significant inspiration, but others are announced in the dedication of the book: "for Jane, Charlotte, Georgette and Dorothy," acknowledging Austen, Brontë, and Sayers as well as Heyer. The book was provisionally called *ImpWed*; Bujold could not think of an appropriate title. *Rules of Engagement*, suggested by Mike Ford, sounded perfect until Bujold discovered that Baen was going to publish a novel of that name by Elizabeth Moon. There was no other book called *A Civil Campaign*, however, and it had the advantage of recalling Georgette Heyer's *A Civil Contract* (1961) (though the plots of the two novels have nothing in common). *A Civil Campaign* is a very apt title for a book in which Miles plans his courtship as if it is a military campaign, and in which he finds what an extremely inept idea this is. The actual literary connections, however, are more with Jane and Dorothy than with Georgette. Bujold acknowledges that Miles's abrupt and inappropriate marriage proposal, and his subsequent letter, owe much to Mr. Darcy in *Pride and Prejudice*. The connections with the courtship of Lord Peter Wimsey and Harriet Vane are even closer. The three-novel structure of meeting (*Strong Poison*; *Komarr*), proposal (*Gaudy Night*; *A Civil Campaign*), and postmarital business (*Busman's Honeymoon*; *Diplomatic Immunity*) are mirrored in the two series, and the characters of Wimsey and Vane are closer than one might think at first sight to Miles and Ekaterin. Physically, Miles and Wimsey are as different as it is possible to be (Wimsey is a champion cricketer, after all). But, as John Lennard puts it:

> Both are aristocratic chatterboxes, nervous, witty, and war-wounded imperial soldier-diplomats and investigators, born of tradition to face a damaging modernity, who in the end find happiness in marriage to injured, inhibited, and sharply intelligent women whom they nurture.[36]

Jane Eyre is there as well; and Shakespeare. Nikohl and Lennard's *Reader's Companion* to the book explores all these connections in great detail, illustrated with numerous comments from Bujold herself, drawn from her online mailing list.

A Civil Campaign is a much more complex novel than anything Bujold had attempted before, thanks in part to the multiple viewpoints: we witness the events alongside (in order) Miles, Kareen Koudelka, Ekaterin, Mark, and Ivan. But the complexity also arises from the way in which Bujold weaves various plots together: the story of Miles's appallingly ill-conceived bid to prepare Ekaterin to accept a marriage proposal (not that long after the death of her husband); the plot against Miles (accusing him of securing the removal of Ekaterin's husband); Mark's bid to establish butter-bug vomit as a commercially viable foodstuff; the various political issues that run through the book (three separate cases involving Donna/Dono Vorrutyer, René Vorbrettan, and Lord Vormuir). Jo Walton points out how the book contrasts dramatically with its predecessor in one significant way:[37] in *Komarr* Miles is the only character whom we have met before, but in *A Civil Campaign* almost every Barrayaran we have ever met makes an appearance, and Barrayaran society itself is given a depth and a reality that it has never had before.

Butter bugs were inserted when the editor, after reading over the early chapters, thought that the book was simply not science-fictional enough. Butter bugs play an important part in the set piece of Miles's totally disastrous dinner party, which is so painfully embarrassing that chapter 9 is difficult to reread. The production of food via genetic modification is certainly topical enough, and the whole enterprise adds a good deal to the humor of the book. Bujold herself, remembering her earlier days as a biology major (her adviser was an expert in insect toxicology), clearly enjoyed writing this part of the book. She has remarked, online, that one feminist critic saw the butter bugs as a symbol for oppressed womanhood (kept just for breeding). Quite the opposite is the case, as Bujold commented acerbically: they symbolize fertility, and sex, which is "really" what this book is about. "You have to come see my butter bugs [. . .] Open your mouth and close your eyes, and you will get a big surprise [. . .] *Does he really want me to touch that thing?*" are all sentences from the book that carry sexual innuendo. Bujold "had to point out [to the unnamed critic] that an ugly alien creature that, when petted, barfs a dubious thick white liquid into one's hand, but at the same time, if one can get past the biological squick factor, promises a greatly enhanced future life, is not a symbol of *female* anything. Everyone reads through their own filters, it seems."[38] I shall leave to others a full Freudian analysis of the public appearance of large numbers of uncontrollable penises at the climax of the novel: not to mention the bug butter fight . . .

"Winterfair Gifts" (2004), a direct sequel to *A Civil Campaign*, is a novella that has Armsman Roic as the focalizing character rather than the usual Miles. Roic is still smarting from the humiliation described in *A Civil Campaign* (being discovered by Lord Vorkosigan half-naked and smeared in bug butter—all in perfect innocence). He is assigned to look after Sergeant Taura, a guest at the wedding of Miles and Ekaterin, as well as play his part in the security of

Vorkosigan House. The novella was published in a volume of sf and fantasy romances and has its own bittersweet romance, between Roic and Taura, who has not long to live. It has pleased Bujold's fans by the introduction of many previous characters: after all, who wouldn't want to go to Miles's wedding? But it has, yet again, a mystery plot, which gives it shape and suspense, and it adds to our understanding of Barrayaran society by providing as our focalizer, for the first time, a man who is not a Vor aristocrat.[39] Roic is working-class, a provincial, feeling slightly humiliated because he has a background as a policeman and not a soldier like most armsmen: a new and refreshing voice, after our prolonged exposure to the aristocracy.

The action of *Diplomatic Immunity* (2001) takes place more than a year later; the first two babies of Miles and Ekaterin's are incubating in a uterine replicator. Miles is sent as imperial auditor to sort out a problem on Graf Station (named after Leo Graf, hero of *Falling Free*) in the area known as Quaddiespace. Like *Cetaganda*, *Diplomatic Immunity* is constructed as a detective story. Lieutenant Solian (a Barrayaran officer, but Komarran by birth) is missing, and a pool of his blood is found in a cargo bay: has he been murdered, and if so, by whom? Who tries to kill Miles, and why? Miles finally unravels the most significant of the various tangles and discovers that a Cetagandan neuter called Ker Dubauer (the third time that Bujold has used that surname) has stolen a shipload of Cetagandan fetuses, planning to set up its own Cetagandan colony. With the spirited help of Ekaterin, Miles manages as usual to save the day; both of them are honoured by the Cetagandans.

The quaddies were introduced in Bujold's fourth novel, *Falling Free*, and we meet two other old friends of Miles's: his former shipmate Bel Thorne and the quaddie Nicol, whom we (and Bel) first meet in the story "Labyrinth." Bujold saw the opportunity of Miles's newfound freedom as imperial auditor to look at the colony that was founded thanks to Leo Graf's engineered escape at the end of *Falling Free*. The imaginative creation of a society of people engineered for life in zero gravity is wonderfully symbolized in chapter 6 by the detailed description of a free-fall ballet. The book was also an opportunity to revisit Bel Thorne, who had not been seen since the end of *Mirror Dance*; indeed, in *Diplomatic Immunity* the hermaphrodite Bel played a larger role than it had in the early Admiral Naismith novels. Its sexuality, which veered alarmingly (Miles, at least, was alarmed) between male and female in the Naismith years, had settled down into an emphasis on the male, thanks to Bel's involvement with the very feminine Nicol.

CryoBurn (2010) was published after a nine-year gap in books about the Vorkosigans. In the scramble following Jim Baen's death in 2006, editor Toni Weisskopf asked Bujold to write another Miles book, and Bujold agreed, but only after she had finished her four-volume Sharing Knife sequence. In *Cryo-Burn* Miles is sent by the emperor to the planet Kibou-daini ("New Hope"), ostensibly to attend a conference on cryonics but in reality in order to investigate the situation on that planet. One of several large cryonics corporations that make their money from freezing the ill and dying for future resuscitation is planning to open up a branch on Komarr. Miles is kidnapped at the conference, along with Roic and Raven (a specialist from the Durona family: see *Memory*). He manages to escape, and, while recovering from his ordeal, he is taken under the protection of Jin Sato, a young boy who is living in an illegal cryonics facility. Miles shares focalization with both Roic and Jin. Jin and his sister Mina are very plausible young children, and very cute: arguably (as noted in a review by Kelly Jennings in *Strange Horizons*), this helps to give what could have been—or *should* have been—a dark novel, dealing for almost the first time in Bujold's work with a society with serious structural problems and a great deal of hopeless poverty, a much lighter tone.[40] Even so, the darkness creeps in, when, for instance, we see Miles blissfully unaware of the effect of his enormous wealth and power on members of an impoverished community. Miles shows to Jin and Mina photographs of his four children, their ponies, and their large mansion in the country.

> What was that line of Uncle Hikaru's? *Them what has, gets.*
>
> And those that didn't have, didn't get, Jin supposed, was the unspoken half of that lesson. He looked at those other children, and at Miles-san, so obviously pleased and proud, and didn't doubt that Mina probably felt like crying. His own throat was tight with envy and ridiculous anger (Cry 227).

The two children do end up better off than they were at the beginning: Miles finds the hidden and frozen body of their mother, revives her, and reunites her to her children. But he leaves Kibou-daini with only hints that some sort of justice might be brought to the planet. Mark, who has a higher sense of injustice than Miles when it comes to Jacksonian clones, is even more oblivious than Miles to that fate of those who simply cannot afford to have themselves frozen:

> Medtech Tanaka said, "But what about the poor?"
> Lord Mark gave her a blank look. "What about 'em?" (Cry 266).

Miles has just done what his emperor wants. He does indeed unravel the plot that he was sent to deal with, and another one in addition. (Had he gone home after solving the task the Emperor had set him, he might have seen his father again, as Miles noted.) The cryonics corporations virtually run the planet, thanks to their exploitation of the laws. Those who are frozen are not legally dead: their heirs cannot inherit, but their votes can still count—and their votes are held, in proxy, by the corporations that froze them. They have gradually taken over the planet, and they have the long-term plan to do the same on Komarr. But Miles also uncovers a much more immediate plot: to stifle knowledge that an unspecified number of people have been frozen using a defective chemical preparation, meaning that they have really died and cannot be resurrected, thus undermining (to an unknown extent) the voting system that keeps the cryonics corporations in power. But Miles has no plan to exploit this situation. He recognizes (Cry 350) that the planetary society might melt down, but he tells himself that clearing up the mess is the job for the consul (318): *"Better him than me."*

At the very end Colonel Vorventa arrives, wearing formal uniform, and delivers to Miles the devastating last three words of the narrative proper: "Count Vorkosigan, sir?" (334). The reader thus knows that Count Vorkosigan—the Aral who has been with us, if often in the background, since the very first chapter of *Shards of Honor*—has died, and Miles has inherited the title. The book ends with five drabbles (stories exactly one hundred words long) detailing the reactions of the five people closest to Count Aral Vorkosigan: Mark, Miles, Cordelia, Ivan, and Gregor.

Aral Vorkosigan has been a powerful stabilizing force in all the Vorkosigan novels and in Miles's own life. If Bujold chooses to write a Vorkosigan novel set after Aral's death, she will be writing about a very different Barrayar. This is certainly consonant with the way she has developed the series. Miles has so far had three careers. Two of them he held simultaneously, combining the careers of military officer attached to Imperial Security with his role as

Admiral Naismith of the Dendarii Mercenaries; soon after those two careers collapsed, at the beginning of *Memory*, he took up the role of imperial auditor, which gave him almost as much freedom to explore new environments and new problems as he had when he was Vorkosigan/Naismith. Now that he is count the horizons might seem to have shrunk, since he will have political duties within the empire, duties in his district, as well as continuing duties to his family and heirs. However, this is not inevitable; after all, Count Aral Vorkosigan could desert his district for years at a time when he was viceroy on Sergyar (Cry 211).

The most recent Vorkosigan novel, *Captain Vorpatril's Alliance* (2012), breaks the patterns of recent novels by not immediately following on from the action of the previous one. It cannot do so, really, without revealing the change that will come to Miles and perhaps to all those close to him after Aral's death. As a consequence, the book is set after the events of *Diplomatic Immunity* and before those of *CryoBurn*. The book is structured as a romance: near the beginning Ivan Vorpatril finds himself in a position where he has to get married, in a purely temporary manner, to Tej, a young woman he is trying to rescue from a dangerous situation, and the rest of the novel is about how they slowly come to realize that they actually like being married to each other. It is close in structure to Georgette Heyer's *Cotillion* (1953), in which hero Freddie Standen—good-looking but by reputation dim, eventually proving himself resourceful and extremely kind—bears a close resemblance to the Ivan encountered in this novel. Freddie agrees to marry the somewhat flighty Kitty Charing to get her out of an awkward situation, on the understanding that they will go their own ways as soon as possible; in the end, of course, he finds that he rather enjoys being married to her. Freddie and Kitty go through precisely the same dance (a cotillion is a country dance) that Ivan and Tej experience here.

Ivan is in a brief posting on Komarr when Tej comes into his life, together with her half-sister Rish. They are from a displaced House on Jackson's Whole; they have lost the rest of their family, which includes a dancing troupe, the Jewels, to which Rish belongs. The Jewels are genetically engineered so that each resembles in color the jewel they are named after—Rish's full name is Lapis Lazuli. After having married Tej, Ivan is able to take her off Komarr and away from those who are chasing her (including Komarr's police). On Barrayar he is faced with the much more difficult task of explaining his new marital state to his mother and to the Vorkosigans. The situation gets more chaotic when the rest of Tej's family turns out to be alive after all. Her formidable grandmother is Cetagandan and old enough to remember where the departing Cetagandan occupation force had hidden its treasures years earlier. The family conspires to recover this treasure (unfortunately left in underground tunnels adjacent to ImpSec HQ), and both Ivan and Simon Illyan get embroiled in the plot. The treasure is recovered, the family is deported back to Jackson's Whole to rebuild their House and serve as allies of Barrayar, and Ivan and Tej get sent off to Illa by Gregor. "Where the hell is Illa?" Ivan asks. It turns out to be a distant planet, and Ivan is military attaché at the consulate: the start of what might be a distinguished diplomatic career as well as a blissful marriage.

The book has its farcical elements, and although Ivan distinguishes himself as an action hero, it is primarily a romance, or a comedy of manners, which appeals particularly to those many Bujold fans who have wanted her to write more about Miles's much-put-upon cousin, Ivan. In the preceding novels we have learned to see Ivan as a lazy, unambitious, womanizing idiot; he has long been the bane of his commanding officers' lives, in part because he allows himself to be sucked into Miles's madcap (and frequently insubordinate) schemes. But now, having largely escaped Miles's shadow, he flourishes, showing dash and initiative. His commanding officer values him, too, for a perfectly rational reason: his social and political awareness (CVA 230). It was hardly surprising that Ivan had learned something from his supremely astute mother the Lady Alys Vorpatril; thinking back from this to earlier novels, one can see that this had been part of Bujold's view of Ivan for a long time. And something else about Ivan is also revealed, which, in retrospect, might seem obvious: "What I like best about you, Ivan Xav, is that you're *nice*. And you make me laugh" (CVA 363). A crucial part of the book is to reveal the Ivan who emerges once he is removed from his cousin's shadow.

Having now written her "Ivan Vorpatril novel," it may be that, if Bujold wishes to continue working in the Vorkosigan Universe, a book about Lord *Mark* Vorkosigan is to be the way forward, rather than beginning to explore the life of Count Miles Vorkosigan. For the moment, however, we have to accept that the sequence may be finished.

CHaPTeR 3

FANTASY WORLDS

Although the series in which this book is published is about science fiction, it is impossible to understand Bujold without looking at her fantasy too: there is the standalone novel *The Spirit Ring*, the Chalion trilogy, and the four books of the Sharing Knife sequence. Since the turn of the millennium Bujold has produced seven fantasy novels and just three science fiction novels. Bujold is not, of course, alone in being a science fiction writer who has turned to fantasy: some of the best known American fantasy writers in the field—Fritz Leiber, Andre Norton, Poul Anderson, Orson Scott Card, and many others—started as science fiction writers. Sometimes what these writers bring to fantasy is a science-fictional approach to world building. If there are systems of magic, for instance, they tend to be imagined as if they were scientific laws operating in a different universe, with a logic about them that makes using reason and deduction as important for the fantasy protagonists as it is for any characters in a science fiction novel. As we shall see, Bujold is no exception to this: her fantasy novels revolve around one major "What if?" from which the rest of the novel proceeds.

Her first fantasy novel—and indeed her first hardback publication—was *The Spirit Ring* (1992), inspired by Agricola's treatise on metallurgy and the autobiography of Benvenuto Cellini, both written in the mid-sixteenth century. The flavor of the story is more fifteenth century than sixteenth, however, and the two real historical figures who are mentioned, including Lorenzo de' Medici, both flourished in the later fifteenth century. This is a world in which magic works and in which Fiametta's father Prospero Beneforte is a noted magician (like his namesake in *The Tempest*) and metallurgist. The heroine, Fiametta, is his daughter, and her magical gift (as her name, Italian for "Little Flame," implies) is pyrokinesis.[1]

The opening scene gives much of the background. We see Fiametta acting as an apprentice goldsmith to her father and hiding from him the fact that she is experimenting with magic other than her allowed fire spell: she is putting a love spell on the gold ring she is making. She brings a gold saltcellar from her father's chest to show the messengers from the Duke of Montefoglia: it is commissioned for the marriage of the duke's daughter to Lord Ferrante of Losimo. Early in the book, therefore, we are alerted to Benvenuto Cellini as an inspiration: Cellini's saltcellar, completed in 1543, is in the Kunsthistorisches Museum in Vienna and is very like Beneforte's, except that Beneforte's saltcellar provides salt that nullifies poison and dispenses pepper that compels truth. One of the duke's messengers is a Swiss mercenary, Uri Ochs, whom Beneforte is using as a model for his statue of Perseus holding the head of Medusa: a reminiscence of Cellini's *Perseus*, which has stood in the Piazza della Signoria in Florence since 1554. Fiametta fancies Uri, and she gives him the gold ring, knowing that if he puts it on he would reveal himself to be her true love (as she hopes). He fails to do so.

The book is written in third-person limited subjective mode, and the chapters are divided equally between the viewpoints of Fiametta herself and of Thur Ochs, Uri's brother. He is a Swiss miner, down on his luck, who eagerly accepts an invitation to go south and become Beneforte's assistant. In the meantime, however, Lord Ferrante has staged a coup against the Duke of Montefoglia. The duke and Uri are both killed, and Fiametta's father dies not long afterward. When Thur Ochs meets Fiametta and rescues her from an innkeeper who wants to steal her gold ring, he puts on the ring himself, and it fits. The reader knows that, whatever vicissitudes occur, the two are fated to be together at the end of the novel. The bulk of the narrative concerns the efforts of Thur, Fiametta, and others to recover Montefoglia for its citizens. There are some ingenious elements introduced by Bujold, which draw this novel out of the ordinary. Thur is sent into the castle at Montefoglia as a spy, posing as a foundry master looking for work, carrying little parchment tambourines that resonate with their twins in the abbey: they are the magical equivalent of bugging devices. He discovers the bodies of Beneforte and his own brother Uri, preserved by magic and salt, who are clearly going to be used in a magical ritual, perhaps, as Fiametta fears, forcing her father's spirit into a spirit-ring. Thur is captured by Nicolo Vitelli, Ferrante's cunning and unscrupulous adviser, whose real name is Jacopo Sprenger, who in both the real and fictional world was co-author of the notorious *Malleus Maleficarum*, the witchfinder's handbook, printed (in our world) in 1487. The denouement involves Fiametta's managing the animation of Beneforte's statue of Perseus by the ghost of Uri Ochs: the huge bronze warrior (a golem of sorts) proves a match for Ferrante and Vitelli / Sprenger. Evil is discomfited, order restored, and Thur and Fiametta happily go through with the long-anticipated wedding ceremony.

Renaissance Italy as a venue for fantasy had been attempted before and since *The Spirit Ring*. R. A. Macavoy's Damiano series (*Damiano* [1983], *Damiano's Lute* [1984], and *Raphael* [1984]), about the adventures of a young alchemist and lutenist, is the most obvious example; but there are also Michaela Roessner's *The Stars Dispose* (1998) and *The Stars Compel* (1999), where the only alchemy on view is culinary in nature, and Midori Snyder's *The Innamorati* (1998), which took its cue from the Commedia dell'Arte. K. J. Parker's Fencer trilogy is also set in a late medieval or Renaissance world: *Colours in the Steel* (1998), which focuses on swordmaking, *The Belly of the Bow* (1999) centering on the technology of archery; and *The Proof House* (2000) on the making of armor. Every one of these novels, it may be noted, shares with Bujold's book an interest in exploring a particular craft or skill. Although *The Spirit Ring* is a fast-paced adventure story with a clear plot and a number of imaginative ideas, one of its attractions for readers is surely the insight it offers into the connected crafts of sculpture and metallurgy. The practical aspects of preindustrial living clearly do have an interest for fantasy readers: *The Spirit Ring* is the fantasy equivalent of *Falling Free*, in which, despite ourselves, we are drawn into the technology of welding. The books by Cellini and Agricola were found by Bujold on her father's shelves; welding, and hence metallurgy, was his métier, as we have seen.

Bujold's next fantasy venture was likewise modeled on fifteenth-century Europe, but very much more obliquely. Bujold had attended a university course in medieval Spanish history a few years before writing the series and there discovered a treasure trove of colorful characters and incidents that she was able to develop in her own way. In the Chalion trilogy (2001–2005) Chalion is a disorienting version of Castile, in the generation before a queen of Castille set about the unification of Spain through a marriage alliance. Our world is systematically distorted. The points of the compass have been reversed, for instance: the Roknari princedoms to the north correspond to the Muslims of the south of the Iberian peninsula (before 1492), with elements of Viking, while Darthaca in the south corresponds to France. A map on Bujold's official website makes the whole geographical slippage very clear.[2] To disorient us further, there are some obvious late-medieval European titles that are not "translated" into English. Thus, a monarch is a *roya* and not a king; his wife is the *royina*, and their son and daughter are the *royse* and the *royesse*. Spanish history supplied real historical characters to inspire some of the fictional ones. Ferdinand and Isabella are mirrored by Bergon of Ibra (Aragon) and Iselle of Chalion (Castile). Iselle's father Ias has a parallel with King Juan II of Castile; Juan's favorite Alvaro de Luna inspired Arvol dy Lutez; and the sad figure of Juana la Loca, Joanna the Mad, could be the model for either Ista or Cattilara (the latter in *Paladin of Souls*). The world seems carefully and meticulously planned, unlike the Vorkosigan universe, although Bujold maintains to me that it was actually stolen wholesale, "which saves a lot of steps."

With many fantasy novels, the way the author has developed a unique magical system is often the major point of interest; with Chalion, however, it is Bujold's imaginative theological system that sets it apart from its rivals. Chalion and its neighbors worship five gods who form a family: Father, Mother, Son, Daughter, and the Bastard. Bujold said in her talk at the 2004 Book Festival in the Library of Congress that there were intended to be five volumes in the Chalion series, one "dedicated" to each of the gods, although at the moment there are only three: *The Curse of Chalion* (2001), concerned above all with the Daughter; *Paladin of Souls* (2003), which is the Bastard's book; and *The Hallowed Hunt* (2005), which is the Son's.[3] The religion of Chalion and most of its neighbors is referred to as *Quintarian*; the Roknari, however, regard the Bastard as a demon and accept only the other four gods and are hence *Quadrene*.

The centrality of religion in Bujold's presentation of the world—the action of all three novels is directed at a crucial stage by the intervention of a god—is refreshingly different from the bulk of modern fantasy. Gods may appear occasionally in modern fantasy, though often in ironic or satiric guise (as in the wonderful Discworld novel *Small Gods* (1992), by Terry Pratchett). But much high fantasy seems to follow the lead of J. R. R. Tolkien himself who, although he declared *The Lord of the Rings* to be "a fundamentally religious and Catholic work," puzzled his readers by seeming to remove religion almost entirely from the life of his characters.[4] In the Vorkosigan books, religion as such is very rarely discussed, and when it does appear, it is not necessarily treated sympathetically: one might think that Bujold agreed with Emperor Ezar, who noted that theists were much more ruthless than atheists, and that he found atheism a comforting faith (CH 230, 235). In Chalion, however, as in medieval Europe, religion is omnipresent, and atheism would hardly seem a sane response to the world. Chalion has five gods, and Bujold's protagonists have direct encounters with them.

One can see orthodox Quintarianism in Chalion as a distortion of orthodox Trinitarian Christianity, which one might (incorrectly) regard as having three gods (Father, Son, and Holy Ghost). Instead of crossing themselves like traditional Christians, the Chalionese make the Sign of the Five, the thumb and first two fingers of the right hand briefly touching the forehead (dedicated to the Daughter), the mouth (the Bastard), the belly (the Mother), and the groin (the Father): the hand has the fingers closed, until it spread out over the heart (the Son). Just as Christianity has, typically, churches with a nave and two aisles, which might be interpreted as symbolizing the Trinity, so the Chalionese recreate their theology in stone, with their temples having four lobes, with one lobe dedicated to each of the four equal gods, with a separate building, behind the Mother's lobe, dedicated to the Bastard. (In the Weald, in *The Hallowed Hunt*, Quintarian buildings are five-sided.)

Quintarianism holds up a distorting mirror to the prevailing Trinitarianism of the Christian tradition, but in its details one may see a critique of traditional Christianity. The gods did not create the world; the world created them, and continues to do so, as souls flow out to join them. Divinity is not wholly male: there is a Mother and a Daughter as well as the familiar Father and Son. The largely characterless Holy Spirit of the Christian tradition is balanced by the Bastard, who is everything the Holy Spirit is not: the offspring of a demon, the patron of the outcast. There is no hell for the wicked in Quintarianism, merely a chaos, which sustains the demonic. The Chalionese gods do not see the material world as inferior or "fallen"; they are fascinated by the "stubbornness of matter." Nor can they intervene in the material world unless they are called upon to do so; thus, in a sense they depend on human agency rather than on any control of human beings, by threats or by "acts of God." They do reflect the material world, however. The four seasons are introduced by religious rituals that make it clear that the four gods each preside over one of the seasons. Near the beginning of *The Curse of Chalion* we witness the ceremony at the start of spring, where someone dressed as the Father of Winter leads a young woman dressed as the Daughter, in her capacity as the Lady of Spring, to the temple. The Bastard is in charge of what is regarded as out-of-season: bastards, orphans, homosexuals, natural disasters, and leap-year days. As befits his outsider status, he is a capricious joker, although not without a sense of real humor. When Ista says to his face, "Lord Bastard, you *bastard!*" he just grins (PS 170).

The three books of the Chalion sequence are linked rather than strictly linear and are immersive rather than quest fantasies: their characters are embedded in the world and their stories stem from the world rather than from an exploration of it. This allows Bujold to step away from character sequels and instead offer sequels of world events: what happens next in the world rather than what the character does next (authors such as Steve Cockayne, Diana Wynne Jones, China Miéville, and K. J. Parker use this form). The main character in Bujold's first novel is barely mentioned in the second. Although the events of the second novel follow on almost immediately from those of the first, the main character of the second is a previously marginal figure; the action of the third novel takes place apparently several hundreds of years earlier.

Although the stories are of the world, the Chalion novels themselves remain character driven, and the two characters who dominate the first two— Cazaril in *The Curse of Chalion* and Ista in *Paladin of Souls*—must rank as two of Bujold's best-conceived and attractive characters. Many Bujold fans (myself included), however dedicated they may be to the admiration of Miles Vorkosigan, rank one or the other of them as the best of all Bujold's novels.

Cazaril, who is the focalizer of *The Curse of Chalion* (2001), is first seen plodding wearily toward the castle of Valenda. The Dowager Provincara dy Baocia recognizes him to be a former page of the late Provincar: Lord Lupe dy Cazaril. It is only gradually that we learn his history: he was a career soldier in the endless wars against the Roknari, but, when the castle of Gotorget was ceded to the enemy, he was not ransomed along with the rest of the garrison's knights; he was instead sold to the Roknari corsairs as a galley slave. After eighteen months of appalling treatment he was freed. On reaching Valenda, his one desire is to be left in peace and to avoid confrontation with the man he believes has betrayed him: Dondo dy Jironal, the powerful brother of the most powerful man in Chalion, its chancellor, Martou dy Jironal. The Provincara makes Cazaril tutor to her young granddaughter, the Royesse Iselle, and her companion Betriz (ages sixteen and nineteen, respectively). When Iselle and her brother the Royse Teidez are summoned to the royal court at Cardegoss, Cazaril must accompany them, knowing he is bound to encounter Dondo dy Jironal.

Once at Cardegoss the Royse Teidez—heir to the royacy since the roya Orico, his half-brother, has so far failed to produce children—finds himself embroiled in politics, as are Iselle and Cazaril, in different ways. Cazaril becomes the victim of slander; Teidez's tutor is killed and replaced by one of Martou dy Jironal's creatures; and Orico is persuaded to give Iselle's hand in marriage, not to a foreign prince (as she expects) but to Dondo dy Jironal. Iselle is at the end of her tether, as is Cazaril. All he can think of to do, on the eve of the wedding, is to kill Dondo by death-magic: an act that, if successful, always results in the death of the magician as well as his target. Cazaril performs the ritual, lives, and finds out to his surprise that Dondo has indeed died through death-magic. Dondo's brother Martou is convinced that Cazaril was behind it, even though he is still alive. Cazaril discovers that two of the people present at the funeral—including Umegat, Orico's zookeeper—are glowing; more disturbing, he sees that members of the royal family also show an aura, but a dark, unpleasant one. He talks to Umegat, whom he discovers is a divine of the Bastard (a priest), and learns much from him. The royal family is subject to a curse (the eponymous curse of Chalion), which is perceptible only to those who have been marked by the gods as their chosen, the living saints: Umegat himself, and now Cazaril. The curse is multifaceted: it brings ill luck, bad counsel, failure, ill health, and early death. As for Cazaril, he has not only been given powers of perception (he finds the castle's ghosts really annoying), but, by a miracle of the Daughter, Cazaril's own body has become a prison for both Dondo's spirit and the demon who captured him at the point of death. Cazaril, in the last half of the volume, has a double task to fulfill: to rid the royal family of the curse and to rid himself of the internal presence of Dondo and the demon. A doctor believes his condition to be an inoperable and fatal tumor, but a reader of fanfic is likely to be reminded of the motif of male pregnancy.

Cazaril does not immediately tell anyone of what he has learned. Teidez, who has realized that Orico's weakness is not natural, is led by ill counsel to the belief that Orico's animals, and Umegat, have been a malignant force. He and his men kill the animals and severely wound Umegat; Orico, without the calming influence of the animals, collapses.[5] Cazaril tells Iselle and Betriz everything; but it is too late for Teidez, who has been scratched by a leopard as he tried to kill it and dies of sepsis. Iselle becomes the Heiress. Iselle decides that she needs allies and sends Cazaril to Ibra to try and arrange a marriage with Bergon, royse of Ibra, whom she had already earmarked as the most eligible Quintarian prince. Cazaril's quest for a marriage alliance is swift and successful, thanks to the discovery that the young royse had been the fellow galley slave whose life Cazaril had saved. The marriage takes place, promising an eventual union of the two kingdoms, but it does not end the curse; Iselle's black aura now surrounds Bergon of Ibra as well. The denouement comes rapidly: dy Jironal attacks the palace where the married couple were and thrusts his sword into Cazaril's belly. The demon escapes and consumes dy Jironal and is apparently neutralized by the Daughter, who makes her presence felt. Cazaril has now offered his life three times for the House of Chalion (on the galley, while saying the death spell, and in this moment); the Daughter offers Cazaril's life back. Cazaril loses his glowing aura; the black aura surrounding those of the royal family disappears; and Orico dies. Cazaril is briefly disturbed to find that he has been replaced as Iselle's secretary, only to discover that this is because he has been nominated as chancellor. The book ends with a touching meeting with the grateful Ista.

A summary like this, however long, does not begin to display the richness and variety of this book or the delight of some of the set scenes. Cazaril himself is one of the most sympathetic of all Bujold's characters, partly because of his palpable humanity and goodness (and, indeed, saintliness), but also because of his down-to-earth sense of humor. He has the habit, apparently picked up from Miles Vorkosigan, of describing himself in his thoughts in ironic terms and in the third person. He pictured himself in Iselle's inventory: "*Sec't'y-tutor, One ea. Gift from Grandmama. Aged thirty-five. Badly damaged in shipping. Value . . . ?*" (CC 63). When his friend Palli tries to suggest that Cazaril would be an ideal person to publicly discredit Chancellor Jironal because he is utterly indifferent to wealth, Cazaril contradicts him earnestly: "No, I'm not. [. . .] I just dress badly. I quite like wealth" (CC 267–68). In fact, we have already seen that he is impervious to bribery. Given his Spanish antecedents, it is not implausible to see Cazaril as an incarnation of Ignatius Loyola, a soldier turned unlikely saint. Cazaril, too, is a former soldier and perfectly capable of violence (not just at the urging of his internal demon). He has sexual desires and, as this is not a world that requires celibacy of its saints, marries the young Betriz; and he is no prude—at the end of the book he receives from another "saint" a collection of pilgrimage tales, some "very, ah, holy," and some "very lewd," clearly Chalion's version of Chaucer's *Canterbury Tales* (CC 439). But he is a saint because he is God-touched, the recipient of the Daughter's grace; and he always retains that modesty, restraint, and self-doubt, which endear him to the reader.

The stereotypical "hero" of a medievalist fantasy is, of course, male, young, athletic, and quite possibly muscular. The stereotype remains, even though it has been subverted countless times, not least by Tolkien himself, whose heroes are not Aragorn and Faramir but a fifty-year-old hobbit and his gardener. Cazaril, like Frodo, is middle-aged and a lover of peace (despite or because of his years as a warrior). But *The Curse of Chalion*'s sequel, *Paladin of Souls* (2003), subverts the hero stereotype even more successfully: its heroic protagonist is a middle-aged mother of two who for years had been dismissed as mad by most of Chalion. Ista is not mad, however; she is God-touched and under a curse, and there has been little to distinguish between her state and madness. After Cazaril has freed her family from "the curse of Chalion," she decides to leave the castle. Her main aim is to escape the endless surveillance of her stuffy attendants, but she is inspired to take the route of pilgrimage after meeting a three-times widow, herself on pilgrimage (transparently Chaucer's Wife of Bath). Her entourage includes the two dy Gura brothers (Ferda and Foix) who had accompanied Cazaril to Ibra in the previous book.

Ista's adventures start almost immediately. Foix dy Gura is possessed by a demon; Ista is convinced that she is being sent dreams by one of the gods. Ista is rescued from a group of Roknari raiders by Arhys dy Lutez, March of Porifors, the son of Arvol dy Lutez, the chancellor who had died in disgrace when Ista had been royina. As we had learned in *The Curse of Chalion*, dy Lutez, the lover of Ista's roya, had actually sacrificed himself in an attempt to lift the curse; as far as the world knew, he was disgraced because he had fallen in love with the royina Ista. There are mysteries: Why is it that Arhys lies in his tent at noon with a bleeding wound (just like the one Ista had seen in a dream) and yet is whole in the mornings? Why is an empty place laid at dinner for Arhys's half-brother Illvin dy Arbanos, who, according to Arhys's wife Cattilara, had been found unconscious some months before with the dead body of his Roknari fiancée? Ista is sure that these bizarre events that she has been involved in show the interference in her life by one of the gods; it is not until she has a vision of the Bastard that she realizes which god it is.

Ista is taken to see the apparently dead body of Illvin, laid out on his bed; it is the wounded man she has seen in her dreams. She is told that when Illvin awakes, which he does once a day, he asks after Ista; each must have each been dreaming of the other. Ista begins to suspect that Cattilara is keeping Illvin unconscious, and, investigating her with newly restored Sight, she can see that there is a demon hiding within her. She realizes that Cattilara is keeping the two brothers from seeing each other, and Ista wonders what Cattilara is hiding. But when she next sees Arhys, she is able, with her Sight, to unravel the mystery. Arhys is dead. He is being kept animate by Cattilara's demon, which is borrowing Illvin's life forces: when Arhys is wounded, it is Illvin who bleeds. What was a mystery becomes a problem: How can Cattilara and Foix be rid of their demons, and how can both Arhys and Illvin be saved? No solution is found before a large Jokonan force turns up, headed by Regent Dowager Joen of Jokona and her son Sordso, both of whom are clearly powerful in sorcery. Joen controls fourteen other sorcerers, used to good effect when the Jokonan force besieges Porifors: they lob sorceries into the castle, causing bowstrings to disintegrate and good meat to seethe with maggots. In desperation Ista decides on a sortie: Arhys is to pick off all the sorcerers, guided by Foix. who with his demon's help can see them. Ista meets the Father God, who passes on the message to Arhys that he will guide him and see him soon, that is, in death. The attack is launched, and a number of sorcerers are eliminated, but not enough. Ista is visited by the Bastard again, who gives her the power to drag demons out of people and take them inside herself, through her mouth. She frees Cattilara of her demon. And she decides to meet Joen face to face by surrendering. They meet, and Joen welcomes her: "I am the Mother of Jokona." Ista feels the god enter her again and replies: "I am the Mouth of Hell." She takes the demons one by one into her mouth and feels the Bastard dispose of them.

Ista is reminiscent of Cordelia, whom many readers see as their favorite Bujold character. As the fantasy writer Sherwood Smith puts it, "Ista is, like Cordelia Naismith, a grouchy, funny, smart middle-aged heroine, not beautiful, but eminently lovable, even when she is angry and soul-parched and must rediscover love."[6] Her strength is shown above all in the denouement: just as Cordelia confronts Vordarian, and returns with his head, so Ista confronts the demons—and eats them. In *The Curse of Chalion* Ista had been a failure: relegated to madness and isolation because of an ill-judged attempt to rid the royal house of its curse. In *Paladin of Souls* she is reborn and learns to be her own agent. The love she finds with Illvin is satisfying; but the romance is far from being the strongest part of the novel, nor indeed the most interesting relationship that Ista discovers. Her interchanges with the Bastard God seem much more real—earthy, and emotionally and erotically charged.

The third novel in the Chalion sequence, *The Hallowed Hunt* (2005), takes place in a different part of the world, the Weald, to the west of Darthaca (a distorted and inversed Germany, as Darthaca is a distorted version of France).[7] The events take place perhaps centuries earlier than the two earlier novels in the Chalion sequence. The protagonist Ingrey arrives at a hunting lodge to investigate the death of Prince Boleso, the youngest son of the "hallow king."

Boleso had been exiled to this place for a while as punishment for his brutal murder of a manservant; now he had been found murdered, alongside a dead leopard. The perpetrator is Lady Ijada, a handmaid to Princess Fara, and she tells how Boleso had intended to use her in a magical ritual to catch the spirit of the leopard. We soon learn that the possession of animal spirits had been common in the old days, before the Darthacans had conquered the Weald; that the Darthacans, as orthodox Quintarians, suppressed the practice. Ingrey himself possesses a wolf spirit but has a license from the divines, since this possession was forced on him by his late father. In the course of the novel he discovers only two others in the Weald who have animal spirits: Lady Ijada, who has acquired the spirit of the leopard that Boleso had killed, and Ingrey's own cousin Wencel, who has a horse spirit.

Wencel turns out to be a devotee of the customs of the Old Weald, deeply hostile to the Darthacan conquerors. He knows that neither he nor Ingrey bears the spirits of ordinary animals, but of animals into which, through sacrifice, other animal spirits have been taken, again and again, until they have become much more than animals. Because they bear the souls of Great Animals, Ingrey and Wencel are both shamans. In addition, Wencel bears in him the souls of all his ancestors, over many centuries; he cannot die, for his essence passes into his blood heir and takes that person over. At present, since he has no children, his blood heir is Ingrey himself. Because of his ancestry, he is the last of the "real" hallow kings, individuals who possess some spiritual power over the land, unlike the current kings, who owe their position to the Darthacan conquest. Wencel binds Ingrey and Princess Fara to his will and takes them with him toward the Wounded Woods. At this point we have no idea what Wencel is trying to achieve. He is driven by his nationalism and his pride; it seems that he may be trying to break the power of the Darthacans and restore the Old Weald.

The truth, when it finally emerges, is far more touching. Wencel has discovered that the only way to free himself from the pain of eternal life is to bring himself, Ingrey, and Fara to the Wounded Woods, property of Ijada and reputed to be Bloodfield, the site of a shrine where, generations earlier, several thousand warriors of the Weald were massacred by the invading Darthacan forces. (Bujold was inspired by reading about the massacres of the pagan Saxons by Charlemagne at the end of the eighth century.[8]) "'That's what this has all been about, then? An elaborate suicide?' said Ingrey indignantly" (HH 377). When Wencel dies, the power of the hallow-king falls on Ingrey, but he does not inherit the countless lives held in Wencel's body or that of his horse spirit: Wencel's "suicide" has ended the cycle of reincarnation, rescuing Ingrey as well as Wencel. And Ingrey realizes he has another task: to free the two thousand or more ghosts who have been kept within the Wounded Woods and send them to the gods. He has five helpers who take the place of the animals; at a Quintarian funeral, they indicate which of the five gods an individual soul must go to. Ingrey sends the ghosts, one by one, to their rest. At the end Ijada and Ingrey speculate upon what he might do, as the last shaman, to bring change to the Temple and the kingdom.

As in the other two Chalion novels, much of the plot revolves around solving a mystery; and as in the other two, the activity of the gods is crucial. Ingrey is spoken to by the Bastard, but the key member of the Five Gods in this novel is the Son, the God of Autumn, who first appears to both Ingrey and Ijada in a vision on the occasion of Boleso's funeral.

Bujold makes the climax of her story a version of the tale that Tolkien buried inside *The Lord of the Rings* and brought in almost as an aside: the moving story of the army of ghostly traitors whom Aragorn frees by taking the Paths of the Dead (*The Return of the King*, ch. 2, "The Passing of the Grey Company"). *The Hallowed Hunt* is not as immediately appealing as the two Chalionese novels, largely because the characters of Ingrey and Ijada are not as well developed or as immediately attractive as either Cazaril or Ista. The real interest of the novel lies in its expansion of the theology, introducing the whole idea of animal spirits. We have yet to see whether the "missing" two volumes of the five-volume Quintarian sequence will make an appearance; after *The Hallowed Hunt* Bujold turned her attention to a very different exercise in world building.

For each of the four years from 2006 to 2009, Bujold published a volume in a new sequence, each of them with the title *The Sharing Knife* followed by the volume number and the single-word volume name: *Beguilement*, *Legacy*, *Passage*, and *Horizon*. Bujold refers to this sequence not as The Sharing Knife but as The Wide Green World. The books follow the adventures of two people traveling through a world far removed from either the Vorkosigan or Chalion universes. The focalizer of the books alternates, within chapters, between

Fawn Bluefield, an eighteen-year-old farm girl, and Dag Redwing Hickory, a fifty-five-year-old one-handed Lakewalker. Fawn has traveled very little, and the world has to be explained to her (and therefore the reader) frequently by the much more experienced Dag. In that sense the series operates very like a portal-quest fantasy, as defined by Mendlesohn, where the "portal" is the gateway out of Fawn's family farm, which she leaves (shortly before the action of *Beguilement* begins) and thereby encounters the wide green world, with which she is largely unfamiliar. As she learns about the world of the Lakewalkers, so do the readers. The four books are, as John Lennard notes, "paired diptychs": *Beguilement* and *Legacy* are a continuous narrative, uniting the couple and casting them adrift; there is a short gap in time and space, and then *Passage* and *Horizon* are likewise a continuous narrative, showing Dag and Fawn returning to a new home.[9]

Beguilement (2006) begins with the first encounter between Fawn and Dag. Fawn is running away from home after discovering she is pregnant, and Dag saves her from an attack by two "mud-men": former animals who had been reshaped into man-form by what Lakewalkers call a malice and farmers call a blight-bogle. Although they get very little thanks for it, Lakewalkers protect farmers from malices by seeking them out and destroying them before they can grow too large and powerful. Having rescued Fawn, Dag goes back to hunting this particular malice but is horrified to discover that its mud-men have recaptured Fawn and brought her to the malice's lair. He throws her his knife, and with it she kills the malice. Only a sharing knife can kill a malice: that is, a knife made of human bone, primed with the dying spirit of a human. Dag discovers that his second knife has now been primed too—with the spirit of her unborn baby, which died under the claws of the malice. When Fawn has recovered from her miscarriage, Dag takes her back to his group of Lakewalkers, who are recuperating in a small town nearby, and then they go back to her family. Despite warnings from those who think that Lakewalkers and farmers cannot mix, they become lovers. Fawn's family finds this very difficult to accept, but eventually Fawn and Dag persuade them to allow them to marry, which they do at the end, in a mixture of farmer and Lakewalker custom.

Near the beginning of the novel we see Dag use his "groundsense" to cure, or perhaps even bring back to life, a young patroller who had been severely wounded by a mud-man's sledgehammer. We see something more of

Dag's groundsense at the Bluefield residence: he is able both to put together a smashed glass bowl and (with the help of a wasp nest) to put to flight a bunch of thugs who wanted to stop the wedding. We learn that the title of the book is ambiguous. Clearly, Dag and Fawn are beguiled with each other, in standard romance fashion. But Lakewalkers are thought to be able to take over or otherwise affect the minds of farmers, putting "persuasions" into women's minds to aid a seduction, for instance. This was called *beguiling* and was disapproved of by both Lakewalkers and farmers alike. Dag's wooing of Fawn was thus a matter of suspicion for everyone in both societies, just as much as the large disparity of their ages was. Of the latter, Fawn's brother Whit commented, "Actually, I'm not sure if *he's* robbing cradles, or *she's* robbing graves!" (SK1 273).

Legacy (2007) begins almost immediately after *Beguilement*. Dag has taken Fawn home, and in the first half of the book he tries to get the Lakewalkers to accept his new wife and begins to experiment with his groundsense. When the Lakewalkers refuse to accept Fawn, and she manages to use a sharing knife to heal an injury, Dag decides to leave Fairbold before he is thrown out for trying to share knowledge with the farmers; he and Fawn leave to catch a riverboat to start their travels.

Before the river trip that occupies most of *Passage* (2008), the couple visit Fawn's family and try to teach them about malices and the groundsense of the Lakewalkers: when they leave, they take Fawn's brother Whit with them and begin the kind of river trip common in American sf and fantasy, which has long admired the work of Mark Twain. Dag has problems along the river, both with farmers who are suspicious of him and from Lakewalkers, who particularly resent the way he uses his groundsense to cure a young farmer injured by Dag's own horse. Lakewalkers are too busy, he is told, to take time off to heal farmers. Dag's continued experiments prove useful when they meet up with a band of ruthless and murderous river pirates led by a renegade Lakewalker called Crane. One of the band is the boat owner's missing fiancé. The band boards Berry's boat, but Dag paralyses Crane with his ghost-hand, and his crew manage to overpower the pirates. Dag gives a very public demonstration of the normally very private knife-making ceremony, when Crane agrees to be executed in such a way as to prime a sharing-knife. The boat reaches the sea at Drowntown; Whit and Berry agree to marry.

Horizon (2009) begins with the wedding and with Fawn searching out a Lakewalker healer, Arkady Waterbirch, who might take Dag on as apprentice: Arkady is reputed to be skilled at *groundsetting*, or healing. Dag wants to know how to control those powers or even extend them further. Dag is also experimenting with producing "amulets" that will protect farmers from Lakewalkers' attempts to beguile them but will also, he hopes, protect them from being controlled by malices. Arkady does eventually take Dag as his apprentice, recognizing his talent, even though he distrusts Dag's desire to treat farmers as equals of Lakewalkers. When Dag decides to go north, Arkady follows him. Fawn and Dag settle in the north, and Fawn gives birth to a daughter. Patrollers and farmers begin to live together in cooperative harmony, thanks to Dag, who has become something of a messiah figure. Fawn talks with the healer Arkady, who tells her,

> "Dag [. . .] walks with a foot in each world. He straddles things. Outside and inside. Patroller and maker. North and south." He glanced at her. "Lakewalker and farmer. Knife maker and medicine maker, gods. He may be the least simple man I've ever met."
>
> Fawn had no argument with that. [. . .] "It goes with his knack for mending things that are broken, I guess. Bowls. Bones. Hearts. Worlds, maybe. To fix things you first have to walk all around them, see them whole" (SK4 148).

The story is about the growing-up of Fawn; but above all it is about Dag's discovery of his world. If this were a science-fiction sequence, one might categorize it as "conceptual breakthrough." Of this Peter Nicholls writes, "Of all the forms which the quest for knowledge takes in modern sf, by far the most important in terms of both the quality and the quantity of the work that dramatizes it, is conceptual breakthrough"; he adds that "few sf stories do not have at least some element of conceptual breakthrough."[10] Either the world is not as it seems, or our knowledge of the world is incomplete. The characters, and through them the readers, want to understand and to discover.

All reviews of the Sharing Knife books place them within the fantasy category, although noting that they are also in a sense Westerns, as well as romances.[11] This is not how I read the books.

The sequence is about the relations between farmers and Lakewalkers, two separate groups of people who share the same landscape and who (until the events of the novels) have very little to do with each other. Lakewalkers on the whole despise farmers; farmers fear the Lakewalkers because they see them as having magical or sorcerous powers. (Taking the Lakewalker as a version of the cowboy, one might say that the theme of the whole series is drawn from the lyrics of *Oklahoma*: "Oh, the farmer and the cowman should be friends.")

To regard the sequence as fantasy is to take the views of farmers at face value. The novels very clearly show that Lakewalkers themselves do not believe that they work magic. It is rather that they have inherited a much deeper awareness of the world around them than farmers can muster; they call this power *groundsense*, and using that power is *groundwork*. "Only you farmers use the term *magic*. Lakewalkers just call it groundwork. Or making. [. . .] Ground is . . . it's in everything, underlies everything" (SK3 9). The rigidly endogamous marriage customs of the Lakewalkers have enabled them to concentrate this power without any genetic dilution.

Bujold has said that the landscape of the Wide Green World is based on the varied landscapes of Ohio, where she grew up; and those who know Ohio have thought that they have recognized specific elements described in the narrative.[12] Her youthful memories of house-boating on the Ohio River were, she says in her afterword to *Passage*, supplemented by accounts of riverboat life in nineteenth-century America, above all on the Mississippi and Ohio Rivers. The culture and language of the farmers are very North American, with "Aunt Roper's cream-and-honey pie [. . .] and Aunt Bluefield's butter-walnut cake, and Mama's maple-hickory nut bars, and my apple pies" (SK1 353). The culture of the Lakewalkers has its parallels with that of Native Americans (and indeed with Tolkien's Rangers),[13] although it is not clear that there is any ethnic difference between them and the farmers. In an online comment following Jo Walton's review of the books, Bujold notes:

> My Wide Green World riffs on the frontier of 1795–1830 or so, when the West began in Pittsburgh, or perhaps Albany, NY, and the body of water bounding the northwest limit was Lake Erie, not Puget Sound.
>
> It's a much-neglected place and period, especially pre-steam, which was part of its attraction for me, as well as being my home turf and full of fabulous forgotten tales.

And to clarify—yet again—the WGW is not, and has never been, our world, past or future. "Inspired by" only, which is writer-speak for "strip-mined for the cool bits." The map of that era has been thoroughly reformatted to fit my screen.[14]

This is not, therefore, an alternative-history fantasy of America, such as in the Alvin Maker series by Orson Scott Card, which the Sharing Knife books very superficially resemble.

However, brought up as I have been on the science fiction of the 1950s, I find it difficult not to read it as a far-future America, or, to be more vague (with John Lennard) to see it as "in one aspect a vision of a far future."[15] Dag explains his understanding of the world to Fawn:

> "'They say we are a fallen folk, and I for one believe it. The ancient lords built great cities, ships, and roads, transformed their bodies, sought longevity, and brought the whole world crashing down at the last. Though I suspect it was a really good run for a while, till then'" (SK1 218).

The Sharing Knife sequence is thus set in some kind of version of North America in a postholocaust or postapocalyptic period. It is undeniable that the Sharing Knife books also share characteristics with certain well-known tropes of science fiction, which were above all popular in the 1950s, in the science fiction that Bujold first encountered. The appearance within the human population of people with extrasensory powers—telepathy, telekinesis, and the like: these were sometimes referred to as psionic or psi-powers—a commonplace of American science fiction in the decade or so after World War II. These psionic powers may be the result of random evolution or of mutation after exposure to radiation; but sometimes this evolution is initiated or developed by scientists. The classic story of this kind is A. E. Van Vogt's *Slan* (serialized in *Astounding* in 1940; in book form in 1946), in which the Slans are persecuted by normal human beings out of fear for their superior powers. Sometimes radiation merely enhances intelligence, as in Wilmar H. Shiras's *Children of the Atom* (short stories in *Astounding* from 1948 to 1950, assembled in book form in 1953). After Hiroshima, however, with increased awareness of the possibility of radiation-induced mutation, a new strand developed: psionic powers develop after a holocaust of some kind, usually a nuclear war, and these new humans, or posthumans, help develop a new and more utopian society. Stories about extrasensory perception (ESP) were famously encouraged by the influential sf editor John W. Campbell Jr, editor of *Astounding Science Fiction* for more than thirty years, who seems to have believed firmly in the scientific possibility of psi powers. He was supported by the researches of apparently reputable scientists, notably J. B. Rhine of Duke University, who popularized such terms as "ESP" and "parapsychology." ESP stories abounded in *Astounding* in the 1950s and early 1960s; we may remember that Bujold was given her subscription to *Astounding* (by then renamed *Analog*) in 1962, but that before this she had been reading her father's copies.

Bujold implies that the powers of the Lakewalkers were deliberately developed in the distant past by sorcerer-lords rather than being the result of random mutation caused by radiation. Again, it would seem from *Beguilement* that the first malice, from which all the others hatched, came at the time of the scientists (which is how I am translating "sorcerer-lords") before their dominance was destroyed during the first malice wars. If we are to think of The Sharing Knife in science-fictional terms, then these malices either derive from a scientific experiment that went badly wrong or involved aliens from another planet or dimension. Bujold regards them as a hybrid between something alien (immortal and insectoid) and human ("but not, for all of that, SF-nal"), and she notes that most of the bad habits of malices come from their human parts.

My difference with Bujold on this issue may stem from nothing more than the always-contentious problem of defining the terms "science fiction" and "fantasy." But if we view the Sharing Knife sequence as science fiction rather than fantasy, at least we are more easily led to realize that scientific inquiry is one of the main plot drivers of the four books. Dag's curiosity about how groundsense works results in prolonged experiments on himself in *Passage* and in *Horizon*; those experiments result in an effective way to protect farmers from malices. The experiments Dag conducts to learn how to control his "ghost hand" (the hand that he can still perceive, where farmers can see only a stump and Dag's range of prostheses) inescapably recalls the experience of Gil Hamilton, Larry Niven's science-fictional detective in *The Long ARM of Gil Hamilton* (1976) who had lost an entire arm. But it is also significant that Dag's experiments move from developing his ability to use his groundsense for medical purposes (which he has already displayed in the first novel, *Be-*

guilement, when he brings his colleague back from apparent death) to seeing the possibilities for gaining an advantage in the prolonged war against the malices. It is in a sense the reverse of the trajectory that Terrence-C goes through in *Ethan of Athos*, the only other book by Bujold that deals with telepathy: Terrence is taught initially that his powers should be used for military or espionage purposes, but he comes to realize their medical value through talking to Ethan Urquhart.

The sequence describes the prehistory of the revival of science in this world: Dag and his mentor Arkady are both protoscientists, and the novel finishes with a sense of optimism. Lakewalkers will learn more about how groundsense works and will educate farmers about it (explaining groundsense in nonmagical terms). Lakewalkers and farmers will learn to cooperate, and together they will learn how to protect themselves and control the world. The whole project is thus closely analogous to the project of science itself, as we have understood it from histories of the Scientific Revolution.[16] It is interesting, too, that the process occurs in the Wide Green World in a society that—unlike most fantasy—has no gods: or, rather, there is a memory of gods, but they are absent and have no place in people's lives. This, Bujold admitted to me, "can be read as another covert SF-nal marker."[17]

There is no hint that the scientific revival will follow a similar trajectory to that described by Walter M. Miller in *A Canticle for Leibowitz* (1960), which derived its historical framework from Edward Gibbon's *The Decline and Fall of the Roman Empire* (1776–1789): the gradual collapse from civilization into barbarism, and the even slower rebuilding of civilization from the ruins. Bujold seems to share some of the rather more modern suspicion of civilization and distrust of civilization's disparagement of "the barbarian." Civilization itself—the sorcerer-lords, or scientists—had, after all, got Dag's world into its current plight; and despite relatively primitive technology, its culture was far from conventionally "barbaric." One of the aspects of the learning curve that Dag experiences through the four volumes was his discovery that the traditional contempt that Lakewalkers felt for so-called "farmers" was quite misplaced: many "farmers" were in fact merchants, manufacturers, engineers, and builders. Lakewalkers themselves have become so concentrated on their war with the malices, which made them into forced itinerants, wandering on one patrol after another in search of blight, that they had come to distrust the settled life of farmers and the "civilization" that this brought with it. Lake-walkers like to be mobile, to follow and to avoid malices: barns and houses were "targets" (SK1 297) and therefore traps, unlike camps. Meanwhile, the "farmers" are busy building towns and starting an industrial revolution; and Dag's own prosthesis was designed and made by a "farmer."

At the start of the quartet, we have two worlds: that of the Lakewalkers and that of the farmers. By the end of the fourth volume, *Horizon*, the two worlds are beginning to come together, with a bravely new and united world on the horizon. In the foregoing paragraphs I have implied that this was the work of Dag—or, to use his full name, Dag Redwing Hickory Oleana (Redwing is the family name; Hickory is for Hickory Lake Camp, his patrol's main base; Oleana is the hinterland name) (SK1 305). But in fact this was as much the work of the woman he came to marry, Fawn Bluefield. Had he changed his name according to Lakewalker practice, he would have become Dag Bluefield West Blue Oleana, West Blue being the Bluefields' nearest settlement. They discuss what name they should take in marriage: Redfield? Bluewing? (SK1 306). The matter does not appear to be settled until events settle it for them: in *Passage* Dag introduces himself as Dag Bluefield, and it is clear that he has decided this because, effectively, Hickory Lake Camp has thrown him out (SK3 83). All this is significant because the reconciliation of the two hostile groups in a sense begins because of the need Dag and Fawn have to win acceptance for their marriage from both their families and communities. Neither the Bluefields nor the Redwings can initially accept this marriage. Some of them, perhaps, cannot stomach it because (like some modern readers of the Sharing Knife books) they view with great suspicion relationships between eighteen-year-old women and men aged fifty-five. (The age difference is much more marked than that between nineteen-year-old Betriz and thirty-five-year-old Cazaril in *The Curse of Chalion*.) But mostly there is the gut instinct that farmers and Lakewalk-ers must remain separate. Both sides have their irrational suspicions of the other, enhanced by mutual ignorance, while the hostility of the Lakewalkers is enhanced by the fact that the farmers do not realize the dangers from which the Lakewalkers are protecting them and therefore show no gratitude. The Lakewalkers respond with contempt and treat all "farmers" as indistinguish-able from each other. As Fawn realizes very early on, "*Farmer* to a Lakewalker didn't mean someone who grew crops; it meant anyone who wasn't a Lakewalker. Townsmen, rivermen, miners, millers—bandits—evidently they were all farmers in Dag's eyes" (SK1 43). It takes her much longer to realize that the arrogance that Lakewalkers displayed toward farmers was in part discomfort at being among people who see them as weird and different (SK4 2). The strains that their cultural baggage put on the relationship between Fawn and Dag continue through all four books. Much of the burden falls on Fawn: after all, Dag has a great reputation among the Lakewalkers as a slayer of malices, and that (for the Lakewalkers only, of course) was a measure of worth. It is characteristic that Dag uses this as an argument in support of Fawn's acceptance among the Lakewalkers: "Fawn's a special case anyway. She's not just a farmer, she's the farmer girl who slew a malice. As contrasted with, for example, your malice count. What was it, again? Oh yes—none?" (SK2 126). As Kate Bonin has pointed out, Fawn is to some extent a Cinderella figure: an obscure farm girl chosen by a romantic figure who is a kind of celebrity within the warrior class to which he belonged.[18] But what she is actually doing is exchanging a comfortable and prosperous family existence for a life of uncertainty.

In the end it is Fawn's courage, good judgment, and intelligence that save the day: it takes her a while to find herself, but she ends up as a strong woman worthy to be placed alongside Cordelia Naismith, Ekaterin Vorsoisson, Elli Quinn, Elena Bothari, Betriz di Ferrej, or the Royina Ista. Although Dag can be roused to eloquence if absolutely necessary, Fawn is the better salesperson for what Dag wants to sell: the chance to remove the barriers between farmers and Lakewalkers. "But Dag's a doer, not a talker" (SK4 8): Fawn, who is often more aware of social subtleties than Dag (particularly around farmers), becomes a persuasive speaker. And she is always there to lend a hand—quite literally, since Dag has only one: "My wife partners me when I need two hands" (SK4 367). Dag is the more powerful of the two in their partnership, but his disability cuts him down to size in a way, making their relationship much more equal and reciprocal than it might have been otherwise.

One other element of *The Sharing Knife* is worth mentioning. In a comment on Jo Walton's review, Bujold noted that she was "tussling with Tolkien. Aren't we all?"[19] It is possible to see the Wide Green World as a deliberate commentary on, and in many cases inversion of, Middle-earth. Instead of a pseudo-medieval Europe, we have a pseudo-Western America. The Lakewalkers are like Tolkien's Rangers; Berry, the riverboat woman, is inspired by Goldberry, "the river-woman's daughter." There are no kings and aristo-crats in the Wide Green World, just country folk and farmers (who are in short supply on Middle-earth, once one leaves the Shire). There is no huge struggle against a Dark Lord; evil is something encountered every now and then, something that has to be dealt with when it occurs. We do not have a grand tale of wizards, elves, and prophecies; we have the story of a disabled, middle-aged man (a little older than Frodo) who sees what is wrong with the world and tries to deal with it.

Over the course of the four books one representative from each of the two cultures of farmers and Lakewalkers meet, fall in love, learn about each other's cultures, understand how each is misrepresented, and fight for those cultures to come together and live at peace. Nattie-Mari, the baby daughter of Fawn and Dag, named after one member of each of their family groups, represents the hope for the future. When simplified to that extent, one can see how in the Wide Green World Bujold was reworking and exploring in greater depth some of the themes of her earlier Vorkosigan books, in which Miles, born in a marriage between representatives of two separate cultures, also offers a new way forward.

CHaPTeR 4

CULTURAL CRITIQUE

The clash of cultures, between societies and within societies, with both negative and positive results, is an underlying theme in much of what Bujold
has written. This chapter will examine this theme primarily as it appears in
Bujold's science fiction; to some extent we have already, in chapter 3, treated
the theme as found in the fantasy books. We shall see that one of the main
purposes of the theme of culture clash in Bujold's works is to cast light upon
the societies of her readers: satire, in its original and broadest sense, is thus one
of Bujold's concerns. Satire invariably has an ethical or moral dimension (the
humorous dimension is often there in Bujold, but critics have not seen humor
as an indispensable element of satire); and the moral world that Bujold builds
is a significant part of her achievement. In most, but not in all, cases, Bujold
lets us know clearly whose moral point of view we are supposed to support.

Like many of her science-fictional predecessors (Poul Anderson, Jack
Vance, and Gene Roddenberry, for instance), Bujold has tended to envisage

largely monolithic planetary cultures on the worlds described in the Vorkosigan books, all of which were colonized ultimately from Earth. Earth had
thousands of languages, and hundreds of different cultures; its colonies tend
to have one language, and one culture each (although class differentiation
might provide variations on that one culture, and Barrayar at least does have
more than one language). By contrasting planetary cultures (Barrayar, Beta
Colony, Komarr, Cetaganda, Jackson's Whole, and others) Bujold is able to
comment in different ways on the politics and prejudices of our own contemporary world. The culture clash found in most of the Vorkosigan books in
some cases provides a plot driver and in all cases operates as a way of getting
readers to think about their own cultural assumptions and prejudices. Often
the culture clash results when an individual from one culture is brought into a
very different cultural environment: in rhetorical terms this equates to Farah
Mendlesohn's "portal-quest fantasy," in which the appearance of an outsider
demands an exposition of the culture that the outsider finds herself or himself
inhabiting.[1]

In *Shards of Honor* a woman from the egalitarian society of Beta Colony
(Cordelia Naismith) comes to know a Barrayaran man (Aral Vorkosigan)
from the feudal and militaristic patriarchy of Barrayar, and she then visits
that patriarchy; in *Ethan of Athos* the Athosian leaves his all-male planet to
encounter homophobia—and women—for the first time. In *Falling Free* we
encounter the clash between the naïve, childlike innocence of the quaddies
and the cynical and ruthless attitudes of their corporate masters. Later on
we are introduced to Komarr, Cetaganda, Jackson's Whole, Kibou-daini, and
even Earth, all of which are seen in the light of our Betan-Barrayaran hybrid's
experience. The cultural confrontation most emphasized in the series is that
between Beta Colony and Barrayar. We see this first in the story of the courtship and marriage of Aral Vorkosigan and Cordelia Naismith, but it continues
through the story of their son Miles.

Miles is a hybrid, learning from two cultures as he grew up. As a hybrid he
remains open also to other cultures: this openness helps to bring the possibility
of reconciliation in the future between Barrayar and Cetaganda, for instance,
because of what he has done and learned in the course of *Cetaganda* and *Diplomatic Immunity*. Since he is always acutely aware of himself as the product of
two cultures, Miles operates as a catalyst, helping along the process of social

change that was begun by his parents, not just on his own planet but on others as well. Indeed, the role that he plays in six of the books as the allegedly Betan admiral Miles Naismith allows him to emphasize his Betan persona as a natural foil to the Barrayaran he was brought up to be. The influence of his mother and his own visits to Beta Colony—he is at school there for a year as a fifteen-year-old—give him a sympathy with Betans that seems very rare among Barrayarans, as well as an awareness of the shortcomings of both cultures. When masquerading as a Betan, Miles may not have been good enough to fool every Betan: he flinches when his cheek is touched by the hermaphrodite Bel Thorne (Thorne offers this as evidence that even if Miles had the accent and the inside jokes, he doesn't have the reflexes [BI 106–7]). But Miles can fool most people, in part because he does not have to try very hard: he inherits his Betan culture from his mother as effortlessly as he inherits his Barrayaran culture from his father. Yet in the end Miles can conceive of giving up his Betan persona, and in *Memory* he does so, while he can never give up being a Barrayaran, a Vor, and a Vorkosigan: his romantic pursuit of Elli Quinn founders on that and returns us to an essentialism of identity.

On the face of it, Barrayar (with its Russian and Greek traditions, and its aristocracy) embodies a more European culture. However, the differences between Beta Colony and Barrayar might instead be seen as representing different facets of American society, which may very loosely be regarded as its progressive, egalitarian, and democratic aspects faced with the conservative and hierarchical. In reality, while the two cultures are depicted in such a way as to force us to think about our own cultural assumptions, whether American or European, there is no simple correspondence between any fictional culture in the Vorkosigan universe and the cultures of our own world.

Beta Colony, the only colony directly colonized by the United States of America, is technologically preeminent within Bujold's science-fictional universe, both in military and medical technology; partly as a result of this, the Betan dollar (that is the word used) is the strongest currency of all currencies found in the galaxy's human colonies. Beta Colony is also very egalitarian—absurdly so, in the eyes of some Barrayarans. Beta first appears in the Vorkosigan narrative when Aral Vorkosigan makes fun of its military capacity, since Betan military personnel usually respond to orders by argument and debate rather than obedience: "If your ranks denote anything but pay scale, it's not apparent to me" (CH II). When Cordelia reveals that she had ordered the crew of her ship to use their own initiative, Aral comments, "A safe order to give a Betan. At least you're sure to be obeyed" (CH II). Egalitarianism, however, goes along with a commitment to individual rights. There is an illuminating three-way conversation between Cordelia, Aral, and Aral's father Piotr about poverty. Cordelia is horrified to discover that on Barrayar there are actually people who do not have comconsoles (personal computers). The first article of the Betan constitution, she says, is "Access to information shall not be abridged." Aral is equally amazed to hear that "not owning a comconsole" is the lowest form of poverty that Cordelia can imagine, and he has to explain to her that poverty on Barrayar means barely having access to shelter, food, and clothing, and having no access to medical care. "If they're sick, they either get well or die," and Piotr adds, "Die, if we're lucky. Vermin." Cordelia's first reaction once she realizes that they are not joking) is to comment, "Why, think of all the geniuses you must be missing!" Piotr doubts that there are any, and Cordelia makes what is to her an obvious point—"They have the same genetic complement as you"—without realizing that this, to an aristocrat, is a serious insult. Piotr responds: "They most certainly do not! My family have been Vor for nine generations," to which Cordelia piles on the insult by asking, "How do you know, if you didn't have gene typing till eighty years ago?" (CH 358–59). Cordelia seems to remain ignorant of the effect this question has on the old Vor general, and luckily the topic of conversation changes. Cordelia lives in a world where poverty in twenty-first-century terms is nonexistent (unless she is merely unaware of it) and where medical care is readily available for all: Beta Colony has more in common with various utopian or near-utopian scenarios found in late-nineteenth- and twentieth-century literature than with any real culture on our Earth, let alone the United States. Bujold has remarked to me that few readers spot that "much about Betan culture is explainable by realizing that Beta Colony was settled by sub-light near-generation ships." Presumably the long journey inculcated a strong communitarian spirit and discipline—untreated disease would soon ravage a generation ship—which sustained them on the struggle to live on a planet that turned out to present an environment barely less hostile than outer space itself.

Betans elect their own president and have neither hereditary monarchy nor an aristocracy, as Barrayar does. They have problems with deference, as

Cordelia shows when, admittedly under some provocation and accidentally, she kicks her president in the groin (CH 180). "I didn't vote for him" becomes a catch phrase from *Shards of Honor*, indicating, one presumes, a healthily disrespectful Betan attitude toward their leaders. The Betan lack of deference is well known on Barrayar too. Miles, in his Betan guise, is given advice by a lieutenant on how to treat a Barrayaran count with sufficient respect: Miles translates that in his mind as *"Call him sir, don't wipe your nose on your sleeve, and none of your damned Betan egalitarian backchat, either"* (VG 320). The contrast between the two societies is brought out through a comparison of their public ceremonies. Betan egalitarianism ensures that these ceremonies were covered in detail by "holovid" (3-D television) and were choreographed and commented to death. In the Barrayaran equivalents, the only recordings made are for reasons of security and the general public are excluded from Barrayaran ceremonies, since there is no need to worry about electorates.

Beta Colony is best known around the human galaxy for two other things: scientific advances and sexual tolerance. Its scientific expertise may be partly a result of the constraining environment, which the original settlers of Beta discovered. The sun's rays are too hot and the atmosphere too poisonous to allow them or most other Earth flora and fauna to live outside. Animals such as horses are only found in zoos; wood is a rare luxury; people live underground. "Beta Colony's cities plunged down into shafts and tunnels, many-layered and complex, cozy and safe. Indeed, Beta Colony did not have architecture so much as it had interior design" (CH 313). It was perhaps no accident that one of the technological innovations for which Beta Colony is best known is the uterine replicator, which provides everything a growing fetus needs, secure from a hostile environment. At a party, denied alcohol because of her pregnancy, Cordelia reflects morosely on the fact that "at home she could have poisoned and endangered herself freely, while her child grew, fully monitored round-the-clock by sober techs, safe and protected in the replicator banks" (CH 329).

Beta Colony's medical technology not only ensures long lives to its citizens— "all Betans expect to live to be 120 . . . they think it's one of their civil rights" (WA 47)—but also enables them to experiment with the human form. Bel Thorne, the hermaphrodite and one of Miles's most loyal followers, is the product of one of those experiments. But the general tolerant approach of Betans to sexual relations is no doubt another source of Barrayaran disapproval. The attempt of Vordarian, a Barrayaran nobleman, to sow marital discord between Cordelia and Aral backfires when he discovers that not only does Cordelia know about Aral's homosexual relationship with a fellow Barrayaran, she also accepts the situation with total equanimity. Vordarian is astonished, until he remembers that Cordelia is Betan: "You are, after all, the people who bioengineered hermaphrodites" (CH 331). The existence of Betan hermaphrodites explains in part why one Barrayaran comment on Betans is simply "more frigging weirds per capita than any other . . ." (WA 108). Vordarian's dying words reflect his racist view of Betans, as, in Andrew Hallam's words, "a people that apparently embody a certain kind of non-violent, soft, probably effeminate liberalism that cannot act—that cannot *do*."[2] Vordarian, thanks to Bothari's beheading sword, never gets a chance to complete his sentence, however: "You're a Betan. You can't do—" (CH 554).

Betan sexual customs are very relaxed compared to those of Barrayarans (or indeed those of modern Americans), but reproduction is a different matter. You need a license to be a parent, and until that time girls and hermaphrodites are fitted with a contraceptive implant. Cordelia acquires hers at age fourteen, at the same time that her hymen is cut and her ears are pierced; the event is celebrated by a coming-out party (CH 408). The wearing of earrings indicates sexual availability, as Elena Bothari finds out, to her embarrassment (WA 53). Sexual availability might also be advertised by clothing, or lack of it. The underground life of Beta, on an overheated planet, makes clothing something that is unnecessary simply as a means to keep warm. Sarongs and sandals are ordinary wear for men; but body paint might be all that is required for some occasions. Because of the general permissiveness (and because of an aversion toward exploitation of any kind), the sexual role of prostitutes is fulfilled by LPSTs: men, women, and hermaphrodites who are qualified (via a license and academic training) as Licenced Practical Sexuality Therapists (CH 527) and who are respected for their work. Cordelia is as bemused by Barrayaran sexual customs, in particular the sexual double standard, as Barrayarans are about the sex life of Betans. She finally works out that Barrayaran sexual politics depend on "impeding the free flow of information to certain persons, preselected by an unspoken code somehow known to and agreed upon by all present except her" (CH 311). She ends up by writing down a set of the rules that she has deduced from observation, however illogical they seem to her, and presents them to Aral, who is vastly amused. Thereafter, if she wants him to laugh, all she has to do is mutter, at an appropriate (or inappropriate) time, "Rule Nine, sir" (CH 312).

Unlike Barrayarans, Betans make civil rights something of a fetish. Clones, for instance, are given full legal protection and are the legal relatives of those from whom they were cloned; this becomes important in the rehabilitation of Miles's abused clone, Mark. Betans prefer imprisonment and therapy for criminals, regarding any form of capital punishment as abhorrent. For them, Aral says, crime is a disease, to be met with attempted rehabilitation: "At least we kill a man cleanly, all at once, instead of in bits, over years. [. . .] Beheading. It's supposed to be almost painless." "How do they know?" asks Cordelia (CH 376). There is an amusing scene where Miles explains that the Barrayaran punishment for desertion in the field of battle is quartering. The Betan thought that quartering someone upon another citizen was not too bad.

> "Quartering," said Miles. "Uh—not domiciled. Cut in four pieces."
> Hathaway stared, shocked. "But that would kill him!" He looked around, and wilted under the triple, unified, and exasperated glares of the three Barrayarans. (WA 77–78).

"Betans! . . . I can't stand Betans," says one of the Barrayarans, while Miles hears the Betan say "bloodthirsty barbarians" under his breath.

The most useful touchstone for learning about Betan views of Barrayarans is Cordelia herself. Her favorite expletive is simply "Barrayarans!"; that encompasses a great deal of meaning. At her first meeting with Aral she rails at Barrayarans for shooting Dubauer with a disruptor: "You Barrayarans were nothing but barbarians, scoundrels, and assassins!" (CH 64). ("And fools," adds Aral.) She finds Barrayaran primitive culinary practices, which involve taking protein "from the bodies of real dead animals," thoroughly disgusting (CH 333). She is appalled at how adolescents on Barrayar are supposed to suppress their sexual urges: "I've never understood why these people won't clip their kids' tubes and turn them loose at age twelve to work out their own damnation, like sensible folk. You may as well try to stop a sandstorm with a windsock . . . Barrayarans!" (WA 41–2). Commander Elli Quinn is excluded from a Barrayaran military facility on the grounds that she is a foreigner: "Barrayarans!" (BI 311). Barrayarans have no legal precedents for dealing with clones and other human variants: "Barrayarans!" (MD 210). Exploiting this loophole in Barrayaran law, Lord Vormuir intends to bring up more than 120 babies, produced with his own sperm, as his own daughters: Miles's comment to Mark, made (one imagines) in an imitation of his mother's accent and tone, is, of course, "Barrayarans!" (ACC 93).

A Barrayaran going to Beta Colony will suffer almost the same level of culture shock, although in very different ways. Elena Bothari knows about, and admires, the alleged freedom on Beta Colony; she is corrected by Miles, who has lived there. Betans do not have "freedom" in the abstract. They cannot have children, for instance, without obtaining a license first. And their planet, whose environment is much more hostile than that of Barrayar, imposes its own limitations on freedom: Betans "put up with rules we'd never tolerate at home. You should see everyone fall into place during a power outage drill, or a sandstorm alarm. They have no margin for—I don't know how to put it. Social failures?" (WA 53). Beta Colony is certainly no kind of utopia: we are left in no doubt about that as early as *Shards of Honor*, when Cordelia faces the amoral ruthlessness of the planet's security forces when they suspect her of being a Barrayaran spy.

Nevertheless, Beta Colony can appear positively utopian to some Barrayarans, above all to women. Cordelia is a role model for Elena Bothari because the former Captain Naismith embodies what is impossible for women on Barrayar: not just a military role, but—simply—*choice*. Elena tells Miles, "Once, reminiscing, [Cordelia] went into this sort of litany about all the things she'd ever been. Like astrocartographer, and explorer, and ship's captain, and POW, and wife, and mother, and politician . . . the list went on and on. There was no telling, she said, what she would be next. And I thought . . . I want to be like that. I want to be like her. Not just one thing, but a world of possibilities" (M 20–21). Of course, once Cordelia marries into the Vorkosigan family, however much she might rebel against it, and however much political and social power she actually possesses, as joint guardian of the young Gregor, or as Vicereine of Sergyar, she acquires all that she has essentially as an appendage of her husband (although there is an argument that Ezar appoints Aral as regent in part because of Cordelia).

If Betans stand for a level of liberalism and progressiveness that is much closer to what one might find in parts of Europe (say, Sweden or the Netherlands) than in the United States, Barrayarans are ostensibly closer to the attitudes of the Russians from whom many of them are descended—but Russians at the time of the tsars rather than of the Bolsheviks. Russian is indeed still widely used, even though Standard English is also widely known: in the Time of Isolation, English and the other languages of Barrayar had all been written in a "mutant" form of the Cyrillic alphabet (CH 366). Cordelia seems to have no problem communicating when she arrives on Barrayar and is presumably speaking a future form of English; but one of the first things she does after marriage is to attempt to learn Russian (CH 280). The faux Russianness is what is most immediately visible in the text and may mislead the reader into ignoring how Barrayarans reflect some of the attitudes of the contemporary American Right and the entrenched sense of privilege of the American aristocracy of wealth.

Bujold herself has said that although Barrayar had a multiethnic European culture, in terms of its history and society Barrayar is actually based in part on Meiji Japan (DD 210–11). The regime of Emperor Gregor, under Aral Vorkosigan's regency and afterward, corresponds to that of the young Emperor Meiji, who restored the Empire in 1868, and who came, like Gregor, not long after a Time of Isolation. Meiji ruled until 1912 and presided over a period of rapid social change, which saw the gradual diminution of the power of the military aristocracy and the establishment of more democratic structures in Japan.

The Barrayaran aristocracy—the Vor—are presented as Russian in origin, and some of them preserve Russian names following their Vor prefix: Bujold derived the name "Vorkosigan" from that of the prominent Soviet diplomat of the 1970s, Alexei Kosygin. She invented the prefix "Vor" because she thought it sounded good; only later did she discover that it is Russian for "thief," which she thought thoroughly appropriate for a group of aristocrats (DD 211). On the other hand, she did regret the result: too many Barrayaran names looked superficially the same. Not all Vor-names were compiled of Russian surnames with the prefix, however: some, like Vann Vorgustafson had the Vor- prefix applied to a Scandinavian name, while the Vorsmythes presumably have English ancestry. The putative leader of the French-speaking Barrayarans is Count Vorville (VG 187), and, judging by their names, Etienne

Vorsoisson (Kom) and René Vorbretten (ACC) are other aristocratic representatives of this group.

Greeks form a distinct and disadvantaged ethnic group on Barrayar (although there are some Vor families with Greek-derived names). The first thing that comes to Miles's mind when he reflects on General Metzov's plans to shoot troops who refused to clean up a toxic dump was that half of the soldiers in question were Greeks: "The language separatists would have been rioting in the streets, had it become a massacre, sure to claim the general had ordered the Greekies into the clean-up as racial sabotage" (VG 89). Those of Russian extraction, including Miles himself (VG 89), use the derogatory word "Greekie" quite unconsciously, although it is clearly regarded as rather vulgar. When Lady Alys Vorpatril remarks that a particular custom has died out "except in some of the backcountry districts in certain language groups," her son Ivan earns a disapproving frown from her when he interjects "she means the Greekie hicks" (ACC 41).

The central element of the Barrayaran system is its hereditary monarchy, in which the ruling emperor (or his regent, before an emperor comes of age) has rather more daily contact with government than the English monarchy has had since the earlier seventeenth century. Emperors rule with the help of their counts, which gives the system a suitably military and medieval air. However, early on, Aral tells Cordelia that the word "count" derived from "accountant": "The first 'counts were Varadar Tau's—an amazing bandit, you should read up on him sometime—Varadar Tau's tax collectors" (CH 323–24). Bujold frequently anticipates our assumptions, only immediately to puncture them: the reader should follow the advice of Cordelia, given immediately after this exchange: "Check your assumptions. In fact, check your assumptions at the door."

The development of Barrayar toward more democratic and socially collaborative structures is a major theme of Barrayaran history during the period of the Vorkosigan books. Aral, as regent, has to manage a balancing act, fostering the progress while at the same time trying to make sure that too-rapid progress does not produce rebellion from powerful conservative elements among the Barrayaran aristocracy. He does not wholly succeed, for rebellions happen several times after he takes up political power: in chronological order, there is Count Vordarian, who attempts to overthrow Aral's regency by force, and

Evon Vorhalas, who attempts to assassinate Aral with soltoxin (both in *Barrayar*); Count Vordrozda, who attempts to undermine Aral by bringing charges of treason against Miles (in *The Warrior's Apprentice*); and Count Vortrifani, who is the figurehead for the "far-right blow-up-the-wormhole isolationist loonie faction," as Miles put it (VG 187). Elena finds Vortrifani scary: "It's the suave way he mops the foam from his lips," says Miles, sarcastically.

Bujold sometimes uses Miles, a Barrayaran infused with a healthy Betan disrespect for Barrayaran customs, to get her readers to check their assumptions. He often says things that no other Barrayaran is prepared to say about their own society. For instance, when Ekaterin says that misusing her influence to get a job would be nepotism, Miles responds that the whole Barrayaran system runs on nepotism: "It's not a vice for us, but a life-style" (Kom 51). Miles does have a fondness for the ceremony and ritual with which Barrayar, like many monarchies, abounds. Indeed, the Old Barrayar of feudal traditions and ceremony still has a romantic attraction for many, and not just for conservative Vor lords, but again the focalizer treats this with some skepticism: Ekaterin remarks to her Aunt Vorthys that some girls love playing "Vor ladies of old, rescued from menace by romantic Vor youths. For some reason they never play *dying in childbirth*, or *vomiting your guts out from the red dysentery*, or *weaving till you go blind and crippled from arthritis and dye poisoning*, or *infanticide*. Well, they do die romantically of disease sometimes, but somehow it's always an illness that makes you interestingly pale and everyone sorry and doesn't involve losing bowel control" (Kom 273). Bujold probably knows contemporaries who romanticize the Middle Ages or, for that matter, the parallel universes of Jane Austen and Georgette Heyer.

Aral Vorkosigan—strongly influenced by Cordelia—sees it as his task to reform the Barrayaran system and to make it closer to Galactic standards without undermining the structure that gave it stability: after the invading Cetagandans are expelled from the planet, Barrayar becomes more open to external influence anyway, such that Miles's grandfather Piotr does not blame Aral for importing reforming ideas—he merely blames Aral for not having *stopped* this "imported off-planet nonsense" (WA 15). One of the more subversive ideas that Aral backs was presumably detested by the snobbish Piotr: Vor names are not used in military training, as Aral argues that aristocratic privilege undermines military discipline.

Reform is a slow process, still going on years after Aral resigns as regent. Miles, in the chronologically most recent novel, is in charge of a committee still trying to make Barrayar's laws on reproductive technology as up to date as those in the rest of the galaxy (Cry 21). But Aral does start moving quickly on some of his reforms. One of the constitutional changes he introduces to keep the counts on their toes is to make it easier for ordinary Barrayarans to switch their oaths to a new district count. Counts have great freedom to run their districts as they wish, in terms of taxation and so on, but this gives them a strong incentive to offer attractive and progressive policies. Miles explains it thus:

> The long-term effect, as you can imagine, has been a downright biological com-
> petition. Count Vorenlightened makes it good for his people, his District grows,
> his revenues increase. His neighbor Count Vorstodgy makes it too tough, and he
> leaks people like a sieve, and his revenues drop. *And* he gets no sympathy from
> his brother Counts, because his loss is their gain. (ACC 90)

But as the more entrenched are not willing to accept these consequences—and in a classic reminder of the importance of the uterine replicator in Cordelia's social revolution that continually bubbles under the surface of these books—the reactionary Lord Vormuir is inspired to buy up thirty uterine replicators to start creating a small army of female liege persons who will grow up to increase his subjects. In a brilliant moment of irony it is a traditionally Barrayan ruling that thwarts him: he must provide dowries for all the girls.

Other targets for Bujold's satire or social comment emerge when we extend our horizon beyond Beta Colony and Barrayar. Some planets are more interesting in these terms than others. Culturally speaking, Komarr is a halfway house between Beta and Barrayar. Like Beta Colony, it is a largely inhospitable planet, the agricultural resources of which are negligible, so its wealth (some of which had to be put toward the terraforming project) largely comes from trade: "Its wormholes had made Komarr rich; it was from the power and wealth pouring through them that its jewel-like domed cities sprang, not grubbed up from the planet's dire, barren soil by sweaty labor" (BA 131–32). But because it is a conquered planet, many of whose inhabitants bitterly resent Barrayar, it must be reeled in, both by radical choices—the recruitment of Komarrans into the Imperial Service alienates many Barrayarans who deem them "the Emperor's pets" (DI 22)—and by romantic ones. Perhaps the most successful move that Gregor makes toward greater integration with Komarr is not part of the plan at all: his marriage to Dr. Laisa Toscane, a member of one of Komarr's most wealthy merchant families (and one which early on sees the advantage of collaborating with the Barrayarans). This succeeds because Barrayans view it as romantic, while the Komarrans have their own way of embracing it. Miles's colleague on Komarr, Captain Tuomonen, reports: "Some of them think it's romantic. Some of them think it's sharp business practice on Emperor Gregor's part. Coming from Komarrans, that's a warm compliment, by the way" (Kom 117). More interestingly, Tuomonen notes that Barrayarans on Komarr, who once regarded Tuomonen's own marriage to a Komarran woman as career suicide, are now thinking that Tuomenon had been extremely farsighted (Kom 117–18).

One of the peculiarities of the Komarran constitution is not explained (or invented) by Bujold until late in the Vorkosigan sequence. As is common in Bujold's universe, it is the environment that is the crucial factor. When Komarr is first settled, incentives are needed to encourage the development and extension of the domes under which all people have to live. All Komarrans have a single vote, but those who are willing to undertake the labour and risk of extending living space can acquire additional votes—which are inheritable and able to be sold. "The basis of the Komarran oligarchy as it now stands is clan possession of blocks of these planetary voting shares. The place is putatively a democracy, but some are measurably more equal than others" (Cry 130). The plot, which Miles uncovers in *CryoBurn*, involves an exploitation or subversion of this system. A group of executives who control a cryonics corporation on the planet Kibou-daini plan to establish a plant on Komarr: they will live much of their lives frozen, and with the profits of their enterprise over the generations they will slowly buy up Komarr, its economy, and its votes. In other words, thanks to its environmental policies, Komarr is a flawed democracy, easily manipulated by the political oligarchy, those with the money: the twenty-first-century parallels are easy to find.

Bujold's cultural worlds frequently force us to think about our own world by taking facets of it and exaggerating or extrapolating them to extremes. Jackson's Whole is a nightmare world in which free-market capitalism has been allowed to develop without any legal restraints. Bujold comments: "Everybody says they want a world with no government. Here's a world with no government. How do you like it?" (DD 212). The planet is very useful to the rest of the galaxy because it does offer services and products that are unavailable elsewhere, largely because other planets have criminalized those activities. Bujold continually reminds us that a place such as this cannot exist unless there are customers: it provides a necessary outlet for humanity's baser instincts.

Jackson's Whole is run, if at all, by a relatively small number of desperately competing Great Houses. A century or two before Miles's time it was little better than a base for space pirates. Since then it has "senesced," as Miles puts it, into a collection of syndicates "almost as structured and staid as little governments," and Miles wonders whether one day they will all succumb to "the creeping tide of integrity." Miles lists the main Houses, when he first comes across them, in the story "Labyrinth":

> House Dyne, detergent banking—launder your money on Jackson's Whole. House Fell, weapons deals with no questions asked. House Bharaputra, illegal genetics. Worse, House Ryoval, whose motto was "Dreams Made Flesh," surely the damndest—Miles used the adjective precisely—procurer in history. House Hargraves, the galactic fence, prim-faced middlemen for ransom deals—you had to give them credit, hostages exchanged through their good offices came back alive, mostly. (BI 103–4)

Jackson's Whole is a culture with many skills—just not any sense of corporate or medical ethics. Bioengineering is particularly advanced on the planet, and in the course of the Vorkosigan books we meet a number of its products. Mark Vorkosigan, Miles's clone, heads the list, but there is also Sergeant Taura, who (along with her deceased siblings) is constructed to be the ultimate warrior: when she dies, she says, she wants her ashes to be buried anywhere in the universe—except Jackson's Whole. Gupta, whom we meet in *Diplomatic Immunity*, is an amphibian human, with gills and webbed extremities, created by House Dyan on Jackson's Whole (DI 145, 174). On Kibou-daini, Miles meets a miniature sphinx with a vocabulary of more than a dozen words, manufactured as a promotional giveaway for the company NewEgypt by "some bioengineering company on Jackson's Whole," Miles is told, to which he responds, in his head, "*Of course*" (Cry 255). Jackson's Whole also creates slaves, either by conditioning or by genetic manipulation: they are called jeeveses (possibly

Bujold's only direct Wodehouse reference). "They're said to pine if they are separated from their master or mistress, and sometimes even die if he or she dies" (CVA 41). The jeeves is a symbol of the creative yet totally exploitative and immoral spirit of uncontrolled capitalism on Jackson's Whole.

Miles dislikes the Houses, although it is thanks to the rivalries between them that, in *Mirror Dance*, he is brought back from death. However he does not have the same visceral hatred for them that his clone brother Mark does. While Mark was himself growing up as a clone on Jackson's Whole, he learns about House Bharaputra's life extension business, whereby wealthy people have their brains, with their personalities and memories, transplanted into the bodies of young clones in order to extend their lives. The operation is not always successful, as a certain percentage of the patients die: "'Yeah,' thought Miles, *'starting with 100% of the clones, whose brains are flushed to make room . . .*'" (BI 116–17). Mark, masquerading as Miles, leads a punitive expedition against Bharaputra's cloning facilities in *Mirror Dance*, rescuing some of the young clones before their "flushing"; later, wiser and more mature, he plans to use his very considerable acquired wealth "to support development of an alternative to the clone-brain transplant method of life extension that will knock it out of business" (Cry 264). The Durona clone family, whose medical skills were key to the revival of Miles after his death and freezing (in *Mirror Dance*), are at the heart of Mark's plan; he arranges for their escape from Jackson's Whole and their settlement on the more technologically advanced planet of Escobar.

The most engaging of all Bujold's exercises in world building is probably Cetaganda. Cetagandans appear, at the beginning, in *Shards of Honor* and *The Warrior's Apprentice*, in rather featureless terms, as the instigators of an invasion of Barrayar and as an opponent of Barrayar in the three Cetagandan wars. They make a physical and very striking first appearance in *The Warrior's Apprentice*, when Miles discovers that among the new recruits to the Dendarii are "two dozen Cetagandan ghem-fighters, variously dressed, but all with full formal face paint freshly applied, looking like an array of Chinese temple demons" (WA 212). In *Ethan of Athos*, however, published in the same year, Cetagandans become a major plot element. Again, it is in the shape of the ghem, the military aristocracy. Ghem-colonel Millisor's attempts to capture Terran-C on Kline Station are being tracked by Elli Quinn, as Miles's agent, and intersect with the very different mission of Ethan Urquhart. From Quinn's point of view, Cetaganda is "a typical male-dominated totalitarian state, only slightly mitigated by their rather artistic cultural peculiarities" (EA 65). Genetic experimentation is one of their interests, and since they are militarily aggressive, she wonders if Terran-C is perhaps a member of a battalion of super-soldiers, bred in vats. She and Ethan soon find out that the Cetagandans are breeding a different kind of super-weapon: a new race of telepaths. Terran-C tells them how Millisor uses him to probe the minds of dissidents: a mistake, since he learned for the first time that there *are* dissidents from the oppressive military regime of the ghem-lords. We acquire ideas about Cetaganda through its main representative on Kline station: Ghem-colonel Luyst Millisor, a counterintelligence officer—efficient, ruthless, cruel, and determined. The Cetagandans occupied Barrayar for a generation and were equally ruthless.

The appearance of Cetagandans in subsequent stories emphasized the impression of the Cetagandans as galactic Nazis or WWII Japanese, that is, irredeemable villains. A year after *Ethan of Athos* the novella "The Borders of Infinity" appeared, in which Miles manages to find a way out of a Cetagandan prisoner-of-war camp on Dagoola, which is constructed to be both perfectly in line with the galaxy's equivalents to the Geneva Conventions and yet hellishly cruel (perfectly calculated rations lead to competition and shortage, absence of work leads to insanity). As a result of Miles's success on Dagoola, Cetaganda puts a price on his head, and in *Brothers in Arms* he spends quite a lot of time avoiding ghem-warriors on Earth. In *The Vor Game* Miles foils a Cetagandan invasion of Vervain, which might be the harbinger of a further expansionary policy of Cetaganda, threatening Barrayar once again. In *Barrayar*, the Cetagandans remain a constant, cold-war threat on the horizon for Aral. In *Mirror Dance*, when Illyan and others realize that Miles's body in its cryochamber is missing, an immediate thought is that it is a Cetagandan plot. Mark is convinced it is still on Jackson's Whole, but he cannot persuade Illyan of this: "He's got Cetagandans on the brain" (MD 338). In addition, the Durona family is convinced that the cloning of Miles to produce Mark was a Cetagandan plot (MD 416). If in doubt, blame the obvious expansionist, ruthless, and largely faceless, villains.

Mirror Dance (1994) looks at events around the time Miles was twenty-eight years old; Bujold's next book, *Cetaganda* (1996), leaps back to when

Miles was twenty-two—that is, before he become a Cetagandan prisoner of war on Dagoola and before the Cetagandans went gunning for him on Old Earth. As we have seen, this was the novel that caused Bujold to realize that not writing the story of Miles in chronological order was going to create all kinds of continuity problems. Bujold's main message with *Cetaganda* would appear to be that villains are human too—or, if looked at from their point of view, are not that villainous at all. She had performed a similar sleight of hand with *Barrayar*, which is humanized as soon as Cordelia gets to know Aral and other Barrayarans. The summary of *Cetaganda* in chapter 2 explained the story in the novel, but it did not emphasise how thoroughly Miles (and Ivan) explored the culture of the Cetagandans. Bujold proceeds by some misdirection and teasing, in that the truth is only revealed gradually, and then only after a number of false leads. It is already known to Barrayarans that the Cetagandan Empire is highly hierarchical, but the exact mechanisms of control had, as far as can be seen, been unclear even to people like the Barrayaran ambassador until Miles came to the planet.

The imperial palace is situated on Eta Ceta IV, and from there the empire's eight major worlds and various other dependent planets are governed. We learn nothing about ordinary Cetagandans, only about the two different levels of the aristocracy, and about the ba, who are the neuter servants of the upper aristocracy. The lower-level aristocrats are the only ones whom most outsiders encounter: the ghem, whose men form the core of the armies that established the empire, but who have, in recent years, met with a number of political reverses. As Ethan discovers on Kline Station, ghem warriors are distinguished from each other by bizarre and colourful patterns painted on their faces, which relate to their status and/or their grouping within the armed forces. The ghem are to be found in security positions on Eta Ceta IV itself: Miles finds Ghem-colonel Benin, who interviews Miles in connection with a murder, to be not unlike a senior security man on Barrayar—in other words, a type that Miles had met many times before and whom he therefore finds both congenial and predictable. Benin wears face paint that indicates his imperial allegiance rather than his clan: "a white base with intricate black curves and red accents that Miles thought of as the bleeding-zebra look" (Cet 116). Miles predicts, correctly, promotion in Benin's future, and he thinks that perhaps Benin would be rewarded by having his genes taken up for inclusion in the genome of the upper aristocracy.

Genetic manipulation is at the heart of the Cetagandan system: ghem ladies vie against each other in producing exotic creations, though by using genetic material from animals and plants rather than humans. Miles and Ivan attend an exhibition of these creations (Cet 164–66); Ivan is attacked by a hyperactive climbing rose. When he encounters a tree, from which small kittens hang in pods, he assumes that they are glued in, and he rashly attempts to rescue one: it dies in his hand as soon as he picks it. More serious but equally amoral genetic engineering is carried on by the haut, the upper level of the aristocracy, who seem to be invisible most of the time, as far as ordinary Cetagandans are concerned. The haut are the result of a program of genetic improvement—of eugenics—over several centuries. There is a question as to whether they are actually human any longer, but their long-term goal is certainly to create a posthuman species. It was already flagged up in *Ethan of Athos* and alluded to in *Cetaganda*, that the Star Crèche might experiment with the importation of genes for telepathy into the genome. The genetic work is carried on by the Star Crèche, an all-female and all-haut group of scientists, ultimately under the control of the emperor, but in practice under the direct control of the mother of the emperor, or the mother of his heir. The Star Crèche controls the genome of the haut very strictly, allowing it to develop in part by the insertion of promising ghem genes; their sexless servitors, the ba, were used for (apparently harmless) genetic experimentation. Each year, the Star Crèche on Eta Ceta IV send out haut fetuses to the eight planetary governors and their consorts (who are all themselves haut women closely associated with the Star Crèche). The story behind *Cetaganda* is the plan to decentralize this system and to allow the consorts to take charge of genetic developments on their planet; however, one of the planetary governors wants to subvert this plan, and centralize matters on himself with the help of senior ghem.

Cetaganda is immediately reminiscent of traditional Japanese culture: there is an emperor; there is an apparently rigid aristocratic or caste system, and a military class; ceremony is an important part of aristocratic life; and there is high respect given (by aristocrats at least) to every aspect of art and aesthetics. Bujold has said that it was partly the Japan of Lady Murasaki Shikibu, who wrote the *Tale of Genji* in the early eleventh century, that lay behind Cetaganda (which might explain the importance of haut women in Cetagandan culture), but also Imperial China of the late Manchu period.[3]

There are no apparent clues from Cetagandan names, however. If the name of Luyst Millisor, the first Cetagandan we meet in the Vorkosigan saga, has any ethnic origins, it would appear to be European rather than Asian. (There is a law firm called Millisor and Nobil in Cleveland, Ohio, but Bujold tells me she had not encountered them.) Other names we come across (in *Cetaganda*) are Fletchir Giaja, the emperor; Lisbet Degtiar, his mother; Ilsum Kety; Dag Benin; and so on. These look very much like the made-up names of people in a Jack Vance space opera. If there is a specific Earth culture from which Cetagandans are intended to derive, it is concealed in points of detail. Indeed, that may be the purpose: after all, it is the policy of the Cetagandan Empire to develop and indeed evolve away from its primitive Earth roots, in the direction of the posthuman.

CryoBurn, in which the action takes place almost entirely on the planet Kibou-daini (not mentioned previously in the Vorkosigan saga), was published in 2010. This is the third culture in the Vorkosigan universe with Japanese links, and this one the most direct of all. The planet is not solely Japanese: one of the first things we learn about it is that the local prefecture's capital is called both Northbridge and Kitahashi ("to ensure the confusion of tourists no doubt" [Cry 6]). The first human being that Miles meets in the narrative is Jin Sato, who clearly speaks English; on the other hand, he automatically adds the Japanese particle *san* to names and (in passages focalized on him) thinks of Miles as "Miles-san." Name giving suggests a multicultural society: there are characters such as Yuuichi Matson and Seiichiro Leiber and (swapping the elements around) George Suwabi and Ted Fuwa, but there are names from Chinese, Korean, and Indian cultures as well as Japanese. We do not actually see much of Kibou-daini society, and what we do see only has one significant similarity with twenty-first-century Japanese society: the importance of large and powerful commercial corporations, on the verge of spreading through the rest of human space. The Japanese element is not emphasized, however, and the scam in which the Kibou-daini corporations are engaged has as much application to American society as to Japanese. As Bujold has said, "The underlying theme of *CryoBurn* is death, and all the multitude of ways people dodge or deal with it" (LMB 12), including the establishment of cryonics corporations. And the germ of the plot came from meeting a science fiction fan who was involved with the Alcor Life Extension Foundation (originally the Alcor Society for Solid State Hypothermia), which has been investigating the potential for human cryopreservation since 1972 (LMB 13–14). The materials that he sent to Bujold prompted her to start imagining a society in which everyone learned to desire cryopreservation, and then to musing upon the problem of the poor who were shut out of healthcare and from such procedures as cryopreservation. She added, in parentheses, "If anyone wants to discern any tart observations about health-care distribution in the here-and-now from all this, feel free" (LMB 13).

Of Earth—"Old, romantic, historic Earth, the big blue marble itself" (BA 7)—we learn relatively little. Even though Miles spends much of *Brothers in Arms* on Earth, he does not leave London. If there is a message here at all, it is aimed at the climate-change deniers. Los Angeles is below water (Miles thinks about taking a submarine tour of Lake Los Angeles), and New York keeps the water at bay by "its famous dykes." London's Thames Tidal Barrier (which opened in 1984) is having to do a lot of heavy-duty pumping to keep the high tides from flooding London. It is known to local wags as the King Canute Memorial (BA 271): no doubt, in the thirtieth century as in the twenty-first, the English still get the story of King Canute back to front, believing him to be an idiot who thought he could control the tides, rather than a wise king attempting to shame his sycophantic courtiers. Disappointingly, Bujold does little to describe a far future London save in vague phrases, such as "the spaceport city of London, a jigsaw of nearly two millennia of clashing architectural styles" (BA 12–13). We have a greater feel for how Vorbarr Sultana looks than we have for future London.

Earth does still play a significant role in the Vorkosigan universe, reigning culturally supreme and as technically advanced as Beta Colony (BA 8). An unnamed engineer from Earth tells Miles, in a self-deprecating manner, "We're rather off the main trade routes, except for the tourists and historians," but Miles thinks to himself that it was a planet of nine billion people, and thus, presumably, of economic importance even so (BA 3). Earth still preserves (or thinks it does) some air of superiority because of its history. Commander Tung, for instance, is from Earth "and never lets you forget it" (WA 161). A section of Kline Station has been transformed into an exact replica of "some famous palace on Earth . . . the Elhamburger or something," thus demonstrating that if Earth means prestige and luxury, then the details of its history have been lost, at least in the mind of someone like Elli Quinn (who has mangled the name "Alhambra") (EA 66).

Earth also does still serve as a repository for its diversity of wildlife. Count Piotr Vorkosigan imports a frozen embryo of a horse from Earth for his stud farm (CH 348). But Earth seems to have exported its biota everywhere it can among its colony worlds centuries earlier. There is an enlightening conversation between Jin and Miles in *CryoBurn* (32). Miles says that Barrayar has "the usual Earth imports," which include fish in stocked lakes: the Barrayaran plants and animals—mostly bugs, but larger creatures in the seas—are generally toxic to humans. On Kibou-daini, Jin responds, the native fauna were mostly microorganisms; a lot of Earth plants had been imported to follow the melting glaciers, but not many animals. Miles compares Kibou-daini to Komarr—"a cold world, being slowly terraformed"—and mentions Sergyar, which has "a fully developed native ecosystem, and lots of amazing animals," some of which, of course, in *Shards of Honor*, come close to killing his parents. Jin is disappointed not to learn more from Miles about Earth. It is only on his second trip, Miles says, that he gets out of London, and that visit (with Ekaterin) is mostly to visit "lots of different gardens" (Cry 281).

Running through all these descriptions of planets is the firm sense that for Bujold, cultures shape individuals as much as environmental or genetic determinants do. As we shall see in chapter 5, this is the principle on which she constructs the characters that live on these worlds.

CHAPTER 5

CHARACTER

At the end of *Diplomatic Immunity* Miles visits Cetaganda for a second time. He has yet again been instrumental in defeating a plot against Barrayar's old enemy, the Cetagandan Empire and is again rewarded by the Cetagandan emperor. This time he does not receive a medal that he would never dare wear on Barrayar but is honored by having his genetic material sampled for the Star Crèche, for possible insertion into the haut genome. As his old associate Pel, a haut lady, puts the sampling needle into his arm, Miles mutters: "It's prob'ly nurture not nature, y'know" (DI 297).

The question of whether character is a product of nurture or nature is one that is alluded to often in the Vorkosigan books. There is a crucial conversation between Miles and Elena Bothari, for instance, which hinges on their shared fear of genetic determinism. Elena's father and Miles's bodyguard Sergeant Bothari has just been killed, and both are trying to cope with this. For Elena, it is not just a question of coping with the death but of dealing with the discovery that her father had been a psychotic monster, murdered by her mother.

> "I am a madman's rape-bred bastard, my mother is a murderess who hates the very shape of my shadow—I can't believe I've inherited no more from them than my nose and my eyes—"
> There it was, the dark fear, most secret (WA 228).

This dark fear is one that Miles shares with Elena: the fear that their futures are going to be determined by their genes. Elena feels that as the child of a madman and a murderess, she has no chance in the world. "No!" cries Miles, "You're not them. You are you, your own person—totally separate—innocent." He is trying to reassure her while at the same time trying to reassure himself. He is descended (by two lines of descent) from the Mad Emperor Yuri (WA 229). In a sense, Miles's whole spectacular career is an attempt to prove that he can overcome his genes (his potential legacy of insanity) and his stunted body. That is no doubt why, to begin with, he is so keen to contradict those who regard him as a mutant: no, he does not have deficient genes, but he has been damaged before birth. *"It's teratogenic, not genetic. I'm not a mutant"* (BI 31). Only later does he decide to remain silent when people call him "a little mutant": if he can achieve so much, perhaps others will realize that mutants can be valuable members of society. He knows that he does not owe his deformity to his genes, but most people assume that he does. In other words, Barrayaran society, and not just the aristocrats, values genetic inheritance; but Miles knows that "It's prob'ly nurture not nature, y'know."

In this chapter, one emphasis will be on the depth and complexity of Bujold's characterization, with particular discussion of the relationship between Miles and his brother Mark, and between Miles and his cousin Ivan. But primarily this chapter will examine how Bujold creates and presents character and personality itself. She presents them as created by culture, by nurture, and by experience. Genes, of course, remain at the root; and we are in a universe in which genes can be modified, before and after birth.

The debate about character runs throughout the Vorkosigan books, and it is a political debate rather than a scientific or psychological one. The political elite of Barrayar, which provides us with most of the protagonists in the Vorkosigan novels, is wedded to the ideology of aristocratic superiority, which values nature (that is, genetics) over nurture; but the reader, who sees Barrayar mostly through the skeptical, cynical, and democratic eyes of Cordelia and Miles, soon learns to see the flaws inherent in a system that rewards birth over ability. And, as Cordelia remarks to the scandalized Piotr Vorkosigan, the Vor cannot even be certain that their bloodline is pure (CH 359). Years later that remark comes home, when it is discovered (through a gene scan) that René Vorbretten had a Cetagandan great-grandfather (ACC 44). Nor does Cordelia seem to be very sympathetic to Miles's fears of congenital insanity. As she says, half joking, to Mark, "No one on Barrayar is sane, by Betan standards. Not even you and me" (MD 286). She is not ascribing mental illness to the entire planet, of course; as we see elsewhere, it is above all the institutions and culture of Barrayar that she regards as mad, rather than necessarily those individuals embedded within that culture, who are almost inevitably guided by those institutions.

The significance of the origins of character and personality is even more crucial when we remember that Bujold's novels are very much character driven. Bujold creates character in a number of ways, but above all through two means: the choice of focalization and the description of people's interrelationships. Series novels, in any genre, win reader loyalty not so much for the ingenuity of their plots or the excitement of their action as for the author's ability to engage readers in their characters and the interaction between those characters. Interaction is one key, hence the popularity of stories with a pair of contrasting protagonists: Holmes and Watson, Jeeves and Wooster, Poirot and Hastings, Cool and Lam, Wolfe and Goodwin, Fafhrd and the Gray Mouser, Aubrey and Maturin. A really successful series writer like Bujold can work with a larger palette of characters who all intrigue readers or who offer different things to different readers. Most Bujold readers admit to a fascination with Miles Vorkosigan, but they may also be intrigued by Cordelia, Mark, Ivan, Gregor, and Illyan, or even minor characters (and latecomers to the series) like Byerly or Roic.

The focus in most of the science fiction has been on Miles Vorkosigan. Three early books—*Shards of Honor*, *Ethan of Athos*, and *Falling Free*—do not feature Miles at all; in *Barrayar* we see him only briefly at the end, as a fetus, an infant, and a five-year-old. But in all the other novels until the last, *Captain Vorpatril's Alliance*, Miles is the main character, and the one whom we get to know best. Early on, at least, we are privy to Miles's thoughts and therefore to his self-doubts and his anxieties, which does much to enable us to accept his apparent genius and astonishing success. In the later books, with multiple focalizations, we are sometimes seeing Miles from the outside, a device which Bujold uses to throw Miles's self-evaluation into sharp perspective.

We do get a hint of Miles's impact on the world around him very early on, in the epilogue to *Barrayar* (completed after several books featuring the adult Miles had been published) when we read Cordelia's panted words to her doctor: "You never told me the little bugger was going to be *hyperactive*" (CH 584). Miles's future is in a sense predicted by Cordelia at that stage, for she noted that his months "spent immobilized in that dreadful spinal brace did teach him how to do charm. The most efficient long-term way to control those about you, and thus exert your will. . . . He's the most willful little monster I've ever encountered, but he makes you not notice" (CH 590). Similar evaluations come from his superiors or associates. Arde Mayhew, soon after he has met Miles, discovers that Elena had not been able to see that the hyperactive Miles had been on stimulants: "Mayhew's laughter faded. 'My God,' he said hollowly, 'you mean he's like that *all the time?*'" (WA 98). Miles's own father had no illusions about Miles's dynamism and self-confidence: "I think he will make a terrible ensign . . . but if he can avoid being strangled by his harried superiors for—er—excessive initiative, I think he might be a fine General Staff officer someday" (WA 98). The man in charge of assigning young trained officers learns this from his own experience. Cecil starts by accusing Miles of insubordination. He argues too much, says Cecil, to which Miles immediately and indignantly responds "No, I don't," before realizing what he has done (VG7). Cecil points out that Miles treats his superior officers not as equals (the word Miles volunteers) but as cattle, to be driven to his will. "Whether you were in charge or not, somehow it was always your idea that ended up getting carried out"; moreover, he did it while still concealing his "little arrogant streak" (VG 7).

The person who knows Miles best, apart from Aral and Cordelia themselves, is his cousin Ivan, who is allowed in *A Civil Campaign* to express his own internal view of the "hyperactive little git" in one of the passages in which he is the focalizing character. Miles asks Ivan for a favor, with a smile.

Damn that smile. . . . In between inspiring you to strangle him with your bare hands, he could make you proud enough to cry. At least, Ivan had taken care no one could see his face, when he'd watched from the Council floor as Miles had taken his Auditor's oath with that terrifying intensity, before all the assembled panoply of Barrayar last Winterfair. So small, so wrecked, so obnoxious. So incandescent. *Give the people a light, and they'll follow it anywhere.* Did Miles know how dangerous he was? (ACC 29)

The reader has seen the way Miles is viewed by his associates, but this insight that he is dangerous—that he has all the charismatic qualities required of a dictator or a mob leader—is not something that often comes to the surface in the text. We shall return to that aspect of Miles's character in chapter 8.

Insubordinate, arrogant, manipulative, hyperactive: these are not generally thought to be endearing qualities. One of Bujold's skills is to allow us to see these qualities mostly from the inside, to see them as inevitable parts of Miles's character, and thus to a large extent to forgive them (while, perhaps, being glad that Miles is not one's own colleague or relative). Miles's own self-evaluation sometimes comes in little vignettes: extracts from imaginary CVs, perhaps. Thus, a young Miles, after he has failed a military assault course, muses to himself: "Lord Miles Naismith Vorkosigan. Occupation: security risk. Hobbies: falling off walls, disappointing sick old men to death, making girls cry" (WA 47). Miles is shown to be perfectly capable of analyzing himself, but he tends only to do so when his impetuosity has landed him in trouble again.

There are a number of self-evident factors in Miles's makeup. First, there is his disability (which is discussed more fully in chapter 6). The poison-gas attack on his home by a disgruntled young Vor lord leaves Miles with stunted growth and brittle bones; it is not until he was in his twenties that successive rounds of operations replace most of his skeletal structure with plastic prosthetics. The Durona family on Jackson's Whole do much reconstruction while they revive him from death (in *Mirror Dance*); but even in his late thirties (in *CryoBurn*), Miles is still reliant to some extent on his walking stick. If one wanted to subscribe to Freud's phallic obsessions, one might note that when Miles was young, he could not bear to be separated from his grandfather's knife: as a fellow soldier said to him, "That, ah,—blade of yours came in pretty handy after all" (WA 311). Later on, his cane functions "not just as a walking aid but to substitute for a foot in the door."[1] Miles never uses his disabilities as an excuse, however; they instead provide him with a constant challenge and force him to compensate his physical disabilities by the use of his mind: *"If you can't be seven feet tall, be seven feet smart"* (BI 106–7). He is an overachiever because of his disabilities, but also—and this is closely related—because of a desire to prove himself to his father, and particularly to his grandfather, whose disappointment in the stunted body of the Vorkosigan heir once led him to an abortive attempt at infanticide (BA 201). He strives all the time, from infancy onward, to make his father proud of him: as he put it to the emperor, "to make my life an offering fit to lay at his feet" (WA 297).

This close attachment to his father and grandfather is not merely an exaggerated familial piety because of his own individual circumstances: it is part of his upbringing as a Vor lord. The Vor (or the best of them) have an almost fanatical belief in the importance of family for its own sake, and also of the importance of the Vor for the survival of the imperial system. Miles learns from his Betan mother to view the Vor system with some detachment and cynicism, but he nevertheless offers the system, and the family that was embedded in it, exceptional loyalty. Even so, it is a burden. When Elena Bothari remarked that Miles was "the culmination of your generations . . . the flower of the Vor," he stared in astonishment, and responded:

> The culmination of degeneration, maybe. . . . They do add up, it's true. My grandfather carried nine generations on his back. My father carried ten. I carry eleven—and I swear that last one weighs more than all the rest put together. It's a wonder I'm not squashed even shorter. I feel like I'm down to about half a meter right now. Soon I'll disappear altogether. (WA 228–30)

As this comment suggests, Miles is hardly a model of balance and sanity. When accused by Galeni of being schizoid, he denies it, but then he admits in afterthought, "A little manic-depressive, maybe" (BA 91). One of his coping mechanisms is to try to avoid introspection by engaging in constant activity. When scared witless, he does not show it because, he says, "I've got forward momentum. There's no virtue in it. It's just a balancing act. I don't dare stop" (WA 113). It is a characteristic he shares with the sorcerer's apprentice, of course, after whom the first novel about the young Miles is named. But he also has the ability to avoid introspection by taking on other identities. When he looks into the mirror, he sees Admiral Naismith. But under that surface he is Lieutenant Vorkosigan. Under that is Lord Vorkosigan, and beneath that is Admiral Naismith. A culinary metaphor occurred to Elli Quinn: "Gods, I've fallen in love with a man who thinks he's an onion" (BA 114).

The different layers of his persona are not equal in their significance. As Lord Vorkosigan, Miles wants to prove his worth to the Imperium through service as lieutenant (or, he hopes, as captain), although all the while knowing that his fellow servicemen despise him for his physical inadequacy and because he has *clearly* succeeded through social and family connections. It is Miles's masquerade as Admiral Naismith, which he achieves through purely instinctive forward momentum—"The Dendarii Mercenaries were an accident. I didn't plan them—they just happened, in the course of scrambling from crisis to crisis" (WA 297)—that provides him with a defense against the strains of trying to prove himself in a world where physical prowess is valued and where anything resembling a mutation is both feared and despised. It is no accident that he takes his fictional surname of Naismith from his mother's maiden name and that the fictional Naismith is, like his mother, a Betan. Beta Colony represents all the freedom, opportunity, and tolerance that is denied to Miles as a Barrayaran. When Gregor comments to Miles that he appears weird in his Naismith persona, Miles remarks, "I guess Naismith is me with no brakes. No constraints. He doesn't have to be a good little Vor, or any kind of a Vor. He doesn't have a problem with subordination, he isn't subordinate to anyone" (VG 193). At times the two personae may not appear very different from each other.

When Miles has to play Admiral Naismith in front of Elena Bothari and Count Vorkosigan, he warns them that Naismith is not very deferential: Elena and Aral, knowing Miles's own lack of deference very well, both burst out laughing, to Miles's discomfort (VG 328–29). Bujold herself has put it in a different way: when describing the two personae as "the constrained Lord Vorkosigan and the active Admiral Naismith," she added: "I leave it as an exercise for the reader to figure how this relates to Mrs. Lois Bujold, housewife, and Lois McMaster Bujold, successful science fiction writer" (VC 14). At an early stage, however, she knew which side of Miles to privilege, perhaps aware that the Naismith phase could not last forever: when *Brothers in Arms* came out, Jim Baen was in favor of putting a banner on the front cover, announcing it as "A Miles Naismith Adventure"; Bujold held out for "A Miles Vorkosigan Adventure" and got her way (VC 14).

Cordelia is perfectly aware of Miles's problems, as she reveals in a conversation with Count Vorkosigan and Miles's clone brother, Mark. She argues that Miles was so stressed he created an alternate personality and then persuaded thousands of mercenaries to support his psychosis, and the Imperium, into paying for it. He's a genius, but maybe not sane. "No. That's not fair. Miles's safety valve works. I won't really begin to fear for his sanity till he's cut off from the little admiral." (MD 216–17). Mark is seriously unsettled by these comments. He had thought of Miles as perfect, never as "seriously crazed." Miles himself occasionally worries about whether he is wholly sane; but it is a question that recurs much more often to those close to him, particularly Mark (who resembles him in all sorts of ways, above all by not being wholly sane himself). This passage is interesting in relation to Bujold's strategy for focalization, which I shall discuss shortly: we learn about how someone as clear-sighted as Cordelia views Miles only after Miles ceases to be the primary focalizing character.

Bujold writes a Miles who is a natural actor. Jo Walton, in her retrospective review of *The Warrior's Apprentice*, commented on how he play-acts, and not only when he is Naismith.

> He gets out of bed to mime the mutant villain, he pretends to be rehearsing Shakespeare with Elena, he plays the Baba in the Elena and Baz's betrothal scene. Clearly acting parts has been part of his life for a long time, and that explains (partly) how he can take on roles so easily.[2]

Being Admiral Naismith, however, is rather more than acting. There are perhaps echoes here of one of Robert A. Heinlein's greatest science-fiction novels, *Double Star* (1956), in which an actor takes on the persona of a major politician and becomes so involved that his act becomes inseparable from reality and indeed makes its own reality. (Another [non-SF] novel that investigates this phenomenon is R. K. Narayan's *The Guide*, 1958.) Becoming Naismith was not so much playing a role as adopting a different personality. As Miles walks into a transfer station ready to rejoin the Dendarii, he "could feel Naismith refilling his skin, generated from somewhere deep in his psyche right out to his fingertips. Goodbye, dull Lieutenant Miles Vorkosigan, deep cover operative for Barrayaran Imperial Security (and overdue for a promotion); hello, dashing Admiral Naismith, space mercenary and all-around soldier of fortune" (MD

27). At that moment, he seems to be like any teenage boy—acting out the role of "Lord Vorthalia the Bold, Legendary Hero from the Time of Isolation" (with whom he had been obsessed as a child: ACC 259), with himself as the hero. But when Illyan asks him to "play the part of Admiral Naismith again," Miles thinks to himself, "*It wasn't just a part, Illyan,*" and adds out loud, "I could play Naismith again, sure. It's *stopping* playing Naismith that scares me." Illyan thinks this is a joke, and Miles knows that he has not understood what it was like: "Three parts fakery and flim-flam, and one part . . . something else. Zen, gestalt, delusion? Uncontrollable moments of alpha-state exaltation" (VG 115).

Miles betrays his ambivalence about the balance between his two roles when talking to Duv Galeni on Earth in *Brothers in Arms*. He tells Galeni he cannot neglect the Dendarii "even to play the part of Lieutenant Vorkosigan."

> Galeni rocked back in his chair, his eyebrows shooting up. "*Play the part* of Lieutenant Vorkosigan? Who do you think you *are?*"
>
> "I'm . . ." Miles fell silent, seized by a sudden vertigo, like falling down a defective lift tube. For a dizzy moment, he could not even make sense of the question. The silence lengthened.
>
> Galeni folded his hands on his desk with an unsettled frown. His voice went mild. "Lose track, did you?"
>
> "I'm . . ." Miles's hands opened helplessly. "It's my duty, when I'm Admiral Naismith, to be Admiral Naismith as hard as I can. I don't usually have to switch back and forth like this" (BA 79–80).

It is clearly an unsettling experience.

Crucial here, for an understanding of Miles, is his last comment: about *duty*. His father, too, has an overwhelming sense of his duty—to his family, to his district, and to the emperor. It is something inculcated in the Vor (and, tellingly, something not shared by his Betan mother). Part of Miles's problem is that his duty is to both the Dendarii and to the empire; but, more specifically, he seems to have felt his duty not as an abstract thing, which he owes to an institution, but as something he owes to the people he knew. But the passage above uses the word "duty" twice. The first time relates to Miles's feeling that he has a "duty" to play Naismith as well as possible. This is not a duty that he owes to others—although his friends among the Dendarii will suffer if he wavers in his masquerade; it is a duty he owes to himself and his own sense of honor.

Bujold's women tend to be more psychologically perceptive than the men. Elli Quinn offers an analysis that supplements Cordelia's, one that Miles clearly finds all too accurate. Cordelia, Elli thought, had been exhausted by the demands of Barrayaran society: "Barrayar is her cancer. Killing her slowly" (MD 26–27), and adds that it was happening to Miles as well. As Naismith he can live without the restraints that being a Vor on Barrayar require. Naismith may be a maniac, but, Elli concludes, "He is my kind of maniac. Lord Vorkosigan is a dull and dutiful stick by contrast. I've seen you at home on Barrayar, Miles. You're like half yourself there. Damped down, muted somehow. Even your voice is lower. It's extremely weird." Elli has fallen in love with Naismith; but she cannot love Lord Vorkosigan. It is entirely predictable that when Miles eventually marries, it is to a Vor woman emerging from a marriage to a Vor lord who is even more "dull and dutiful," at least on the surface, than Miles himself.

The prediction that Miles needs his Naismith role in order to retain his sanity was perceptive but, as it turned out, wrong. When Miles is dismissed from the imperial service (for hiding the extent of his medical problems after being resuscitated from cryonic freezing), he does indeed plunge into despair. But that is something he has done before, as Naismith, when he finds himself in a crisis (most notably in the days following Bothari's death). His real despair in *Memory* relates to being deprived of any role or purpose that will serve to give him identity. He has lost his role in ImpSec, and he stands little chance of becoming Naismith again. Once he is given the problem of trying to understand what has happened to the hitherto impeccable memory of his former boss Illyan, he recovers his equanimity. When Haroche eventually offers him the chance to return to the Dendarii and to his Naismith role, he is tempted. But *"I elect to be . . . myself"* (Mem 387), he tells himself. It is a crucial moment in the novel—indeed in his whole life.

But the decision proves less crucial than expected, for when Miles is given the official chain of imperial auditor, he has the authority to investigate the situation properly (Ivan remarked that it was a choke-chain that Miles had always needed [Mem 230]). Miles is able to reincorporate his discarded Naismith person into the role of auditor, unaware of this until Ivan (far more perceptive than Miles ever acknowledges) points out how he is playing the little admiral again. "Wasn't it on purpose? You're acting just like you do when you play Admiral Naismith, except without the Betan accent. Full tilt forward, no inhibitions, innocent bystanders scramble for their lives" (Mem 235). Naismith is, of course, a much more authoritative persona than he has ever been able to display as Lieutenant Vorkosigan. The post as auditor gives Miles back what his role as admiral bestowed: an opportunity to avoid his problems of insubordination by having no one to be subordinate to. As auditor, he is answerable to the emperor, but an auditor can act as if he *were* emperor, independent and entirely responsible for his own decisions. Innocent bystanders scramble for their lives.

Miles's character develops in response to his circumstances: his disability, his status as only son and heir, his intelligence, and the various crises into which he throws himself. But Bujold also emphasizes that it develops in interaction with those around him. His mother and his Betan grandmother help give him horizons that are much wider and more tolerant than the average Barrayaran's, whether Vor or not. His relation with his father develops in reaction to his father's guilt about not protecting him from terrorism and for taking on the sort of job that attracts terrorist attacks; in addition, there is the guilt involved in taking a job that requires so much time spent out of the home. That guilt poisons his relationship with Miles—or threatens to do so. "My work has been a blight on you from the very beginning," Aral says. And Miles responds, although only after his father has left the room: "I'll make you take back that apology! I am all right, damn it! I'll make you see it. I'll stuff you so full of pride in me there'll be no room left for your precious guilt!" (WA 49). We have seen how Bujold brings her father into her stories, as Leo Graf and as Auditor Vorthys; but there is clearly something of the relationship between herself and her father in this relationship between Miles and his father, at least in terms of her desire to prove herself.

Bujold develops and expands on Miles's character across the whole Vorkosigan sequence, in part as she develops and expands her own narrative techniques. All Bujold's novels are written in the narrative mode of third-person limited subjective: that is, at any point we are vouchsafed the thoughts of only one individual, and that individual is always on stage. Anything that happens outside that person's direct experience is not directly reported in the novel. The two novels that deal with Cordelia's experience up to and just beyond Miles's birth are focalized entirely through Cordelia; *Ethan of Athos* is focalized solely through Ethan; the first five books that deal with Miles are focalized solely through Miles. That gives a very particular flavor to Miles's characterization. Even though comments critical of Miles's position are embedded in the narrative, it is only when the focalization moves away from Miles that we begin to see clearly how Miles is viewed by those around him. Once Bujold develops this use of the third-person limited subjective mode, above all in the direction of multiple focalization, she develops and deepens the character of Miles and others.

It is *Mirror Dance* that breaks with the rather simple pattern of focalization that Bujold has used in the early Vorkosigan books. Bujold has called *Mirror Dance* "Mark's book" (VC 17). It begins by focalizing on Mark; for the next six chapters the point-of-view character alternates between Mark and Miles. Then, as Miles lies in a portable cryo unit, technically dead after his chest is shredded by a needle grenade, the novel is perforce focalized through Mark. Miles is resuscitated in chapter 19, and thereafter the focalization roughly alternates between Mark and Miles, though they are both allocated pairs of chapters. *Memory*, the next novel in the chronological sequence of Miles's career, is again a third-person limited narrative focalized through Miles. But the next two novels extend the experimentation that began with *Mirror Dance*. *Komarr* is told with a strictly alternating focalization, chapter by chapter, alternating between Ekaterin and Miles, but the first and last chapters are both given to Ekaterin, just as the first and last chapters of *Mirror Dance* are given to Mark. The decision to focalize in this way allows us to understand that Ekaterin is very different from the woman imagined by Miles in his own focalized chapters.

A Civil Campaign, the novel detailing the next period in Miles's life, is the most complex and varied of all the Bujold novels in terms of its focalization. The first chapter has Miles as the only focal character; thereafter, the only chapter in which Miles is the sole focal character is the long, central chapter 9, in which Miles's fateful dinner party is described. Apart from that there are at least two focal characters in each chapter (the change of focalization marked typographically by a line of space). There are, in total, five characters whose viewpoint we see: in order, Miles, Kareen Koudelka, Ekaterin, Mark, and Ivan. Three focalizing characters is the maximum for any single chapter, until we reach the epilogue, where the focalization shifts from Miles to Kareen, to

Mark, to Ivan, and finally to Ekaterin.[3] Thereafter, Bujold experiments a little more with focalization. The novella "Winterfair Gifts" takes a single focalizing character, Armsman Roic—the first time that the narrative is focalized through someone who is a working-class Barrayaran in origin. (We have had two focalizing characters before who are not technically Vor—Mark and Kareen Koudelka—but Mark is treated as Vor, and the Koudelkas have lived alongside the Vor all their lives.) *Diplomatic Immunity* reverts to the old pattern of having Miles as the sole focalizer. But *CryoBurn* focalizes through three characters, one of whom, Jin Sato, is not only *not* a Barrayaran at all, he is also a child: a double first. The other two focalizing characters are Miles and Roic. Shifts in focalization are clear: Miles almost always appears as Miles-san when the narrative is focalized on Jin, while, for Roic, Miles is always *m'lord*, except for one occasion when even the calm Roic gets exasperated, and Miles becomes the "little gi—m'lord" (87). Each chapter has two of those three characters as the focalizing character, except for chapter 7, which has Miles alone, and chapter 19, the penultimate chapter after the action has wound down, when all three are taken in turn as the focalizing character.

Bujold continues this more complex approach to focalization in her most recent novel. *Captain Vorpatril's Alliance* starts, predictably, with Captain Ivan Vorpatril as the focalizing character. But already before the end of chapter 1 our second main focalizer makes an appearance: Tej, Ivan's future wife. Thereafter, most chapters feature both of those focalizing characters. There are exceptions: the fourth chapter is focalized through Tej alone; chapter 21, the fourth chapter from the end, through Ivan alone. The symmetry is presumably not accidental, as there are signs that Bujold is thinking much more about the structure of her novels. In this most recent novel it is also apparent that Bujold does much more to cue her readers into the changes of focalization. In almost all cases the change is marked by not just by the insertion of a blank line but by the use of the new focalizing character's name, either in the opening word or at least in the opening sentence; an additional clue is that whenever Tej is the focalizing character, Ivan is invariably referred to as Ivan Xav.

Bujold usually seems completely in command of the choice of focalization, and she clearly gives a lot of thought to the effect of her choice. Bujold's first experiments with focalization in her early novel *Falling Free* (her fourth) show what happens when she is *not* in command. Leo Graf is the default focalizer, and chapters 1, 2, 6, and 8 are given to him alone. The two quaddies Claire and Silver are the other main focalizing characters, which allows the reader to see how the action in the novel is actually viewed by the quaddies as opposed by those who are in one way or another trying to manipulate them or change their lives. In chapter 4 there is a brief change of focalization to Bannerji, the security chief who only plays an intermittent role in the action ("her Security captain, what's-his-name, oh, yes, that idiot Bannerji," as Van Atta, the focalizing character of chapter 13, puts it). The "villain," Van Atta, makes his first appearance as a focalizing character as late as chapter 10. In the last chapter the focalization shifts from Leo to Van Atta, back to Leo, back to Van Atta, and then back to Leo again. At times it is not at all clear through whose eyes we are seeing the action. As Bujold notes, the spine of this book was the plot, which dictated the movement of focalization; normally the spine of her books is character development.

With this one exception, however, Bujold uses focalization as a very effective way of building the reader's knowledge of character. It is insidious, in that in the first seven books about the Vorkosigans we are led to empathize uncritically with our two focalizing characters, Cordelia and Miles, and implicitly to share their view of the world, which (given their closeness) is not very different from each other. It is only in the more recent books that Bujold has widened our perspective and thus deepened our knowledge of her universe and given us external perceptions of our two earliest focalizers. Our view of Cordelia does not really change, although our view of Miles certainly does, and so does our understanding of characters who were initially seen only through the lens of Miles.

There is no space here to examine in any detail the host of other characters in Miles's world, but it is worth our while to look at three people who are close to the adult Miles: his clone, Mark Vorkosigan; his boss, Simon Illyan; and his cousin, Ivan Vorpatril.

Bujold has said more than once that her main plot-generation technique has been to ask, "What's the worst possible thing that I can do to these people?" (with the necessary addendum " . . . that they can survive and learn from") (VC 6). Of all the characters that she has mistreated and tortured, probably the most unfortunate is not Miles, but Mark. He has been cloned to resemble Miles; in his childhood he goes through just as many surgical operations as Miles, but in a reverse direction. Miles has operations to remove deformities; Mark to supply them. Cordelia, who has read the medical reports in detail, explains the effects of these interventions to Aral and Mark (MD 253). The Jackson's Whole surgeons cut Mark down to Miles's size, but they do not genetically retrofit his metabolism. Mark is a very short man; but his metabolism is that of someone much taller. As a result, he finds it very easy to put on weight, a lot of weight: which, as Cordelia recognizes, also fulfills his psychological desire to distinguish himself from Miles. She sees rebellion and fear as the two components of his weight increase: rebellion against the destiny that the Jackson's Whole surgeons had intended for him, and fear of being overwhelmed by Miles. The "weight ploy," Cordelia thinks, has the same kind of "half-cocked, half-conscious brilliance" that Miles displays (MD 254).

Mark is indeed Bujold's test case for the nature versus nurture debate. He shares Miles's genes, but his upbringing is totally different. He is brought up to think of himself as Miles, his only name until the end of *Brother in Arms*, and even then, the name he is given, Mark, is his by virtue of being Miles's brother: he cannot completely escape the relationship. But Miles is brought up not in a supportive family environment but initially by staff in a facility on Jackson's Whole, then with a foster parent on the same planet, and finally by a half-crazed terrorist who drills into young Mark that his destiny is to be an assassin and the new emperor of Barrayar. He is trained to be not himself but Miles's double, and he learns whatever of Miles's gestures and habits he can. At some level Mark remains fascinated by this project, as emerges when he meets Illyan and tells him about Miles's death. Illyan, shocked, carefully places his hands flat on the desk in front of him: *"So that's where Miles picked up that gesture*, Mark, who had studied it, thought irrelevantly" (MD 199). Miles realizes that Ser Galen, the terrorist (or Komarran patriot, if you will), is not going to make Mark the emperor: he merely wants to use Mark as a dispensable agent to create chaos. The clone, just as bright as Miles, has already worked this out for himself. But, when he first has a conversation with Miles, he seems to think of himself as merely the product of his genes. Miles tells him that this is not true: "You are what you do. Choose again, and change" (BA 202).

In the same conversation Miles gives his clone an opportunity to develop his own personality and identity by giving him a name. Up to that point the clone is called Miles: that, after all, is his role, just as, in a sense, Miles's was to play Admiral Naismith. But he has a name, Miles reminds him: not one he can choose, but one that he was born with, since a second son acquires the second names of his two grandfathers just as the eldest son, in this case Miles, inherits the first names of his two grandfathers (BA 198). Thus, the clone is Mark Pierre Vorkosigan; and the status that goes with that gives him a position high within Barrayaran society and thus the power to choose a life for himself—to become a star pilot, to get involved in the family wine business, to go and live with his grandmother on Beta Colony. Choice, of course, is what is initially being denied the clone, as he lives out the destiny planned for him by Ser Galeni. Neither the destiny of genes nor the destiny of "parental" plans count for anything for Miles, since there is a great vista of choice and an opportunity to make the life he wants. Events much later, on Kibou-daini, suggest that Miles did not think long on the fact that he was in a hugely privileged situation, as a Vor lord, and that choice was not in great supply for the average farmer or lowly soldier.

Whatever Miles believes about the freedom to choose one's own destiny, Bujold shows us that, like identical twins, the genes that Miles and Mark share often provide them with similar reactions. When a Komarran guard asks Mark whether he needs help in his interrogation of Miles, they say, almost in unison, "I don't need help" and "He doesn't need help" (BA 195). They certainly do share above-average intelligence, though Mark's actual age is several years younger than Miles's, with a concomitant lack of experience. But in many other ways they are shown to be very different. That is perhaps best expressed in their disparate preferences in women. Miles's girlfriends—Elena Bothari, Elli Quinn, Ekaterin Vorsoisson, Taura—are all tall, elegant brunettes, often women whom other men find scary (though none more so than Taura). When Mark first meets Ekaterin, he judges her "pretty enough, in that elegant brainy-brunette style Miles liked. Calm? Perhaps. Guarded, certainly. Not very expressive. Round blondes were much sexier" (ACC 96): round blondes, that is, like Kareen Koudelka and, for that matter (though this is no doubt irrelevant), like the emperor's wife Laisa. In his early days as Mark, he almost raped someone close to his ideal: "Somebody short, soft, pink, timid, somebody who wouldn't kill and eat him after they mated" (MD 145). He is terrified by Elena and by Elli. Mark's ideal woman is as far away from Miles's as possible.

Bujold inflicts appalling suffering on both Miles and Mark,[4] and she is realistic enough as a writer to understand that such suffering is bound to leave traumas behind. But as the suffering is different, so is the trauma. Shannan Palma has noted that a key difference between Miles and Mark is that Miles's bones are brittle and break easily by accident; Mark's have been broken for him.[5] As a result, she argues, Miles knows that pain waits for him whenever he takes a risk; he chooses "forward momentum" in part because that means he has no time to reflect. Mark, on the other hand, has never had the option of self-directed movement and has simply learned to endure. The torture inflicted on Mark by Ryoval in *Mirror Dance* is one of captivity and suffering; Miles, Palma suggests, would probably have babbled uncontrollably before going to pieces primarily *because* there was no option for movement; his resources do not include the ability to take no action or to cope with disempowerment (something we also see in *Memory*).

As we have seen, Miles works through his traumas with the help of Admiral Naismith, and once married to Ekaterin and given freedom of action thanks to his auditorship, he appears by the end of the sequence (as we currently have it) reasonably balanced and sane. Mark, on the other hand, when we see him in *A Civil Campaign*, is still in therapy, still struggling with the demons he unlocked when he was being tortured by Ryoval. As a defence mechanism Mark's personality splits into five parts. There is Gorge, who handles the force-feedings; Grunt, who copes with the sexual assaults; Howl, who positively *wants* to be punished; and one who hides away until needed, the Other, who would eventually be revealed as Killer. Mark hides away too, protected by this "ugly, grotty, hard-bitten bunch, these psychic mercenaries of his" (MD 461).

Mark's mental condition seems to be within an area of modern psychiatry where there is considerable disagreement as to the causes and treatments, or even as to the nomenclature. It used to be known as MPD (multiple personality disorder), but is generally now known as DID (dissociative identity disorder). It was once thought to be to the result of trauma, particularly childhood trauma, but there are now suggestions that psychotherapeutic techniques can cause the disorder, or that it relates to memory-processing problems induced after childhood. There are different terms used to describe aspects of the disorder as well. The psychiatrist Paulette Gillig contrasts an "ego state," whose behaviors possess permeable boundaries with other states (although each possessing a common idea of self), with "alters" (a plural noun), meaning the other identities, each of which may give a separate "autobiographical memory" and initiative, and "a sense of ownership over individual behavior." Ellert Nijenhuis and colleagues suggest that there is a distinction between the personalities that control day-to-day behavior, though with reduced emotional reactivity, which they refer to as "the apparently normal part of the personality" (ANP) and the personalities that emerge in survival situations, which form the "emotional part of the personality" (EP).[6] Clearly Gorge, Grunt, Howl, and the Killer are those personalities who emerge in the "survival situation" in which Mark found himself on Jackson's Whole; subsequently, when he finds himself in a safe environment again, his task is to reintegrate. There is very little certainty in the whole academic area of multiple personality disorder, and Bujold's take on it would probably not be accepted by all in the field, but it is a plausible take, and an effective one in terms of the narrative arc: as Bujold has pointed out, Mark fractures along fault lines already set up in the books.

The disintegration of the personality clearly interests Bujold, although in the cases of both Mark and Miles there is a fascination with reintegration as well. In the same vein is the consideration of Simon Illyan, above all in *Memory* and thereafter. This novel was written at the time Bujold's sister-in-law Trudie was trying to cope with her mother's Alzheimer's disease and focuses on the effects of such problems on people's careers as well as their sense of identity.

At the beginning of *Memory* Miles is sacked from ImpSec by Simon Illyan because he has lied about his history of seizures (a side effect of his revival from cryogenic stasis); shortly after, Simon Illyan is hospitalized and relieved of his duties because of the failure of his memory chip. The latter is a shock to readers of the Vorkosigan books. Illyan had been a stable character—in every sense of that phrase—since *Shards of Honor*, the very first Vorkosigan book. He is utterly dependable and efficient, as well as entirely loyal and personally unambitious: the perfect public servant. Illyan's phenomenal memory, the product of an implanted eidetic memory chip, increases his value, first to Emperor Ezar and then to Aral: "You may think of him as a recording device with legs, which the Emperor may play back at will," Aral says, as he first introduces Illyan to Cordelia (CH 122). His forbidding list of accomplishments is enough to terrify most of those who work for him; Miles, and thus the reader, knows that behind his official persona hides someone with real personal kindness and a dry sense of humor.

The disintegration of Illyan's memory is discovered to be the result of deliberate sabotage; however, it mimics the appearance of Alzheimer's both in the behavior of the patient and in the reactions of those around him, who have to live through the disconcerting and distressing process. In the case of Illyan, of course, an operation serves to solve the problem: the memory chip is removed, and slowly his old brain—and to some extent his old, natural memory—returns. The new Illyan is one of the most sympathetic characters in the whole Vorkosigan saga: a gentle, retiring man. In *Captain Vorpatril's Alliance*, four years after his retirement and now married to Ivan's mother, Lady Alys, he is coping well with his continuing memory problems, and enjoying his leisure. His sardonic humor is well to the fore and sometimes seems to be playing with the formidable reputation he had earned for himself. He congratulates Ivan's wife Tej for having a father who "could sell elephants to circus masters." When Tej, puzzled, replies that circus masters would *want* to buy elephants, Illyan responds, with a broad smile, "Quite so" (CVA 264). His enigmatic demeanor, once supplied professionally in support of ImpSec's goals, now seems to be employed for his own amusement. Illyan's transformation from the efficient and even sinister spymaster to a relaxed elderly man delighting in his new life is perhaps the most satisfying piece of character development in Bujold's fiction.

If one wants to find a character in the Vorkosigan universe who may stand as a model of social normality, in contrast to Miles and Mark or even Illyan, then Ivan Vorpatril might be the obvious choice. Bujold's construction of Ivan has emerged, we can see now (with the recent publication of *Captain Vorpatril's Alliance*), as one of the more complex and successful of her characterizations. Ivan is born amid the civil war fomented by Vordarian and is alarmingly brought into the world by Sergeant Bothari; his father was killed only minutes before his birth. We first meet "the open, annoyingly handsome face" of Ivan at a gathering in Vorkosigan House for Grandfather Piotr's funeral rites (WA 42); Miles and "that idiot Ivan," as Miles and Aral both think of him, grab food and wine and retire to Miles's room. Thereafter, for a number of books, we see Ivan almost solely through Miles's eyes. Little of what we see is favorable. Under fast-penta (a drug with truth-serum properties), "You can fool all of the people some of the time," chirped Miles, "and some of the people all of the time, but you can fool Ivan anytime. He doesn't pay attention" (BA 172). "Nobody gets to choose their relatives anyway, clone or no," Miles tells Mark, "I mean, given a choice, would you pick Ivan Vorpatril for your cousin?" (BA 198). "Do me a favor, Ivan. Don't try to think. You'll hurt yourself. Just follow orders, huh?" (Cet 192). Cordelia is one of the few people shown (at a time when Mark, not Miles, is the focalizer) to understand Ivan, to some extent. She sees him as struggling against a micromanaging mother, Lady Alys, doing whatever his mother wants (out of geniality or laziness), except giving her grandchildren (MD 295).

Bujold's skill lies in persuading most readers—those readers who do not read between the lines—that Ivan is not very bright, a thoughtless womanizer and partygoer, someone who would be quite at home in Wodehouse's Drones Club, except when he has to play the role of Miles's unwilling sidekick. He does not even do that very well, in Miles's opinion, in that when the two of them are together, Ivan's tall, handsome figure reminds Miles too much of his own physical defects. Miles is furious when the Cetagandan rebels take Ivan to be the senior figure in the team just because of his imposing appearance: he rants to them (admittedly, partly to gain time until a rescuer arrived), "What did you think? That because he's taller, and, and cuter, he had to be running this show? It's the haut way, isn't it? You—you *morons*! *I'm* the brains of this outfit!" (Cet 239). But in certain circumstances Miles is happy to defer to Ivan: when he gets dressed for his disastrous dinner party, for instance, he decides what to wear by thinking what Ivan would find acceptable (ACC 159).

Ivan, in his youth at least, is not a paragon of virtue: Elena Bothari, after she has left Barrayar, calls him a jerk, and when Miles offers mild protest ("He's not such a bad sort"), Elena reveals that Ivan used to corner her when her intimidating father was not around and try to "feel her up." She never told anyone, but now says, "I almost wish I could go back in time, just to boot him in the balls" (WA 230–31). Elena does not have the social status of the Koudelka girls, or their self-confidence: Kareen Koudelka advised Mark, "Ignore Ivan, we all do" (MD 306). Ivan is presented not just as a jerk but as a rather gauche one at that. He manages to describe Elli Quinn's face, after her plasma arc injury, as being like an onion; this is within earshot of Elli, although at least Ivan has the grace to be embarrassed when she indignantly reminds him of it later (BA 27). One of Ivan's endearing features—his sense of humor—is also one of his irritating characteristics. His mother berates him for a comment he makes about Lord Mark. "'It was a joke,' Ivan muttered defensively. 'How do you expect us to all get through this alive if we're not allowed to have a sense of humor?'"—only to receive the brutal advice from his mother: "Exert yourself" (ACC 48). But, as Miles later remarks to himself, Ivan's wit is bearable because it is so often ingenuous, while unlike Ivan, "Byerly never insulted anyone unintentionally" (ACC 52).

When we have been with Miles and Ivan for long enough, we begin to appreciate the complexity of the relationship that Bujold has devised for them. To begin with, Miles's treatment of Ivan, since childhood, is mostly dreadful. Ivan well remembers the occasions when he suffered as a result of Miles's plans: at age eight, getting Ivan and Elena to dig an "escape tunnel" in the garden, only to have the tunnel collapse on Ivan (Cet 191); at age ten, persuading Ivan to help him activate an old hover tank and drive it into a barn (Cet 162); taking Ivan through a winding gorge in a lightflyer at night and without lights, without telling Ivan that he had been practicing for the previous three days (Mem 139). In their adult life, Miles constantly puts Ivan down, both in and out of Ivan's presence. It is not surprising that when we first get to share Ivan's thoughts, in *A Civil Campaign*, we discover that they are not always very charitable toward Miles. When Miles tells him about Ekaterin, Ivan thinks of "every bit of chaff his cousin had ever inflicted upon him for his numerous love affairs. *Did you think I was a stone, for you to sharpen your wits upon?*" (ACC 26). Ivan soon realizes that he has got into another of those "Miles-arguments again, which always seemed to result oh-so-logically in Miles getting whatever Miles wanted. Ivan recognized the pattern; it hadn't changed since they were five years old" (ACC 27). That same passage offers some of the epithets Ivan applied to Miles: "the hyperactive little git," "the dwarf," "the little paranoid," "Miles the maniacal."

At the same time, Ivan admits to himself that Miles was extraordinary: "In between inspiring you to strangle him with your bare hands, he could make you proud enough to cry" (ACC 29), and Bujold shows the very real depths of Ivan's care for Miles, as when she has Ivan, assisted by Galeni, quickly and efficiently shock Miles out of his catatonic fugue after being sacked from

ImpSec. He is concerned about his cousin and acts sensibly, and he hardly reacts when Miles subsequently punches him in the jaw (for the first time in Miles's life). But Ivan also finds himself in a position to order Miles around and lay down the law, possibly for the first time in *his* life. Miles obeys but grumbles, "You enjoyed that," only to get the response "Damn straight" from Ivan (Mem 98).

Bujold makes us appreciate the position of someone who grows up very much in the shadow of a hypersuccessful and charismatic cousin. From childhood Ivan recognizes that he is inferior to Miles in many ways, while at the same time feeling guilty that he is whole and unharmed while his cousin's body has been so damaged. Miles is himself jealous of the handsome Ivan's ability to charm the ladies, as we are privy to in Ivan's unspoken musings: "The little paranoid actually believed Ivan had the magic to entice any woman Miles really wanted away from him. His fears were more flattering to Ivan than he would ever let on" (ACC 29). Ivan does put a lot of emotional effort into finding women to go out with, almost as much effort as he devotes to avoiding marriage with them. He has a "steady allegiance to a few simple rules" (CVA 19): "First rule of picking up girls, y'know; she laughs, you live" (CVA 14).

Ivan is always unnerved when Miles becomes deeply involved in high politics. He does not run away screaming when those issues arise, as that would attract unwonted attention: "Saunter away slowly, that was the ticket" (ACC 28). Ivan does not like to be noticed, and those who are too close to Miles (and Emperor Gregor, who is also Ivan's cousin and foster brother, something Miles often forgets) tend to attract attention. It is not wholly clear why Ivan is reluctant to be involved in politics: perhaps a facet of his laziness, of his caution, or of the alarming fact that he stands in line of imperial succession and the antenatal death of his father, Padma. Even prior to *Captain Vorpatril's Alliance* there is the suspicion that Ivan plays the silly ass in order to be pigeonholed as someone not worth involving.

Yet there are glimpses: when Ivan shows Byerly that he knows about the significance of Komarran trade, Byerly expresses surprise that he know things like that, and Ivan hastily denies that his comprehension is anything out of the ordinary: "It's common knowledge" (ACC 220). Aral thinks that Ivan would make a decent average sort of count; Cordelia, more perceptive as usual, notes that he is "the invisible average man." He could do a lot more, but he stands so close to the imperial throne that if he were visible, he would soon be pressured into standing as a figurehead—"a handsome figurehead"—for some faction or other. "He only plays the fool. He may in fact be the least foolish one among us" (MD 256–57): the foolish, in Cordelia's eyes, may be those who, out of a sense of duty, stand up as a target to those wanting to bomb you or poison your unborn baby. She is thinking, of course, of her husband Aral.

Toward the end of the existing Miles novels, Ivan does develop what might seem to be uncharacteristic virtues: he seems to act efficiently as aide to his mother, Alys, in the affair of the royal wedding, despite his reluctance, and he comes into his own when Lord Dono Vorrutyer is hijacked by gunmen. It is Ivan's swift action that turns that would-be disaster into a political triumph—and one, moreover, that completely surprises Miles. Ivan exults in the "look of complete crogglement on his cousin the Imperial-Auditor-I'm-in-Charge-Here's face." Miles greets him with "Ivan, you idi—," and Ivan responds with "*Don't* . . . say it. [. . .] I just saved your ass, again. And what thanks do I get, again? None. Nothing but abuse and scorn. My humble lot in life" (ACC 366). The only thing that dents Ivan's exhilaration is the nod of appreciation that Gregor gives him; after a lifetime of trying to avoid attention and responsibility, Ivan has made himself all too visible at the center of power. Bujold shows us, near the very end of *A Civil Campaign*, that Ivan has indeed become so involved in the political intrigue that he badgers Byerly until he finds out the truth of the attack on Lord Dono—and discovers to his astonishment that his own mother is the agent who serves as the link between Byerly and ImpSec.

In *Captain Vorpatril's Alliance* Ivan is working as aide-de-camp to Admiral Desplains, who explains later to Ivan's new wife that he valued him. "What Desplains had actually told her was, *Despite Ivan's erratic personal life, he's never once made an error in identifying hidden political stakes. Rare talent, that.* Or had that been *political snakes*? Confusing" (CVA 230). The reader is left wondering whether that was "stakes," which of course makes perfect sense, or "snakes." The latter would have been a reference to Ivan's own metaphor for his job: When he gets into his office in the morning, and after his first coffee, he opens the admiral's inbox. (Nobody had a digital inbox when Bujold started writing the Vorkosigan series, but computing is clearly developing along the same lines on Barrayar as it has done on Earth, and at about the same time-scale.) Ivan thinks of it as being left with a large pile of boxes, each marked "Urgent." When Ivan metaphorically opens each box, he finds that they all contain snakes, some of them venomous and agitated, some venomous and quiescent, some nonvenomous, some dead, and some perhaps not snakes at all, but worms. Ivan forwards the venomous and agitated ones to the admiral, keeps the quiescent ones for later, and sends the dead ones and the worms back to the senders with a variety of standard answers, ranging from patient explanation to cutting remark. The admiral seems very happy with Ivan's capacity to sort the snakes, and with Ivan's metaphor: at one point he opens the morning's proceedings with "Ophidian census today, Ivan?" (CVA 81).

Finally, a character manages to find the word that sums Ivan up. It comes toward the end of *Captain Vorpatril's Alliance*, when Ivan's wife asks him if he knows what she likes best about him. He asks, joking, "My shiny groundcar? My Vorish insouciance? My astounding sexual prowess?" No, she says: "What I like best about you, Ivan Xav, is that you're *nice*. And you make me laugh." Ivan is a bit taken aback, thinking that this is not much: "Yes," she sighed, "but consider the *context*" (CVA 363). The *context* in question presumably relates not only to the tragic circumstance of Tej's family and the plight in which Tej has found herself, but also the whole background of her upbringing on Jackson's Whole, perhaps the nastiest and most insecure society in the human galaxy.

In reality, however, Bujold has shown Ivan to be *nice* for some time. He has been remarkably good to his irritating cousin for much of his life: as Miles belatedly acknowledges, he has saved Miles's neck, or tried to, a dozen times (ACC 29). Ivan tries to protect Miles from his native rashness, and when he fails, he tends to keep Miles company in the hope of at least keeping him alive. He gets very nervous when Miles's actions verge on illegality, and this has as much to do with his honesty as his caution. As Ivan tries to restrain his cousin from hacking Galeni's computer, Miles says, "You have the instincts of a gentleman, Ivan. . . . How did you ever get into Security?" (BA 126).

Ivan is a gentleman and, like his mother, Lady Alys, has an extremely highly developed sense of social and political niceties. When Donna Vorrutyer comes back from Beta Colony transformed into Lord Dono, it is Ivan who understands the imperative of seeking an audience with Emperor Gregor before he hears about the sex change from someone else. Byerly and Dono

Vorrutyer, who are experienced Vor politicos themselves, think of Gregor as being easygoing, as that is the persona that Gregor projects. Ivan knows that he is not easygoing, merely quiet: when really pissed, he looks exactly the same—"that's the scary part" (ACC 140). Ivan is in a position to give his advice, and he does so, forcefully and accurately. "I didn't do anything," he declares after the meeting with the emperor (ACC 156), but that is not true: he acted as a successful intermediary in a social situation that threatened to be very awkward, even though it thrust him into that very visibility which he hates.

Captain Vorpatril's Alliance shows us an efficient Ivan and a nice Ivan; but it also shows us an Ivan who, despite the immense superficial dissimilarity to Miles, displays some of Miles's own characteristics. This is hardly an argument for nature over nurture, however: Ivan is not that closely related to Miles (his father's mother had a sister who married Count Piotr Vorkosigan). It is much more likely that the Ivan of *Captain Vorpatril's Alliance* acquires his own forward momentum, his fast decision making, and his relative lack of caution from being overexposed, for more than three decades, to Miles's own personality. His social and political skills, however, must owe much to his Lady Alys, who is a powerful political figure, though within fairly well-defined boundaries, and who has demanded his presence at public affairs for years.[7] Although unconscious of it, Ivan has served his own apprenticeship.

This chapter began with Miles's genes being taken for the gene bank on Cetaganda, yet the books conclude overwhelmingly with an argument for nature. There is a discussion in *A Civil Campaign* between Miles and Richars Vorrutyer that is, in part, a discussion about genetics. Richars says of René Vorbrettan, who is one-eighth Cetagandan: "He's *Cetagandan*" (ACC 234). Miles's straightforward response—"I am trying to think by what possible criteria anyone could sanely describe René Vorbretten as a Cetagandan"—is met by the unhesitating reply: "Blood." Richars is following the one-drop rule, the legal principle of racial classification found only in the United States, which so bemuses the rest of the world: "one drop of Negro blood" in one's ancestry makes one a Negro. Vorrutyer is a Conservative in Barrayaran politics: an aristocrat who sees "blood" as one of the main determining factors of social worth and political power. He would no doubt have been furious had he heard his cousin Dono airily dismiss the attack on Vorbretten with "we all have our little genetic handicaps" (ACC 158). Miles, even more than Dono, cannot accept that "blood" counts for much: his Betan mother has brought him up not to believe that, and his Barrayaran father is genuinely wedded to breaking down the old social order, so that some day Barrayar would be as much a meritocracy as an aristocracy. "Nature" versus "Nurture" is a debate that, in our world too, is as much political as scientific.

CHAPTER 6

DISABILITY AND GENETIC MODIFICATION

At the time of the London Paralympic Games in September 2012, the magazine *SFX* published a list of "10 Inspirational Disabled Characters from Sci-Fi
and Fantasy."[1] Given the bias of the magazine toward the visual media, *SFX*
naturally led with the autistic Gary from *Alphas* and the blind Geordi LaForge
from *Star Trek: The Next Generation*. Indeed, there was only one inspirational
disabled character from books: Miles Vorkosigan, coming in at number 7. The
authors noted that they could not find an illustration of Miles from any book
cover (they did not look hard enough), and so they had to use pictures from
Steve Jackson's role-playing game based on the Vorkosigan books[2]; they end
by remarking that this is "a sad comment on what publishers think is sellable." Sellable or not, disability is something that permeates Bujold's work,
and numerous readers have found inspiration in what she has written. Bujold
has said that when she realized how her work resonated with the disabled, she

was "croggled."[3] She has rationalized it as simply "good characterization," thinking herself into someone else's skin.

> I've had engineers ask if I was an engineer, mothers ask if I was a mother, medical people ask me my medical background, military men ask me in which branch I served, gay men thank me for "getting a gay man right."[4]

Typically she adds a caveat: reader feedback is not a good sample, as a writer hears from those who like the stories a lot and not from those who throw the book across the room "or, worse, wander away bored." However, Bujold is being somewhat disingenuous here: after all, she was close to her engineer father and brother, she has been a mother, and she worked in a hospital for years. She has used whatever experience she could to help her. What remains is thus not just "good characterization" but "empathy."

For the remaining chapters of this book I have selected a number of themes Bujold explores throughout her fictional work. This chapter is about disability, including attitudes toward disability and ideas about deviations from the bodily norm. It is interesting both how rarely disability is treated in science fiction and fantasy and how ubiquitous it is in Bujold's work. Most visible is Miles Vorkosigan himself, whose fetus was damaged by an insurgent's attack and who struggles with his brittle bones and other problems throughout the early decades of his life. But to Miles can be added many other characters whose physical or mental disabilities are a crucial part of the narrative, from the brain-damaged Dubauer in *Shards of Honor* to the one-handed Dag in the Sharing Knife sequence, and Cazaril, with a mutilated hand and a demonic stomach tumor, in the first Chalion book. Bujold has declared that she was never writing books about issues: they are about character. The disabilities with which her characters have to cope "do not comprise the sums of their characters nor the reasons for their existences, but are just plot-things that happen to them and with which they must deal, daily or otherwise," and she adds that the letters she gets from disabled readers suggest that they prefer that approach.[5]

The definition of disability is problematic, of course. In *Falling Free* Bujold examines a genetic experiment to produce the quaddies, who are highly adapted for a free-fall environment in space: Bujold has said that when she created them, she thought of them as superadapted rather than handicapped.[6] Nevertheless, they *are* handicapped if placed on a planetary surface, and they are certainly perceived as "freaks" by those who are "normal." Miles Vorkosigan (regarded as a "freak" himself by some) has no problem in accepting these people as fully human; with similar acceptance of difference, he befriends Bel Thorne, a Betan hermaphrodite, and takes Taura, the fanged and clawed female who is the last survivor of an experiment to produce a breed of supersoldier, as his lover.

"Disability," as the term is now used by governmental organizations, covers a wide range of physical and mental problems. The U.S. Social Security Administration, for instance, uses fourteen categories for adult disability, including impairment of the musculoskeletal system, the sensory system, the respiratory system, the digestive system, the endocrine system, and so on. The Canadian government categorizes it quite differently, in advice to employers, listing forty-one different types of disability, under main headings: cognitive impairment, deaf-blind, dexterity impairment, elderly, hearing impairment, learning disability, mobility impairment, speech and language impairment, and visual impairment. (They do not seem to list impairment brought about by serious diseases, as the American categorization does.) But all this is just to underline the wide range of conditions that can be subsumed within the word "disability." Sergeant Bothari's psychological problems, exacerbated by his medication, count as a disability; so do Mark Vorkosigan's physical and psychological problems; so, certainly, do Miles's seizures and Illyan's erratic memory loss, which are the twin plot drivers of *Memory*.

Many readers, perhaps—myself included—initially assumed that Bujold must have some close, personal experience of disability. But she has said that Miles's disability, at least, was a direct result of trying to think of the worst thing that she could do to her characters: and the worst thing she could do to the physically very active Aral and Cordelia, in a highly militaristic society, was to give them a physically handicapped child.[7] However, she had come across many disabled people while working as a pharmacy technician in the Ohio State University hospitals in Columbus. Indeed, her physical model for the adult Miles was a hospital pharmacist with whom she worked: his head barely reached her shoulder, and from him she "stole the hunched appearance, the limp and leg braces, and not a little of the charm and brilliance."[8] Bujold also wonders, as we shall discuss further, whether her interest in disability is in part perhaps "a personal metaphor for being born female."[9]

A space opera story might not be thought of as somewhere a wide range of disabilities would be found, except perhaps those created as casualties of war; but that would be to forget, most notably, a character in Robert A. Heinlein's oeuvre, namely Waldo Farthingwate-Jones. The story "Waldo" was published in *Astounding* (August 1942) under Heinlein's most usual pseudonym, Anson McDonald; it is about a scientist who suffers from *myasthenia gravis* and who copes with his extreme muscular weakness by living on a satellite, in zero gravity, and by inventing what in the story—and subsequently in our real world—is called a "waldo," a device for mechanically amplifying weak muscular movements. It is an integral part of the story that Waldo does not think of himself as disabled; indeed, because of his intellect and the physical strength given to him by his waldoes, he thinks himself superior to the "smooth apes" who lived below him on Earth.

Bujold, a Heinlein reader, might have had "Waldo" at the back of her mind when she created her own anomalous "disabled characters," the quaddies, in her novel *Falling Free*. The history of the quaddies was the reverse of that of Waldo: he found an ideal home for his own body in zero gravity, whereas their bodies were created, by genetic engineering, to form ideal types for zero-gravity conditions. They do not get motion sickness, they are much more resistant to radiation than standard human stock, and, most visibly, they have arms where legs should be (hence "quaddies"). On a space station, of course, they are not disabled at all; they are far better adapted for those conditions than standard humans are. But on planets they suffer from severe mobility impairment: they can move around only with difficulty, by crawling on all four bare hands, as Claire and Tony have to do when they escape to the planetary surface. An official Barrayaran report mentioned in *Diplomatic Immunity* refers to them as "horrible spider mutants" (11): "The difference between deleterious mutation and benign or advantageous modification was not readily grasped by Barrayarans from the backcountry," comments Miles's narrating voice. But prejudice seems ubiquitous in the galaxy. The ghastly bureaucrat Van Atta who controls the quaddies in *Falling Free*—he's from Earth and may be Bujold's most comprehensively nasty villain—comments: "I about puked when I first saw one, and I was prepared. You get used to the little chimps pretty quick, though" (FF 7).

In the Vorkosigan universe there are two reasons why deviations from the human norm are regarded with horror. There is a general fear, throughout human space, of genetic manipulation of the human body; Van Atta remarks that this was particularly "after that Nuovo Brasilian military cloning fiasco" (FF 15), an event otherwise not mentioned. On Barrayar specifically, however, there is a real fear of genetic mutation, following a radiation event when the wormhole collapsed, ushering in the Time of Isolation. This explains the comment about "deleterious mutation" in the quotation above. Even in Miles's day it is by no means unknown for minor disabilities such as a hare-lip to be the occasion for infanticide: how Miles copes with that is the theme of the novella "The Mountains of Mourning." One look at Miles Vorkosigan—a hunchback, less than five feet high—convinces most Barrayarans that he, too, is a mutant. When he was young he would explain that, no, his disabilities were the result of poisoning in the womb, the result of an attack by political opponents of his father, having nothing to do with genetic mutation. Even before he is out of his teens, however, he realizes that he could be a role model for other mutants, and in his maturity he accepts the insult "mutant" without bridling, since his achievements and high social status could demonstrate to everyone that a mutant could be a valuable member of society.

Bujold has written about her attitude to disability in her introductory chapter to *The Vorkosigan Companion*. It is possible that some of her disabled characters in the Vorkosigan books (Taura, Elli, Bel Thorne, Mark) are "got up as plot-mirrors for Miles" (VC 7). But that does not explain the quaddies, who are independent of him. And so, she says, "I've sometimes wondered if this theme is a personal metaphor." This seems to boil down to her feeling wrong in her own body. "I grew up in a family with a remarkable father, strong older brothers, a close grandfather, and a mother whose attempts to feminize me I fought from the age of two onwards."[10] As she sees it now, there was nothing wrong with the body; it was the status granted to it in the 1950s and 1960s that was the problem. Miles grows up in the "wrong" body, for without the soltoxin attack he might have been more Ivan's shape and size, as Cordelia comments to Aral (MD 253). Bujold writes: "The sense of being 'wrong' is deeply inculcated in females in our society."[11] Miles was Bujold in reverse: he grew up as a male, with male role models (above all his father) but smaller than all those around him, fragile, a "wrong"-shaped body, forced to rely on wit and charm to deal with (and manipulate) those around him. Bujold, early on in her writing career, called Miles "a female in disguise," someone socially disadvantaged by disability "just as women in patriarchal society are made to feel deformed."[12] This will be discussed in the next chapter; but it is worth underlining here that being disabled and being female are often closely linked concepts in Bujold's worlds.

Miles learns to cope with his own disabilities. He experiences open revulsion on Barrayar but maintains that he finds that preferable to the reactions he encounters on Beta Colony when, at age fifteen, he spends a year there. He hopes to have sex with beautiful young Betan girls, but they are all taken; instead, he has "good Samaritans, the kinky/curious, hermaphrodites, and boys." He does have a short affair with a kinky/curious girl and finds her fascination with his odd body to be very unsettling: "Anyway, after finding his sexual parts disappointingly normal, the girl had drifted off" (WA 54). He hopes to achieve social acceptance within the Barrayaran military, and when that does not work, he carves out a different career in space, using nothing more than his own native chutzpah. His entire career is a personal response to his disability. And that disability gives him a very particular position in his universe. As Sylvia Kelso puts it, "For most of his life Miles has been an exemplary Harawayan cyborg, a pleasurable confuser of boundaries, . . . a stubborn solvent of established Barrayaran categories."[13]

However, in her books Bujold is not interested just in how disabled people cope psychologically but also in how other people react to the disabled. This goes back to the very beginning of the Vorkosigan saga, when Cordelia's officer Dubauer is hit by Sergeant Bothari's nerve disruptor (CH 9). His brain is permanently damaged. He is cared for by Cordelia and Aral, and then disappears from the story; only much later do we learn that Dubauer has survived, "sort of" (CH 281), but needs permanent care. Bujold has said that she wrote the story of Dubauer's assisted passage through a hostile landscape while her second child was very young; she thought about how it would be to maneuver a 180-pound toddler through rough country.[14] The reaction to Dubauer's disability separates the Betan from the Barrayaran. The Betan instinct is to care, regardless of how difficult and impractical that might be (and caring for him as they trek across a hostile planet could have been fatal to his carers, Cordelia and Aral); the Barrayaran attitude is much more harsh (or, if you wish, pragmatic)—Aral offers to put Dubauer out of his misery with the help of his combat knife (CH 13). In the end, however, Aral accedes to Cordelia's wish to look after Dubauer, partly because Dubauer has changed his status in Aral's mind. He is no longer a liability: he is a prisoner, and Aral has proclaimed, "I do not kill prisoners" (CH 14). When they finally reach the Barrayaran camp, Dubauer is taken by some Barrayarans, and they attempt to question him through torture (a version of water-boarding). "You Barrayarans are nothing but barbarians, scoundrels, and assassins!" cries Cordelia; "And fools. Don't leave out fools," Aral adds, before he bawls his men out for mistreating *his* prisoner (CH 64).

We next meet disability in the character of Koudelka, who is wounded by disruptor fire in the course of the shipboard mutiny against Aral Vorkosigan. He is not as badly hurt as Dubauer, but he has to submit to a complex set of operations to restore his mobility, which nevertheless leaves him lame and (a crucial plot element later on) with possible penile dysfunction. He faces dismissal from the army: but Aral (regent-elect) makes him his personal secretary. Not long on Barrayar, Cordelia rather naively remarks on how one sees only healthy-looking people on the streets. Aral (looking grim) said that detectable problems were eliminated before birth—or after. But war injuries are a different problem: "As for injuries like Koudelka's, or worse . . . the social stigma is very great. Watch him in a larger group sometime, not his close friends. It's no accident that the suicide rate among medically discharged soldiers is high" (CH 281). Cordelia regards this as "horrible," and clearly the reader is meant to agree. Indeed, most readers will realize that this is a commentary on contemporary attitudes. In America and elsewhere the prejudice against handicapped veterans, from employers and others, is deeply rooted, despite the legal protection that veterans are afforded. In 2012 a U.S. veteran committed suicide every eighty minutes.[15] There is another relevant statistic from the United Kingdom, reported in September 2012, immediately after the London Paralympic Games: at a time when the government has argued for the reclassification of many with disabilities as "fit for work," a comparison between 2010 and 2011 showed that hate crime in the United Kingdom directed at disabled people had increased by more than a third.[16]

Not long after the discussion about Koudelka in *Barrayar*, Cordelia overhears two young Vor officers. She was amused by their comments about Aral and herself until one of them asked about "the three-legged spastic" trailing after Aral.

> "You'd think he could do better than that. What a mutant. Surely Vorkosigan has the pick of the Service, as Regent."
> She felt she'd received a body blow, so great was the unexpected pain of the careless remark. (CH 291–2)

Later in the same novel Koudelka, accompanied by Sergeant Bothari, is set upon by a gang of Barrayarans and beaten up because he "walked funny" (CH 364).

The prejudice of Barrayarans toward "mutants" is actually a prejudice against all those who depart too far from the body norm. The battle against this kind of prejudice is one of the themes that span several novels of the Vorkosigan series. Barrayaran society is going through the same kind of development that Western society in general went through, or is still going through, in terms of treatment of all minorities, including the disabled. Some of that change on Barrayar is perhaps to be seen as inevitable evolution, as the real threat of genetic mutation diminishes; but the attitude of progressives (like Aral) in the heart of government has an impact as well. Progress, of a sort, is happening, but it is slow. When a crippled man is castrated by a gang of drunks in Vorbarr Sultana, "it was considered Progress that it was a scandal, and not simply taken for granted" (VG 11). Miles can be remarkably self-centered and blind to matters of social justice, but on this matter he is a zealot, above all after the experience related in "The Mountains of Mourning": just as Mark's whole childhood experience inspires him to bring about an end to the cloning business on Jackson's Whole, so Miles becomes concerned about ending prejudice against perceived mutants on his own planet or, at least, in his father's county.

"The Mountains of Mourning" is set in the period of Miles's life between completion of his military training and his first assignment. Aral sends him to deal with a problem of infanticide in the backwoods of his own county, in Silvy Vale—sends someone, that is, regarded as a "mutie" to deal with the widely prevalent feeling that "muties" should be killed at birth. The dead child is Raina, a baby with a harelip. Even Pym, his own father's armsman, who accompanies Miles, shares the common mindset: he makes a distinction between infanticide and murder (*Oh my poor Barrayar*, Miles comments to himself [MM 48]). Miles gives his best shot when trying to explain the crime to the twelve-year-old Zed, who had commented that "she was only a mutie" (MM 55). Miles explains it in terms of *honor*. Barrayar's honor suffers when people from other planets hear that these things happen and therefore regard all Barrayarans are savages. "A soldier gets honor by killing an armed enemy, not a baby. This matter touches my honor as a Vorkosigan, Zed." But he adds an additional, very personal, touch: "You will all be astonished at what *only a mutie* can do. *That* I have sworn on my grandfather's grave." And Bujold makes this incident a significant one in Miles's life. Even at the time, Miles regards it as life changing: Raina, the dead girl, replaces his grandfather as the symbol of what he is fighting for; the story starts at his grandfather's grave and ends at Raina's, with the concluding words: "He knew who he served now. And why he could not quit. And why he must not fail" (MM 100). And the dead Raina is indeed not someone that Miles forgets. He provides money for developing the area and for providing education (the founding of the Raina Csurik Primary School, for a start). It is the memory of Raina and the knowledge that Miles was too busy being Admiral Naismith to remember her properly that ten years later helps to reconcile him to having lost his Naismith person. "Raina was the one symbol of his service that still made sense" (Mem 145). He revisits Silvy Vale to burn an offering on Raina's grave, and he discovers that her grave is now underwater. A hydroelectric scheme has brought power to the remote area and, though computers are in schools and elsewhere, has provided the locals with access to the world around them and to new ideas, for effectively the first time: it is a more suitable monument for Raina than a grave. We also see Miles drawing on his experiences and serving as a spokesman for those who might perceive of themselves as "muties" when, in *Komarr* he honestly and openly discusses the genetic disease that Ekaterin's son Nikki has acquired from his father.

Miles's mission is not just dependent on his experience of growing up as a "mutie" and of acting as the Count's Voice in Silvy Vale. It owes much to Cordelia and to Miles's Betan grandmother, whose values were so different from those of Barrayarans. Miles is brought up to have a fellow-feeling for freaks. Indeed, his whole career as Admiral Naismith takes off because he feels sorry for Arde Mayhew, a jump pilot on Beta who has an obsolete coupling system to a spaceship wired into his brain and is thus "a fellow-freak, a loser in trouble" (WA 56). The word "freak" is often used for the quaddies, even by quaddies themselves: Nicol seems to expect to be seen as a freak, but she objects to being regarded as a *"manufactured* freak" (BI 113), which she was on Jackson's Whole, where several Houses specialized in manufacturing them. When she meets Bel Thorne, she knows they have something in common, not as "freaks" but as "genetics" (BI 114). Sergeant Taura, who *is* manufactured on Jackson's Whole, also inevitably sees herself as a freak (Cry 174). We meet other artificially created variants of natural species in the course of the Vorkosigan books: the human with gills in *Diplomatic Immunity*, the sphinx pet in *CryoBurn*, and the kitten-tree in *Cetaganda*. These unhappy beings are invariably created by scientists either on Jackson's Whole or on Cetaganda, planets obsessed by capitalist profit in the first instance and by genetic advances in the second. The message seems to be that both planetary cultures have, because of their obsessions, forgotten the nature of humanity itself.

The "freak" that we come to know the best is the Cetagandan L-X-10 Terran-C, or Terrence Cee, in *Ethan of Athos*, who has so far convinced himself that he is a freak that he doubts his own humanity. "Do you realize that I am not a human being, Dr. Urquhart? [. . .] I have no father and no mother. I wasn't born, I was made. And that doesn't horrify you?" Ethan Urquhart, however, is not only a scientist, all of whose fellow-citizens on Athos have been produced through uterine replicators; he also has a good theological education. (He is one of the few genuinely religious people we meet in the Vorkosigan universe.)

> "Well—you have free will, obviously, or you could not be opposing your creators. Therefore you are not an automaton, but a child of God the Father, answerable to Him according to your abilities," Ethan catechized.
> [. . .] Cee strained forward. "What am I to you, then, if not a monster?"
> Ethan scratched his chin reflectively. "We all remain children of the Father, however we may otherwise be orphaned. You are my brother, of course."
> "Of course . . . ?" echoed Cee. His legs and arms drew in, making his body a tight ball. Tears leaked between his squeezed eyelids. (EA 125)

The difficulty people in the novel have with Cee is fear that the telepath would gain access to their innermost thoughts. It is a fear shared by Cee himself, since he has always been told that he would make an ideal weapon in terms of espionage, and he is clearly reluctant to act as a weapon. But Bujold writes medical sf, not military sf, and Ethan has an inner life that he is comfortable with. Dr Ethan Urquhart opens Cee's eyes to the medical possibilities of his talent, telling him that he will be able to know where babies hurt and what it feels like, and how he could communicate with stroke victims or with paralyzed people: "God the Father," Ethan's enthusiasm mounted, "you could be an absolute savior!" (EA 124). Ethan is falling in love with Cee and imagines taking Cee sailing on the South Province coast. He has forgotten that Cee was telepathic, until Cee whispers that he has never seen oceans before. "Ethan's red went to scarlet. He felt transparent as glass" (EA 154). But he is accepting of Cee's "freakiness" partly because he finds him attractive (the Cetagandan agent Millisor suggests that Cee's talent may operate in both directions, since most people found themselves attracted to him) but partly because he is genuinely open to ideas of difference. Ethan's only failing is that his culture has conditioned him to think of women as repulsive. He can take all of Cee's description of his story without feeling uncomfortable, until Cee starts talking about the sexual relations his scientist-creator had encouraged between himself and his sort-of-sister Janine.

Bujold clearly understands that there may be built-in limits to the amount of tolerance that anyone might feel. Miles has been brought up intellectually, by his Betan relatives above all, to believe that any type of "freakiness" should be accepted, but the hypersensitive Bel tests his limits, which are physical or instinctual rather than intellectual. Bel is a hermaphrodite, one of the products of Betan genetic manipulation, who can emphasize the masculine or the feminine side of its personality and body at will. In "Labyrinth" they are discussing Bel's future: Has Bel thought of settling on Beta Colony with another hermaphrodite? Miles asks. Bel changes the subject abruptly and congratulates Miles on his ability to masquerade as a Betan when playing Admiral Naismith: he is "almost perfect" but gives himself away by flinching when Bel touches him (BI 106–7). Miles does become easier in Bel's company as he grows more familiar with it and accepts that Bel is in love with him. But, although prepared to abandon the rule against fraternizing with the lower ranks when it comes to Elli Quinn or Taura, Miles never progresses beyond a kiss with Bel Thorne. Indeed, his own unspoken comments on this display Barrayaran prejudice rather than Betan tolerance:

> He found Bel Thorne manning the security comconsole. If manning was the right term; Thorne was one of Beta Colony's hermaphrodite minority, hapless heirs of a century-past genetic project of dubious merit. It had been one of the lunatic fringe's loonier experiments, in Miles's estimation. (BA 257)

And again:

> Bel Thorne, the Ariel's commander, was a Betan hermaphrodite, man/woman descendant of a centuries-past genetic-social experiment every bit as bizarre, in Miles's private opinion, as anything rumored to be done for money by House Ryoval's ethics-free surgeons. A fringe effort of Betan egalitarianism run amok, hermaphroditism had not caught on, and the original idealists' hapless descendants remained a minority on hyper-tolerant Beta Colony. (BI 104)

Lunatic, bizarre, run amok, hapless: Miles shows that despite his abhorrence for the Barrayaran mistreatment of mutants, he shares the Barrayaran distaste for deviation from bodily norms and has not truly learned Betan acceptance from his mother. Even when Bel is emphasizing its female side (the neuter pronoun is used by the hermaphrodites themselves), Miles seems to be repelled by it. Perhaps, indeed, Cordelia's own tolerance does not extend to hermaphrodites: after all, her own mother (to whom Miles was very close) has an ambivalent attitude toward them. When a Barrayaran shows distaste for them, she will patriotically defend them; but in private she dismisses them crudely and cruelly as "people who are pathologically incapable of making up their minds" (WA 92).

Elli Quinn is someone else who is a freak, although in a very different way from anyone else in Bujold's work: she is freakishly beautiful. In one of Miles's earlier military engagements, Quinn is one of the casualties: a plasma arc burns her face away. Miles pays for restorative surgery on Beta Colony. Miles, "young and dumb," as he later admits, gives her the most perfectly beautiful face that Betan dollars could buy. It is only later that he realizes it could be a problem (BA 235–36). Miles always treats her the same—with the old face, with no face, with the new face. But other people react very differently: men make passes instead of following orders. Ellie has to use tricks that she has learned from watching Miles to get people to "respond to the inside of me, and not the outside," a classic demand from those who are disabled.

Physical disability, or at least variety of the human norm, is to be found throughout the Vorkosigan universe. Mental disability is something that is much less ubiquitous in Bujold's narratives, but it is there nevertheless. The fear of hereditary mental instability, as we have seen, is shared by Miles and Elena Bothari, and Miles's cousin the Emperor Gregor himself lies awake at night worrying about what he might have inherited from Yuri and from his own equally mad father Prince Serg (VG 334). However, these characters are distant in the narrative. Much more prominent is the figure of Sergeant Bothari. When Mark is discussing him with Count Aral Vorkosigan, Aral comments that "Bothari was . . . a difficult man," and when Mark offers "criminal," Aral responds that this is an "incomplete" judgement (MD 263). Bothari is the bastard son of a prostitute. Bastardy, he points out to Cordelia, is as bad on Barrayar as being a mutant (CH 528). As a teenager Bothari acts a part-time prostitute himself; at the same time, he shows the signs of schizophrenia. To get out of his situation he enlists in the Barrayaran military. He has been attached to Admiral Vorrutyer's staff for four years as the admiral's torturer. He is ordered to rape women for the admiral's delectation and does so until the day he slits Vorrutyer's throat rather than see him rape Cordelia. He goes through therapy after this: not the relatively sophisticated therapy of Beta Colony but the brutal, primitive therapy of Barrayar. When he has partially recovered from this experience, he becomes Count Piotr Vorkosigan's arms-man, but soon he is seconded to Cordelia's service and is then chosen by Aral and Cordelia to be Miles's bodyguard. He serves Miles efficiently for the first eighteen years of Miles's life until he and his daughter Elena go with Miles on what becomes the first of his Dendarii operations. When Bothari encounters Elena's mother, whom he had raped at the time of the invasion of Escobar, he allows her to shoot him; he dies with the ambiguous words "Rest now" on his lips (WA 219).

Aral pronounces what is probably the best analysis of Bothari. He tries to explain to Cordelia why Bothari has become her faithful follower. "He's a chameleon. A mirror. He becomes whatever is required of him." If someone wants a monster or a torturer, or a faithful follower, he will play the part. "You are the only person I know who looks at Bothari and sees a hero. So he becomes one for you. He clings to you because you create him a greater man than he ever dreamed of being" (CH 566).

In his later years Bothari is still coping with his schizophrenia, but he also has to deal with the blocks placed into his memory during his therapy, which are designed to make him forget his actions at the time of the attack on Escobar. He has found ways of partially remembering (taking notes of his partial memories and using them to stimulate further memory). He seems also to have been given drugs to suppress his sadistic and violent urges: when he does commit a violent act, he has a correspondingly painful reaction himself. When he beheads Count Vordarian, on Cordelia's orders, he falls to the ground and screams with the pain: "It was as if Vordarian's death cry had been forced out of Bothari's throat" (CH 554).

As remarked earlier, in Bujold's narrative it is the reactions of able people to the disabled that are of just as much interest as the disabled themselves. In Bothari's case we have a strange web of interrelationships involving Aral, Cordelia, Miles, and also Bothari's daughter Elena. The latter relationship is the most important for Bothari, as it connects him with genuine human concerns; but it is, of course, based on a lie. Bothari and Elena Bothari know that she has been born from a uterine replicator, but Elena does not know that she was the product of Bothari's rape of an Escobaran prisoner, Elena Visconti.

Aral sees himself as Bothari's keeper, in part because he recognizes that he literally owes everything to Bothari, for saving his life. He thinks that wearing a uniform and obeying orders to some extent controls Bothari's schizophrenia. He tries to understand him: "He's a very complex man with a very limited range of expression, who's had some very bad experiences. But in his own twisty way, he's honorable" (CH 46). But Aral also describes him as "a usable madman" (CH 281) and does not hesitate to do so.

Cordelia (when under the influence of the drugs supplied by her interrogator back home on Beta Colony) says of Bothari, "He talks to demons. The demons talk back. You'd like Bothari. Aral does. I do. Good guy to have with you on your next trip to hell. He speaks the language" (CH 190). And when Cordelia takes her trip to hell to try to rescue Miles's fetus from Count Vordarian, she too uses him to do her dirty business, though it is Bothari who reminds her how she can do this legally: "Do you remember, back on the front lawn at Vorkosigan Surleau when we were loading Negri's body into the lightflyer, when my Lord Regent told me to obey your voice as his own? [. . .] He never countermanded that order" (CH 500–501). Koudelka tries to order Bothari around and reminds him that he is Count Piotr's man: "No," responds Bothari, "I am Lady Vorkosigan's dog" (CH 505). It is an epithet that Cordelia adopts for herself. He's a monster, she admits, "but he's my monster. My good dog" (CH 532).

Miles knows Bothari better than anyone, apart from his parents, since Bothari is at his side from his infancy until not long after Miles had put together his Dendarii fleet. Miles knows his voice intimately: "One had to know him a long time to interpret its expressionlessness. Miles knew every minute variation in its timbre as a man knows his own room in the dark" (WA 9). Bothari saves Miles in the cradle by holding Count Piotr by one hand from a third-floor balcony until he agrees not to smother the child (BA 201). He saves Miles from suicide during deep depression when, on Beta Colony as a teenager, he fights to take Miles's dagger away from him (WA 54).

Miles's initial reaction to Bothari's death is shock: he does not cry until three days later, and then the crying lasts for hours. He stops caring about the ship or himself. After days of this, Elena comes in to remonstrate with him. They argue about Bothari: Elena feels betrayed—"It was all *lies*. Faking glory, while all the time underneath was this—cesspit" (WA 228). Miles tries to explain that Bothari "was trying to forge a new truth," that is, to play a useful and even heroic role that would extinguish the memory of his dark past. Miles eventually starts babbling and makes one of the most inappropriately timed and strangely phrased marriage proposals in science fiction: "I love you [. . .] I can't live without my Bothari, marry me!" (WA 229). Linda Wight discusses the possible queer reading of this passage, and indeed the whole of the relationship between Bothari and Miles (LMB 126–27). As she says, although there is no indication that their relationship has a sexual nature, there is nevertheless a homoerotic element in their relationship; and perhaps this adds to our understanding of the odd relationship between Bothari and Aral. After all, Bothari kills the sadistic Vorrutyer, who had been Aral's lover.

If Aral and Cordelia both use Bothari, there is one occasion where Miles uses Bothari just as cold-bloodedly. Miles has captured a ship (his first), and he needs the codes the jump pilot has in his memory. Persuasion and reason get

Miles nowhere, and he hands the man over to the sergeant. Bothari threatens to pull out the brain implant that the jump pilot needs for communicating with the spaceship; and he does so. The pilot spills his information, and not too long afterward he dies of the trauma. Miles is present when Bothari does this, and he puts Arde Mayhew straight on the question of responsibility: "What Bothari does on my orders is my responsibility, not his." "I saw the look on his face," counters Mayhew. "He *enjoyed* that. You didn't." But Miles sticks to his line: "If you have a problem about him, see me" (WA 118). Later on, though, when Bothari excuses himself by saying that the jump pilot's death "saved many and not just on our side," Miles responds coldly: "I'll keep that in mind, when I come to explain to my father how it was we happened to torture a prisoner to death" (WA 127). Although this is a rebuke to Bothari, the significant word is "we": Miles continues to accept the responsibility of command. It is not the only time in the Vorkosigan saga that we are presented with "good guys" making decisions that readers are encouraged to regard as evil.

After Bothari's death, Miles thinks of him frequently. Bujold has Miles remembering Bothari in every single book until Miles is married with children: *Diplomatic Immunity* is the first novel that does not mention Bothari. Parenthood in Bujold's work, for Bothari, for Aral and Cordelia, and for Miles, is an epiphanic event and a key boundary for memory.

There is an idea that resonates throughout the Vorkosigan sequence: a person's humanity can be measured by the way that person regards and treats those who are marked out as different through disability or some other characteristic. The care that Aral, Cordelia, and Miles take to look after Bothari is all one with that with which Cordelia looked after Dubauer in the first book. Betan culture, operating on Aral through Cordelia, changes the way in which Barrayarans regard the other. Miles is an advance guard of changes we see threaded all the way through Barrayaran society. Bujold's message throughout is one of tolerance, empathy, and appreciation of circumstance, a lesson for the twenty-first century as well as for the thirtieth.

CHAPTER 7

WOMEN, UTERINE REPLICATORS, AND SEXUALITY

An earnest young male fan once came up to Bujold and said, "Ms. Bujold, you write like a man." Bujold claims to be slow at thinking on her feet, and only afterward did she realize she should have said, "Oh, really? Which one?"[1] She adds, naturally enough, that she is still trying to work out whether or not the remark had been a compliment. Another of her hypothetical responses was: "I don't write like a man, you just read like one."[2] Although Bujold has claimed to be a "human-beingist" rather than a feminist, throughout her work she has been concerned with emphasizing the equality of women and men and trying to understand the mentality of those who do not accept that equality. She did not react well (though with characteristic good manners) when a Bulgarian interviewer in 2010 asked her, "Have you been accused of feminist tendencies in your works?" After saying, "'Accused?' I wasn't aware it was a crime," she added: "Of course I'm a feminist. A woman who isn't a feminist would be like a slave in favor of slavery."[3]

From the beginning of the Vorkosigan books Bujold has been determined to explore feminist issues. As we have seen, she deliberately sets up the debate between Betan and Barrayaran attitudes toward women. The egalitarian planet Beta Colony is held up as some sort of model in matters of equality, sexual or otherwise; Cordelia Naismith is Betan, and her son Miles is brought up with many of her Betan attitudes and adopts them for his mercenary fleet. However, we see strong women not only in that more egalitarian environment of the Dendarii fleet (notably Elena Bothari and Elli Quinn) but also in patriarchal societies like Barrayar (Alys Vorpatril, Ekaterin Vorvayne), not to mention in Bujold's other work (Betriz, the Royina Ista, Fawn). What Bujold is doing is extremely effective in the science-fictional context in which she is writing. There were stronger feminist voices in science fiction in the decade before Bujold finished her first novels—one thinks of Suzy McKee Charnas's *Walk to the End of the World* (1974), Joanna Russ's *The Female Man* (1975), Marge Piercy's *Woman at the Edge of Time* (1976), and Pamela Sargent's *The Shore of Women* (1986)—but anecdotal evidence suggests that far fewer men read these books than read Bujold. Bujold is perceived as writing space opera, traditionally an almost entirely male genre; and some readers of space opera may well have encountered feminism first in the Vorkosigan books.

Feminism for Bujold involves far more than writing about women. As noted in the previous chapter, Bujold herself wondered if, in her writing, disability works as "a personal metaphor for being born female."[4] Miles is "a female in disguise," someone socially disadvantaged by disability "just as women in patriarchal society are made to feel deformed."[5] Sylvia Kelso speculates that Miles "achieves all the masculine things that women would *like* to do": winning through by intellect and manipulation, retaining his compassion and sensitivity throughout. He is "the daylight version of the codedly feminine." His clone-brother Mark, however, is the nighttime version, "the codedly feminine that women do *not* like to face."[6] Miles is vulnerable, and he builds his sense of identity through family and through achievement; Mark uses greed (for food and money) as a defensive mechanism, has multiple-personality disorder (also a coping mechanism), suffers from extremely low self-esteem, and experiences hate and envy, a response perhaps to the lack of love in his childhood. Miles and Mark have in essence both been abused in childhood by endless and painful medical interventions and, in Miles's, case by frequent accidents involving the breaking of his bones. (In the latter case the abuse is committed by the author: "His bones have a slightly suspicious tendency to break only when I need them to," admits Bujold [VC 7].) Miles compensates by trying to dominate; Mark by trying to accumulate—initially, food and, later, money and influence.

If these two brothers are feminized, then Miles is surrounded by women who are, in part, masculinized, or who at least take roles traditionally held by men: they are mercenary commanders or soldiers. Miles has sex with most of them, including the genetically manufactured supersoldier Taura, who is nearly twice his height. Height difference only matters when you're standing up, Miles decides. But since she was a virgin, Miles warns her that intercourse might hurt. "'That's all right,' she replies. 'I have a very high pain threshold.'" *"But I don't"* is Miles's internalized scream (BI 166). Elena Bothari is one of these masculinized women—but one who only achieves the ability to express that side of her once she has left Barrayar. Before that, she was as (socially) disabled as Miles. When Miles has failed his military physicals, he comments to Elena, "I wish you could have taken my physicals. Between us we'd make a hell of an officer."

> Something of the old frankness they had shared as children escaped her lips suddenly. "Yes, but by Barrayaran standards I'm more handicapped than you—I'm female. I wouldn't even be permitted to petition to take the tests." (WA 18)

Elena does make one hell of an officer, all on her own: but only after she leaves Barrayar.

What makes Bujold's works stand out in the context of contemporary science fiction and fantasy is not the number of women or their strength of personality; it is the importance of pregnancy, childbirth, and motherhood in her narratives. The perspective offered on the final page of the last book of the Sharing Knife sequence is an interesting example of this. Fawn is in the rocking chair, feeding her baby.

> And if hope for their wide green world grew as slowly as a baby grew into a mama, well, no one had ever said raising either was a task for the faint of heart, or the impatient.
> Fawn rocked, and fed the future (SK4 453).

This is reminiscent of the ending of another long saga, when Sam Gamgee takes his little child on his knee and announces "Well, I'm back."[7] A child is the future, of course; Bujold, unlike most genre authors, does not forget this. And, by introducing the technology of uterine replicators (allowing the "test-tube" maturation of embryos), Bujold also introduces a debate about the possible insertion of technology into the process of birth, a debate that joins with the equally controversial debate about genetic manipulation, discussed in the previous chapter. Bujold's own training and her hospital work lead her to a "strongly biological mode of analysis," as John Lennard puts it.[8] "All . . . true wealth . . . is biological," Aral Vorkosigan says, in what were nearly his dying words (MD 278).

The focus on parenting starts very early in the Vorkosigan books. Bujold was caring for her two very young children at the time and chose to incorporate her concerns into her work. In Bujold's first published story, "Barter," a harassed mother opts for a device that temporarily puts her noisy and irritating children into suspended animation. The two books that became *Cordelia's Honor* are "about the price of becoming a parent" (CH 595). Aral and Cordelia are not the only couples involved: "All the other supporting couples took up and played their symphonic variations on the theme"—that is Kou and Drou, Padma and Alys, Piotr and his dead wife, Serg and Kareen, and Bothari and the uterine replicator containing his daughter's fetus. The second of the pair of books, *Barrayar*, is dedicated to Bujold's two children, Anne and Paul, "my teachers in learning about this part of becoming human" (CH 256).

Bujold is unusual, too, within the world of space opera and indeed in the wider world of sf, in creating a number of very plausible and engaging child characters, in particular the two young children in *CryoBurn*, Jin and Mina Sato, and the child of Ekaterin's first marriage, Nicki Vorsoisson, whose decision to contact Emperor Gregor directly is one of the more poignant scenes of *A Civil Campaign*. The Emperor Gregor himself first appears as a young child, in *Barrayar*: again, a very realistic portrayal of a child in the midst of traumatic events.

Women's right to choose whether to give birth or to abort, a matter of intense debate in the United States for decades, is a debate in the Vorkosigan books as well. Quite near the beginning of Cordelia's relationship with Aral, seventeen uterine replicators appear in Aral Vorkosigan's office: the casualties of the war with Escobar, the products, mostly or entirely, of the rapes of Escobaran women by Barrayaran soldiers. Cordelia tells Aral that a couple of the mothers were "pretty emotionally divided about abortions." Aral is fairly certain that they should not take the trouble to keep the fetuses alive: "We usually abort bastards." "Why not just flush them?" the surgeon asks. "Some unmilitary notion about the value of human life, perhaps," responds Cordelia: "Some cultures have it" (CH 166–68). Cordelia's view prevails, and Aral commits to the preservation of the fetuses. When Miles's fetus is damaged in the womb, Aral's father Piotr begs the parents to abort the fetus, and later, indeed, tried to do it himself, by turning off the uterine replicator. Again, Aral and Cordelia resist. Abortion is known on Barrayar (Bothari was surprised that his prostitute mother had not aborted him), but it is clearly resisted by Cordelia. We must not assume, of course, that Cordelia is Bujold (who says, for the record, that she is pro-choice, although knowing that choice has two or more sides). Cordelia comes from a society with almost perfect contraception: all girls are given a contraceptive implant at puberty. Cordelia is not so much opposed to abortion on principle as appalled that it should ever be necessary, and an additional factor for Aral and Cordelia is the concern that Aral—also affected by the soltoxin gas—may no longer be capable of engendering a healthy fetus. Cordelia's choice is not only an ethical one; it is bounded by context (and, as in a kidnap attempt, to abort might be to jeopardize any further pregnancy by telling attackers that they could be successful).

Abortion is mentioned in Bujold's fourth novel, too, in a bizarre way. The quaddies are not, legally speaking, human (according to the corporation lawyers): they are "post-fetal experimental tissue cultures" (FF 112). When Van Atta decides that he has to get rid of them, various options are proposed, including sterilization and euthanasia. "And what do you call murdering them?" asks Leo Graf. "Retroactive abortion?" (FF 112). There is real abortion in prospect, however: fifteen quaddies are pregnant, and Van Atta has no qualms about deciding that there will be forcible abortions if the necessary sterilizations are carried out. On Barrayar, of course, in the backcountry, abortion is not the response to fetuses that are regarded as defective, simply because the technology is not there to detect those defects before birth. The answer instead is infanticide. Miles's commission to investigate an infanticide in "The Mountains of Mourning" is one small part of the attempt by Aral and the Progressives to make infanticide something that will be socially unacceptable.

As we have already seen, one of the main elements in the contrast between Barrayaran and Betan culture that can be found in the early volumes of the Vorkosigan series is the role of women in society. Barrayar is in a rapid process of change from something resembling nineteenth-century Western culture to, let us say, that which existed in the second half of the twentieth century; Beta Colony has already gone far beyond modern America or Europe in terms of women's equality. Cordelia becomes something of a heroine for some younger Barrayaran women, because of the role model of female agency she represents.

Elena is the most significant example of the new possibilities open to Barrayaran women, although she has to leave Barrayar in order to achieve her goals. However, mirroring the development of the many ripostes Bujold later considered to the "you write like a man" comment, some ten years after the start of her new career, Elena reminisces with Miles about her career development. She has been brought up to accept a tenet of Barrayaran society: "Being a soldier was the only job that counted" (Mem 20). By the time that she actually achieves her goal of a military career, her father, a career soldier himself, is long dead. Ironically, according to Miles, Sergeant Bothari might not have disapproved of his daughter's career choice: "Your father once said that if a woman puts on a uniform she's asking for it, and you should never hesitate to fire—odd streak of egalitarianism, coming from him." (WA 173). But by the time Elena achieves her career ambition, she realizes (while talking to Cordelia) how narrow her ambitions have been. Cordelia had managed to have a career and a number of other roles: not just astrocartographer and ship's captain, but mother and politician as well: "Not just one thing, but a world of possibilities. I want to find out who else I can be" (Mem 21). On Barrayar, at least, this remains a utopian desire. Most women, even Vor women, have reduced horizons. Even at the top, their scope for action is limited. Princess Kareen, the widow of Prince Serg, is not even consulted about the regency: she is just a "physical medium of transmission for the genetic material between royal generations."[9] Without her little son Gregor, she has nothing, but even with him she has no life of her own: "Gregor is my hope of survival. And my prison" (CH 335). Elena has learned from Cordelia that she has choice. She resigns her commission with the Dendarii in order to raise a family, but that is not a closing of her ambitions. After that, perhaps, she will become a commercial shipmaster.

Alongside Elena Bothari one could place Droushnakovi ("Drou"). She comes from a family of soldiers; she is trained in martial arts and becomes bodyguard to, first, Prince Serg's wife Kareen and, subsequently, to Cordelia herself. Cordelia persuades Aral to allow her to compete in an unarmed combat competition and, once Aral tells her to play to win, she wins very convincingly (sending her male opponent to hospital). But Drou soon settles down, marries Lieutenant Koudelka (Kou), and produces a family of little girls. However, this is not just a retreat into domesticity. As Regina Yung Lee nicely puts it, "Droushnakovi moves from woman soldier to non-Vor social icon."[10] She is symbolic of the way in which Aral is trying to break down barriers between the classes or castes. Her daughters, the Koudelka sisters, despite their "middle-class" status, contribute to the dissolution of Barrayaran tradition: Delia Koudelka marries Duv Galeni, a Komarran, and her sisters Kareen and Olivia marry into the aristocracy, a Vorkosigan and a Vorrutyer. Yet in Cordelia's terms it is Kareen who is the real success story. She goes to Beta Colony for her education, learns all kinds of unBarrayaran behavior, and becomes partner, in all senses, to Mark Vorkosigan. It is clear that she is going to become one of the first female entrepreneurs operating on a large scale in Barrayaran history. Here, too, the Vorkosigans supply a spark that helps bring Barrayaran women closer to some kind of liberation.

The significant liberating factor is the uterine replicator, working away quietly in the background to revolutionize society. This is a Betan technology that is largely unknown on Barrayar until the time of Aral and Cordelia, but by the end of Aral's regency it is becoming more and more common, at least among the wealthier elements of Barrayaran society. The fetus is transferred to the replicator, an artificial womb, at an early stage of cell division. The fetus grows inside the replicator, in optimal conditions and with due care, until the normal time for birth—called "cracking the bottle" on Beta Colony, Cordelia says (CH 220). When Miles's bottle is cracked, Aral and Cordelia each take a latch, and break the sterile seal to open up the container: "If you can open a picnic cooler, you can do this" (CH 578). Miles later admits to Elena that if he had thought about this earlier, he could have agitated for two birthdays:

one to celebrate when the fetus was removed from his mother (in her case by Cesarian) and a second when it was removed from the replicator. Cordelia and Aral chose Cesarian Day for his birthday (WA 35).

In *Mirror Dance* Mark Vorkosigan has a conversation with Kareen Koudelka that illustrates how things on Barrayar have changed in thirty years (MD 308–9). Kareen asks whether, if he were going to get married, would he be happy for his wife to use a uterine replicator. "Why would any couple not choose to use a replicator?" is his response. When Kareen says, with the inarticulacy of a modern teenager, "To, like, prove her love for him," his immediate response is "Good God, how barbaric!" and suggests that it would actually prove the opposite. But Kareen goes on to explain the demographic problem faced by the upper classes. Soon after Cordelia moved to Barrayar, Barrayarans started using an imported pill that enabled one to choose the sex of one's child. For a time everyone chose to have a boy; and the ratio of the sexes changed. But Kareen and the other Koudelka girls were of an age when there was a serious "girl-drought." As a result, women have the upper hand in marriage negotiations, and go-betweens are not even dealing on behalf of men who refuse uterine replicators. The clear implication is that, if it is their choice, women will choose the replicators—but also that the replicator has enhanced the genetic power and role of the women of the Vor class, bringing their former behind-the-scenes presence into a more public arena.

Ekaterin's dreadful sister-in-law Rosalie Vorvayne sees other advantages in the uterine replicator, particularly if Ekaterin decides on a marriage of convenience with that "grotesque little man" Miles.

> "I mean, he's a mutie, isn't he? High Vor or no, the family would never urge you to match with a mutie just for money, Kat. Put that right out of your mind." She paused thoughtfully. "Still . . . they're not handing out too many chances to be a Countess. I suppose, with the uterine replicators these days, you wouldn't actually have to have any physical contact. To have children, I mean. And they could be gene-cleaned. These galactic technologies give the idea of a marriage of convenience a whole new twist. But it's not as though you were that desperate." (ACC 147–48)

These are thus at least two other possible social consequences of the spread of uterine replicators on Barrayar: the ability to avoid physical contact and the facility of checking for mutation. The latter, indeed, seems to be uppermost in the mind of the Barrayaran scientist, Dr. Henri, who examines his first uterine replicator in Cordelia's presence. When he finds out that Cordelia herself was born with the aid of this technology, he asks whether she was free of genetic defects, and when she responds "Certified," he commented, "We need this technology" (CH 343).

All new technologies result in the unexpected. Another possible use is humorously treated in *A Civil Campaign*. Lord Vormuir decides to solve his district's underpopulation problem. He buys himself thirty uterine replicators, supplies all the sperm himself, and starts producing daughters on an industrial scale. When this is discovered there are 118 (thirty of them still in the replicators), not counting the four that were produced naturally, with the help of his wife. The problem, of course, is that Barrayaran law has not kept up with all the new technology that is being introduced. Miles ends up on a committee to look at that whole problem; Vormuir's own production line is closed down by order of Miles, as imperial auditor, but Vormuir plans to challenge that legally. The children are being well looked after, and so it was not a question of abuse; the children are legally his, so it is not slavery. It is Ekaterin who comes up with the solution, based on historic precedent: since these children are all Vormuir's illegitimate daughters, he should be required by the emperor to provide a suitably high aristocratic dowry for each of them when they come of age (ACC 93). This eventually becomes the imperial decision. Miles hands the official document to Vormuir and then retreats rapidly as Vormuir reads it, but not before he hears Vormuir's "sudden howl of anguish" when he reaches the word "dowries" (ACC 381).

Bujold is hardly thought of as a radical feminist, but it is noteworthy that one of the theoretical progenitors of the uterine replicator was Shulamith Firestone, whose feminist book *The Dialectic of Sex* (1970) was regarded in its day as extremely radical. She took the incubators and bottles of Aldous Huxley's *Brave New World* (1932), generally regarded by (male) critics as thoroughly dystopian, and gave them a utopian twist. Firestone regarded the first of her four "minimal demands" as *"the freeing of women from the tyranny of their biology by any means available, and the diffusion of the childbearing and childrearing role to the society as a whole, to men and children as well as to women."*[11] The childbearing, she says, could be taken over by technology. If this were too much for people to cope with, as it would be at first, then women who bear children should be given adequate incentives and compensation. As for child*rearing*, this had more to do at that time with maintaining power relationships and forcing the internalization of family values than with the happiness of the child, a situation that would change once society had developed so that "the interests of the individual coincided with those of the larger society."[12] At this point, childrearing no longer needed to be restricted to the nuclear family. As far as childrearing is concerned, Firestone is merely echoing what many utopian schemes or intentional community models had advocated; her proposal for childbearing still remains a matter for science-fictional speculation.

It is on the male utopia of Athos, ironically, that something almost approaching Firestone's utopia has been achieved. Uterine replicators are the norm, since there are no women; and thus women, whom the great majority of Athosians have never met, can be dismissed as "uterine replicators on legs" (EA 34). There is a nice satirical exchange between Elli Quinn and Ethan. She wonders if the Cetagandans are breeding a race of super soldiers in vats (she is no doubt thinking of the super soldier under her command, Sergeant Taura). Ethan considers this seriously and then rejects it on the grounds that producing infants is so expensive: "Why, on Athos it absorbs most of the planet's economic resources. Food of course—housing, education, clothing, medical care—it takes nearly all our efforts just to maintain population replacement, let alone to increase" (EA 77–78). Elli is amused, remarking that "people seem to come in floods" on other planets. Ethan is puzzled: "The labor costs alone of bringing a child to maturity are astronomical." Elli explains that labor costs are not included in most people's calculations. Ethan is astonished: "Athosians would never sit still for such a hidden labor tax! Don't the primary nurturers even get social duty credits?" (This, it will be remembered, is precisely what Firestone was recommending.)[13] Elli responds by noting that on other planets raising a child is called "women's work."

The other planet that has become dependent on uterine replicators is Cetaganda, as Miles learns when, in *Cetaganda*, he is introduced to some of the secrets of the female control of reproduction. Cetaganda takes replicator technology to its ultimate ends, as an instrument of eugenics. If it can be used to erase genetic defects on Beta Colony or Barrayar, it can be used also to develop the human genome further in planned evolution.

In the upper echelons of Cetagandan society, natural births have long since been abandoned. When the Cetagandan Lord Yenaro wants to put down Ivan Vorpatril, he mentions to Lady Gelle, a ghem-lady, that Ivan had a biological birth. All births are biological, she says.

> "Ah, but no. The original sort of biology. From his mother's body."
> "Eeeuu." Her nose wrinkled in horror. "Really, Yenaro. You are so obnoxious tonight." (Cet 30)

Among the haut, the upper aristocracy, an embryo is produced after negotiation between the heads of the two genetic lines (or "constellations"; what Barrayarans would call clans). The contract has to be approved by the head of the all-female Star Crèche; at the time of the narrative, this had been the mother of the emperor. If any genetic alternations were proposed, as was often the case, this had to be approved by the Star Crèche. The Star Crèche has authority over haut births on the eight outlying planets in the Cetagandan Empire: the fertilizations take place in the Star Crèche's headquarters, in the Celestial Gardens on Cetaganda, and the growing fetuses in their uterine replicators are sent back to the various planets. Each of the satraps who govern the colony worlds have a haut consort effectively appointed by the Star Crèche. The emperor has supreme control of the genetic engineering project run by the Star Crèche; but in practice the haut women are deciding on the way humans on Cetaganda evolve. Those who are in ultimate charge of reproduction thus have considerable power: not the power to effect day-to-day political decisions, but the power to create the future. Bujold has dubbed Cetanganda an "oocytic empire," as contrasted with the more normal spermatocytic societies. They do not spread their gametes at random but control them very carefully. The egg-shaped float-chair bubbles were intended to have symbolic significance, though Bujold notes that no one seems to have noticed this: "There is, apparently, such a thing as being too subtle."

Ivan asks Miles how long it will be before we no longer consider the haut-lords human; Miles responds that it is more a question of when it will be that "the haut-lords no longer regard *us* as human" (Cet 300). It is clear, to Miles's eyes at least, that haut women have already progressed toward the posthuman. Much is made of the immediate impact their beauty has on those who are not used to them: and even most Cetagandans never see them, as they travel in their opaque float-chairs. When Miles first sees a haut woman, Rian Degtiar, the effect on him is astonishing (and somewhat implausible): he falls to his knees in front of her, unconscious of how he got there, and, just as rapidly, falls in love (Cet 88–89). "Pheromones, probably," Bujold comments to me. But there is a good deal of emphasis on the overwhelming beauty of the haut women. If we are looking for plausibly relevant literary parallels to this, again we need look no further than Tolkien. Sam Gamgee and Gimli both experience the same reaction to Galadriel as Miles does to Rian Degtiar: the ethereal, etiolated beauty of Bujold's haut women and Tolkien's elven women may share common roots.

Beta Colony and Barrayar are a long way behind Athos and Cetaganda in their use of the uterine replicator. Around the time of Miles's birth three times as many children on Beta Colony are gestated in vitro as in vivo (CH 298), with the minority who choose live gestation being convinced of the psychosocial advantages. Cordelia's own Betan sister-in-law boasts that her two children were born the natural way. Even by the time of Miles's marriage, some thirty years after Cordelia and seventeen uterine replicators had come to Barrayar, it is obvious that Barrayar is only one step along this path. Only some women have been freed from "the tyranny of their biology" by the uterine replicator, because replicators are under suspicion and are "hideously expensive." Presumably they were far more expensive two hundred years earlier, when the arch-capitalist in *Falling Free*, Van Atta, made the point that despite the expense "it's probably only a matter of time before rich women everywhere start ducking their biological duties and cooking up their kids in 'em" (FF 17).

In the Vorkosigan saga, Bujold deals with other aspects of gender and sexuality: notably homosexuality and transgenderism. She has by no means pleased all commentators on these matters. It is notable, for instance, that (excluding *Ethan of Athos* for the moment) the most prominent man presented as gay in the early books is Admiral Vorrutyer, who also delights in the infliction of pain and in the voyeuristic contemplation of rape. When Vorrutyer is killed by Bothari, his close associate Vorhalas does not refer to him as someone for whom torture seems a major hobby but simply calls him "that sodomizing son-of-a-bitch" (CH 137). Having sex with other men seems to be a worse crime than being a torturer, in the eyes of Vorhalas at least. But being gay on Barrayar, while not illegal, is clearly not viewed favorably at all. As Bujold commented to me, "The Barrayaran social strictures are pretty much what you would expect from an underpopulated world with a high death rate trying desperately to herd as many people as possible into producing as many offspring as possible." The differences between Barrayaran and Betan attitudes are clear. Vordarian, who will later lead a rebellion against Aral Vorkosigan, tries to undermine Aral's marriage with Cordelia by telling her of Aral's sexual relationship with the late Admiral Vorrutyer. He is disconcerted to find that Cordelia already knows and, as a Betan, dismisses the fact as irrelevant. But she does so in an odd way that is difficult to explain. When Vordarian says thoughtfully, "He's bisexual, you know," Cordelia responds, "Was bisexual. Now he's monogamous" (CH 330). Bisexuals, that is, those who respond both to males and females, can of course be monogamous too: sexual orientation is nothing to do with willingness to conform to social norms (in a monogamous society). Cordelia seems to be trying to put Aral's homosexuality in the past: a youthful peccadillo, or something that he put aside once he had ended his relationship with the singularly perverted Vorrutyer.

Mark has been told about Aral's past as part of his early training. He talks about it with Cordelia, who tells him:

> "I judge him to be bisexual, but subconsciously more attracted to men than to women. Or rather—to soldiers. Not to men generally, I don't think. I am, by Barrayaran standards, a rather extreme, er, tomboy, and thus became the solution to his dilemmas. The first time he met me I was in uniform, in the middle of a nasty armed encounter. He thought it was love at first sight. I've never bothered explaining to him that it was his compulsions leaping up." Her lips twitched. (MD 286)

Aral is thus portrayed not as an enthusiastic homosexual but as someone who to a large extent keeps his secret desires locked away somewhere even he cannot see them, out of shame or guilt. The only hint of a more positive aspect to his love of Vorrutyer is the sketches that Aral made of him as a young man.[14]

We do not meet any wholeheartedly gay men in the Vorkosigan saga except for those who live on the planet of Athos. And it is suggestive that, apart from Aral, all those Barrayarans whose sexual habits are not exclusively heterosexual are from one single family, the Vorrutyers.[15] Vice-Admiral Ges Vorrutyer we have already met. There is also Donna Vorrutyer and Byerly

Vorrutyer, and other family members make an appearance. It is worthwhile dwelling briefly on that family, with the help of Suford Lewis's "Brief Guide to Barrayaran Genealogy" (VC 460–69). One suspects that Lewis knows rather more about Barrayaran genealogy than Bujold does, so one does not need to follow her through all her intricacies. Her argument is partly based on the supposition that madness is inherited, which certainly those on Barrayar believe, or fear. We know about Mad Yuri, the emperor who put to death many of his closest relatives (including Aral's mother). Lewis suggests that Prince Serg inherited that madness through his father Ezar's marriage to a relative of Yuri's, either the sister or daughter. We know that Gregor worried that he too might inherit his father Serg's madness (VG 334). The only other person who is referred to (in passing) as Mad is Mad Miles: that is his nickname among some of the older Dendarii, according to Baz (VG 271), and is also a phrase that subsequently Miles applies to himself ("when I was babbling Mad Miles, hustler of the Dendarii" [DI 51–52]). But we may note that Miles says that he "can trace a blood relationship with Mad Emperor Yuri through two lines of descent" (WA 229). He is also descended from a Vorrutyer, from Emperor Dorca's ruthless supporter Count Pierre "le Sanguinaire" Vorrutyer: "Old Pierre's eldest daughter had married an earlier Count Vorkosigan, which was where the Pierre of Mark's middle name had come down from" (ACC 136). Suford Lewis suggests that the madness in the Vorbarra line may have come from their close connections with the Vorrutyer, and that therefore the genetic source of the madness of Yuri, Serg, and Ges Vorrutyer may be one individual. We may throw in here Ges Vorrutyer's uncle, Dono Vorrutyer, who designed the ImpSec HQ for Mad Emperor Yuri, as well as the Municipal Stadium, which vie with each other for the title of ugliest building in Vorbarr Sultana. According to Armsman Pym, Dono retired to the countryside and built a bizarre set of towers on the family estates (which became a tourist attraction). He wasn't assassinated by the Architectural Defense League, as Mark jokingly suggests; he died stark mad (MD 326).

Madness and homosexuality thus seem to be connected in these books. The only four people on Barrayar who do not exhibit "normal" sexual tendencies are three Vorrutyers and a Vorkosigan, and the families are intermarried and known for their congenital madness. Aral and Admiral Ges Vorrutyer we have discussed. At first sight, Byerly Vorrutyer is a chip off the admiral's block. When we first meet him, in *A Civil Campaign*, apparently as a suitor of Ekaterin, Miles thinks of him as a "town clown" and as having "impeccable taste in everything but his vices" (ACC 50). Ekaterin is rather taken with his outrageous wit; Miles, less charitable, preferred Ivan's wit, as it was ingenuous, while "unlike Ivan, Byerly never insulted anyone unintentionally" (ACC 52). Through the action of *A Civil Campaign* we learn that Byerly is a devious conspirator and that some of this is in virtuous pursuance of his task as a part-time secret operative for ImpSec. What his vices are is never specified, although Ivan's remark to himself that Byerly was no competition for his own amorous intentions is one of several hints (taken up by many writers of Bujold fanfic, and specifically of Ivan/By slash) that Byerly is gay. It is not until Bujold's most recent book, *Captain Vorpatril's Alliance*, that we understand Byerly a little better, although that is not until after Bujold has teased the reader a little. By visits Ivan late at night.

> "Get to the point, By. I want to go to bed. And by the looks of you, so do you."
> By let his eyes widen. "Why Ivan! Was that an invitation? I'm so thrilled!"
> "Someday," Ivan growled, "I might say yes to that old line, just to watch you have a coronary."
> By spread his hand over his heart, and intoned wistfully, "And so I might." (CVA 3–4)

After Byerly has asked Tej's blue-skinned sister Rish to go out with him (for the first of many times), Tej asks:

> "So . . . is By bi? . . . Bisexual, that is."
> "I have no idea what By's real preferences are," Ivan stated firmly. "Nor do I wish to know."
> "What, couldn't you smell him, that first night he came in on Komarr?" said Rish. Addressing Tej, Ivan hoped. "He'd had a busy two days or so. Any lingering scents from prior to that were too attenuated to discern" (CVA 173).

Tej's question is never answered. And by the end of the book, Byerly seems to be Rish's partner. His "vices" are forgotten, and one is left with the possibility that his apparently homosexual behavior—such as the occasional camp gesture (ACC 137)—was, like much of his behavior, a professional mask for his undercover career.[16]

Byerly Vorrutyer's cousin Donna Vorrutyer is a different matter. She has divorced twice and been widowed once; in between two of the spouses she has had a fling with Ivan, ten years her junior. At the time of *A Civil Campaign* she is in dispute with her cousin Richars Vorrutyer over the inheritance of the countship. Count Pierre has died, and she submits to the council a legal objection to Richars's inheritance of the title. Richars shares a lot of characteristics of the nastier parts of the Vorrutyer family, and Donna's hatred of him goes back a long way, at least to the time when she was twelve: he tried to rape her, she said, "and when I fought him off, [he] drowned my new puppy in retaliation" (ACC 132). After the formal deposition of her declaration of impediment she disappears for Beta Colony, and it is assumed that the case will be considered on her return. Miles speculates that perhaps she would come back from Beta Colony with a uterine replicator containing Pierre's clone, which would create interesting legal wrangling. Byerly knows Donna's plan and watches Ivan's amazement at the shuttle-port as he realizes that the smart man who looks like a true Vorrutyer—"that hair, those eyes, that smirking swagger" (ACC 130)—is Donna, now Lord Dono Vorrutyer. Dono explains to the embarrassed (but fascinated) Ivan that the transformation is complete: Dono will be able to father the next Count and do so in the assurance that any offspring will be free of genetic disease or mutation. "The prick's always been the most important qualification for a Countship anyway. History says so" (ACC 135).

Dono has told no one about his trip to Beta, except for Pierre's armsmen, his attorney, and Byerly; but he knows that he has been shadowed by an imperial agent, so Gregor is not nearly as surprised as Ivan expects him to be. For political reasons Gregor is happy not to oppose Dono: Dono is a Progressive, like the emperor, while Richars is a Conservative. After thinking about the situation for a while, Gregor's immediate response is "So . . . what's it like?" Dono explains that apart from his energy (and his temper) being at a higher level than before, it is the world that has changed. On Beta Colony, he sees little change. By the time he gets to Komarr, his personal space has doubled compared to what it was when he was a woman, and people's response time has halved. The effect increases noticeably as soon as he reaches the Vorbarr Sultana shuttleport. "The view from the top of the food chain promises to be downright panoramic" (ACC 156). Gregor concludes the interview with the use of his favorite phrase (of which Ivan later says "I always thought that was an appallingly irresponsible thing for an emperor to say" [CVA 285]): "Let's see what happens." The men who meet Dono are fascinated and amused. Ekaterin's reaction is more interesting: "I should think it would have taken a great deal of courage. [. . .] And anger" (ACC 166).

Richars, who has expected to be the next count, denies that Donna has really become a man. But he is speaking to the wrong person: Miles is perfectly familiar with the efficiency of Betan medical techniques. Richars is then horrified that Ivan, who "used to screw her, you know," has now "climbed into that side of the bunk." Miles accuses Richars of inconsistency:

> "You cannot logically imply my cousin Ivan is a homosexual for screwing Dono, not that I think he is doing so, unless you simultaneously grant Dono is actually male. In which case, his suit for the Vorrutyer Countship holds."
>
> "I think," said Richars primly after a moment, "your cousin Ivan may be a very confused young man."
>
> "Not about that, he's not," Miles sighed. (ACC 233)

Miles is so annoyed with Richars's attitudes and behavior that he decides to abandon any position of neutrality and to start campaigning to get Lord Dono accepted by the Council of Counts as Count Vorrutyer. Bujold goes into some detail in the last third of *A Civil Campaign* about the politics of the Progressives vs. the Conservatives. There are in fact two related issues, both of which stand as touchstones for the differences between the two factions. There is the question of whether gender reassignment can allow someone to become a count (not, as Byerly says, something that hordes of women are going to try [ACC 155]); and second, there is the discovery that René Vorbretten has a Cetagandan great-grandfather who is leading a rival to try to oust him from the countship. In the end, with a certain amount of unethical behaviour on both sides, the Progressives on the council win both votes, and Barrayar discards another part of its irrational and blinkered past. There is little doubt that among the many things that Bujold is doing in this book is to remind her readers that tradition cannot rule everything and that new ideas have to be entertained.

Bujold has, however, disappointed a number of her readers by being, in their view, not Progressive enough. While it is bold of her to have a gender-reassignment operation so crucial to the plot of *A Civil Campaign*, she has been criticized for misrepresenting the usual experience of trans people in our own contemporary world. For trans people, the decision to change their gender is usually the agonized result of a long mental process, when they find it very difficult to cope with living in a body that their mind tells them is alien to them. Donna/Dono Vorrutyer changes gender as a legal tactic. Dono makes the effort to appear male, in terms of body language, for instance; his role model, indeed, is Aral Vorkosigan—ironically, perhaps, given Aral's own sexual history. But it seems to be some kind of game for Dono, not unlike Miles playing at being Admiral Naismith. There are some Betans "who switch sexes back and forth three or four times in their lives," he says; indeed, Dono has met some of them, and he finds them most helpful (ACC 134). Clearly, Dono's case is unique and not intended as representative, but some trans readers have seen it as unhelpful that gender reassignment is portrayed like this, as a simple matter of choice, in its only appearance in Bujold's oeuvre.

Not all gay or gay-friendly readers of Bujold's fiction have been pleased with her representation of homosexuality either. Homosexuals in the Chalion universe are tolerated by Quintarians (for they are protected by the Lord Bastard) but persecuted by Quadrenes (who deny the godhead of the Bastard); the only time we encounter homosexuality itself it is in the form of male rape on the slave galleys. Homosexuality in the Vorkosigan novels, at least among the characters we see onstage, is restricted to males. The openly gay Vorrutyer comes to a nasty end, while neither Aral nor Byerly are *really* gay and are seen to turn exclusively to women. The hermaphrodite Bel Thorne, who embarrasses Miles by its ability to emphasize either of its two sexes according to circumstance, ends happily male, with a female partner. During the Cetagandan occupation, a Cetagandan captain who has fallen in love with a young Barrayaran man dies in the Cetagandan nuclear bombing of the Vorkosigan's district capital (CVA 257). In *The Curse of Chalion* the roya Ias loves his chancellor Dy Lutez, and they form a ménage à trois with the royina Ista (the heroine of *Paladin of Souls*); but Dy Lutez dies, not exactly accidentally, in an attempt to defeat the curse of Chalion, and Ias dies of grief a year later. There are no homosexuals among the major characters in Bujold's worlds (apart from Athos) who live happy and fulfilled lives: the feminist Adrienne

Rich would classify Bujold as one of those collaborating with the patriarchal project of compulsory heterosexuality.[17]

Athos might appear to be the major exception, of course. *Ethan of Athos* was a groundbreaking work, as we have seen, offering a planet of male homosexuals to science-fiction readers who, within mass-market publishing at least, had never experienced that before. Ethan Urquhart himself is a very sympathetic character whose adventures off-planet, in Kline Station, are enthralling. His own cultural assumptions—above all, the one that assumes that any social contact with women could lead to madness—are challenged in amusing ways, without any attempt being made to "convert" him to heterosexuality. But the two homosexual relationships he has in the book—with Janos and Terrence—are hardly enthusiastic descriptions of homosexual love. Janos is depicted as an irresponsible brat: one wonders how Ethan's relationship with him could have lasted a week. The problem is resolved by having Janos run off to the frontier life of the Outlands, leaving Ethan free to express his love for Terrence. He finds Terrence very attractive physically, although he is nervous in his presence because of Terrence's telepathic abilities. Ethan "proposes" to Terrence by saying that within a year the immigrant could have DA status (designated alternate parent), and then he could become Primary Nurturer for Ethan's sons. This would give Terrence the ability to accumulate the credits he needs to become a parent himself. Terrence says that he understands that this relationship is not unlike marriage and asks whether it would involve sexual relations. "Not necessarily," says Ethan (EA 236). Ethan hopes that Terrence might "grow accustomed to our ways," and Terrence admits that he just might. In other words, in the course of the novel Ethan moves from a destructive relationship with one male into a celibate relationship with another. Clearly, there are happy and sexually active homosexual relationships on Athos, although they all appear in the distance. We may presume that Athos and Terrence might live happily together, but Bujold denies the reader the certainty of that.

Ethan of Athos shows Bujold challenging the deep conservatism of much American science fiction; but ultimately, for whatever reason, her other books seem mostly uncomfortable with the positive portrayal of homosexuality. She probably did not want to offend her readership; and the ease with which they *can* be offended was shown by the reaction that Bujold experienced to the mild amount of sexual activity (of the heterosexual kind) in the Wide Green World. Overall, she has explored the problems of alternatives to our own ideas of sexuality with much greater openness and invention than most science fiction writers of her generation. Few other writers, for instance, have created a major hermaphrodite character, let alone one as sympathetic as Bel Thorne. And I cannot think of another writer who has experimented with genuinely neuter characters, like the ba servants of the haut ladies on Cetaganda. Bujold now regrets that she used the pronoun "it" of the hermaphrodites, rather than keeping the word for use with the ba, where it would be much more appropriate. The ba is a fascinating creation, which offers Bujold scope for development if she wishes to take it. They are loyal servants, a science-fictional and genetically engineered version of a Byzantine eunuch, but far more than that. Because they are used for testing out new genetic improvements to the haut line, the ba are siblings, or "children, even" (DI 127) of the haut. And they may be servants, but they are "every bit as smart and dangerous as a haut lord" (DI 127); a ba is at the heart of the plot that Miles sets out to unravel in both *Cetaganda* and *Diplomatic Immunity*.

CHAPTER 8

WAR, LEADERSHIP, AND HONOR

Traditionally, since the days of E. E. "Doc" Smith, a central theme of space opera has been warfare. The earlier Vorkosigan novels do not buck the trend: the very first, *Shards of Honor*, begins in the middle of a war between Barrayar and Beta Colony. The Vorkosigans, from Piotr to Aral and to Miles himself, define themselves or create themselves through military service. It is one of the many frustrations of Miles's early life that none of his military exploits with the Dendarii Free Mercenaries will ever be known to the public, since they are all ascribed to his alter ego, Admiral Naismith (and are all under strict security embargo by ImpSec). Yet the characters we are led to admire (above all Cordelia Naismith and Miles himself) hate warfare and despise violence as a solution to problems.

We can see no evidence in the books that Bujold is a pacifist, in the sense of opposing all war on principle. There is no doubt in the minds of her characters that the twenty-year war to remove the invading Cetagandans was wholly justified. But what seems to interest Bujold most is not the fighting, or even the peacemaking, but the whole question of what makes a good leader, which is perhaps at its most focused and immediate among the military. Bujold's work presents us with models of good leadership, both within the armed services and in civil society, and models, too, of its opposite: mismanagement or, at the extreme, tyranny. Sometimes these models seem a little like caricatures; yet this is offset by an ability to dissect political contests with more subtlety than one finds in any other writer of space opera except for C. J. Cherryh.

In her Vorkosigan novels Bujold undermines one of the most ubiquitous elements of the subgenre of space opera in those early stories, and she undermines it still further later on by leaving warfare behind altogether. Miles's near-fatal meeting with a needle grenade at the beginning of *Mirror Dance* means that his days with the Dendarii are effectively over. Indeed, *Cetaganda*, written after *Mirror Dance* but set several years earlier, retrofits Miles into a civilian position; it introduces Miles the problem solver or detective as a presage of his later career. But Miles's later civilian career is not such an extreme break as it might seem at first sight: after all, Miles never sought war, and he was far more likely to use his Dendarii to prevent warfare and to make peace than the opposite. Broadening our horizons a little, we can make comparisons across other works too: of the male characters in Bujold's fantasy novels, Cazaril and Dag are also reluctant fighters and natural peacemakers. Indeed Bujold herself has called *The Sharing Knife* an epic that (unlike almost all other epics) is "all about waging peace."[1]

Effective leadership for Bujold seems to be very much a question of projecting an image of worthiness and above all trustworthiness to one's followers. That, in Barrayaran society, but also in the preindustrial societies of Chalion and the Wide Green World, is very much tied up with idea of honor.

Let us start this discussion by thinking about the paradox of Aral Vorkosigan. Aral looms over the entire sequence, from the very first chapter of *Shards of Honor* to the very last words of *CryoBurn*, far more authoritatively than does his son Miles. Aral was "The Butcher of Komarr"; he is the admiral whose loyalty to the emperor ensured the deaths of thousands at Escobar, including the emperor's heir himself. After the death of Emperor Ezar, Aral runs the Barrayaran Empire for sixteen years, until Gregor comes of age at twenty; he then governs Sergyar, as viceroy. He is someone highly attuned to his sense of honor yet one who has need of occasional retuning by Cordelia. According to Emperor Gregor, each year Aral gives a lecture about honor versus reputation to the graduating class of officers, a lecture Miles would do well to listen to (ACC 291). "I wouldn't call it a lecture," says Aral (after expressing pleasure that Gregor had remembered), "just a useful distinction, to clarify thought. [. . .] Reputation is what other people know about you. Honor is what you know about yourself. [. . .] The friction tends to arise when the two are not the same" (ACC 293). It is soul-destroying, he suggests, to have your honor shattered while your public reputation stands high; the other way round is just very, very irritating.

Aral's own career suggests he has had experience of both soul destruction and irritation. "The Butcher of Komarr" is how many people think of Aral, and not only on Komarr. Even Miles does not have the whole story explained to him as a child (WA 290; BA 22). Cordelia has the explanation early on in her acquaintance with Aral, as soon as she realizes that her captor is the Butcher. Prisoners were indeed killed: we learn much later that the Solstice Massacre involved the gunning down of two hundred Counsellors, senior politicians, on Komarr (BA 22). Since Aral had given his "word, as Vorkosigan," that they were to be spared, when his political officer had them killed behind his back, he broke the man's neck with his own hands. "It was a personal matter, you see, touching my honor. I couldn't order a firing squad—they were all afraid of the Ministry of Political Education" (CH 22).

The political officers of Ezar's period could countermand the orders of the senior military officer present, so Aral cannot deal with this within the military chain of command. He had, however, given his word to spare the prisoners, and his word has been shown to be unreliable; all he can do is to reveal, as publicly as possible, what happens to those who compromise his word. The value of his "word" is the center of Aral's honor (and that of other Vor): "My word as Vorkosigan" is something that comes to the lips of both Aral and Miles on suitably serious occasions. For Aral, it seems at times that "giving his word" is the reminder to himself that he should behave honorably. When the seventeen uterine replicators were delivered to him, he wondered what he should do with them. Cordelia reminded him that he had signed for them:

He sighed. "Quite. Pledged my word, in a sense." He set the problem up in familiar terms, and found his balance therein. "My word as Vorkosigan, in fact. Right. Good. Objective defined, plan of attack proposed—we're in business." (CH 168)

More than once when Miles is dealing with non-Barrayarans, the significance of a Barrayaran's *word* has to be explained. It is a meaningful oath, the breaking of which is both dishonor and crime.

Through Aral we come to see that "honor" is a vitally important political and social principle on Barrayar. As far as we can see, it only affects the Vor: but the Vor are a large group, who still dominate politics. The story of the Butcher, referred to frequently throughout the saga, shows that it is *not* ultimately a political problem for Aral. Indeed, Aral is happy, to some extent, to keep his horrific reputation. Only when Miles is almost middle-aged, with the title of imperial auditor, does he dare ask his father about the effect of that soubriquet. "I've found it a mixed . . . damnation. But yes, I have used the weight of that reputation, from time to time, to lean on certain susceptible men. Why not, I paid for it." (ACC 294). The Komarr episode threatens Aral's reputation; for those who do not know the full story, it strengthens his political authority; but it also threatens his honor, since the massacre happened under his command. He has to rebuild his honor from that point onward. Aral's final recommendation to Miles is: "Guard your honor. Let your reputation fall where it will. And outlive the bastards" (ACC 295).

Yet there is one truly dishonorable moment in Aral's life, and it is one that affects many of the characters in the books. Prior to the invasion of Escobar, Aral Vorkosigan is on the flagship with Prince Serg, the emperor's son, and Admiral Rulf Vorhalas. Vorrutyer has been killed, and Aral urges Prince Serg to stay on the flagship as senior officer rather than to lead the invasion fleet down onto the planet's surface. With a calculated balance between insult and reliance on regulations—"I must formally protest. By landing with the ground troops on Escobar you are leaving your proper post" (CH 135)—Aral manipulates the vain Serg to play the hero. He knows (as we are later told) that the Escobarans have an effective and secret defence, the latest Betan invention—weapons that "had been bravely convoyed through the Barrayaran blockade by one Captain Cordelia Naismith, Betan Expeditionary Force" (CH 269)—and that he is sending the vile Prince Serg to his death, along with tens of thousands of military personnel and Aral's perfectly honorable friend Vorhalas. The aftermath involves a great deal of lying. Prince Serg is hailed as a military hero, and his death is treated publically as a great loss. Both Miles and Gregor are lied to; and once Miles finds out the truth about Prince Serg, from Elena Bothari's mother, he conspires in keeping the truth from Gregor.

Is Aral's behaviour honorable? This is clearly something to which Aral devotes a good deal of thought over the ensuing twenty years. In the immediate aftermath Cordelia remarks that Vorrutyer appears to her to be the ultimate in evil. Aral, however, thinks of him as just a little villain—"an old-fashioned craftsman, making crimes one-off"—and adds:

> "The really unforgivable acts are committed by calm men in beautiful green silk rooms, who deal death wholesale, by the shipload, without lust, or anger, or desire, or any redeeming emotion to excuse them but cold fear of some pretended future. But the crimes they hope to prevent in that future are imaginary. The ones they commit in the present—they are real." (CH 141)

Emperor Ezar has chosen to put all the bad eggs in one basket, along with many good ones, and drop the basket: it is "the most wasteful political assassination plot in Barrayaran history, and the most subtle, the corpses hidden in a mountain of corpses, forever inextricable." Cordelia muses, "Somewhere in a quiet, green silk room, where a great choreographer designed a dance of death, and the honor of a man of honor was broken on the wheel of his service" (CH 147). Aral reveals not long afterward that he himself sat in that room, with Ezar and Captain Negri, planning to deal out death by the shipload (CH 159). Aral sees the question as an ethical one without answer: "I've always tried to walk the path of honor. But what do you do when all choices are evil? Shameful action, shameful inaction, every path leading to a thicket of death" (CH 162).

Despite the bloodbath of Escobar, Cordelia continues to trust Aral's sense of honor. Mehta, her interrogator on Beta Colony, understandably cannot comprehend this. When she asks Cordelia *why* she believed Aral's word, she could only say, "It—seemed consistent, with what I saw of his character" (CH 189). When asked to explain, she says, "A man's word is something more to a Barrayaran than a vague promise, at least for the old-fashioned types. Heavens, it's even the basis for their government, oaths of fealty and all that." But when pushed, she admits that Aral had broken his word, and that the cost had been huge. Mehta looks at this response from a Betan point of view—"he breaks it for a price, then"—but Cordelia explains that he did not break it for a price, but at a cost. "A price is something you get. A cost is something you lose. He lost—much, at Escobar" (CH 190).

The Vor's first duty is to the emperor. In the case of the Escobaran affair, Aral sacrifices his honor for the sake of the emperor. The reader is certainly told, more than once, that the alternative was worse; but we still have to reckon with the "cost." Cordelia and Aral have a revealing conversation, wherein Aral admits that he has broken his word, that he has lied, that he has killed a man after a summary court martial. "I think you are getting blood-glutted. Individuals are losing their meaning for you," Cordelia comments (CH 158). Aral agrees and says it is time to quit. Cordelia then asks him how the emperor had "bought" him, in this plan to kill thousands for the sake of ridding the universe of Prince Serg. His reply makes him more complicit rather than less; the emperor and Negri convinced him, after a week of argument, that his actions at Escobar were necessary, for the greater good. Perhaps the most honourable aspect of Aral, the aspect that allows Cordelia to accept his actions, is that he is never quite satisfied with this.

Yet despite the challenges to the notion of honor, neither Aral nor Cordelia, nor indeed Miles, confronts the problem of the feudal notion of "honor" and its incompatibility with the kind of warfare that "modern" Barrayar wages. How can bombing ever be "honorable" in the same way that a fight between two individuals can be? (Tolkien had exactly that reaction during World War II.[2]) Bujold has explained this to me in terms of the semantic problem inherent in the word "honor": that it can be used as a synonym for duty, but also a synonym for ego. Aral gradually moves, during his younger life, from honor-as-ego to honor-as-duty. Later, Miles will trace the same trajectory. Self-sacrifice for the Imperium—for all the humans who make up the empire—is one way of proving one's honor. This is a Vor thing, but not restricted to men. Ekaterin unwittingly proves herself to Miles when, after singlehandedly sabotaging the efforts of the Komarran extremists, she hears from Miles that he had been prepared to sacrifice her life, and Madame Vorthys's life, if necessary. "Wouldn't you put *your* life on the line to stop them?" she asks, to which he honestly replies, "Yes, but I wasn't putting my life—I was putting yours." "But I'm Vor," she says (Kom 300). Indeed, Ekaterin and Madame Vorthys have already discussed this possibility of sacrificing themselves to combat the Komarran "terrorists" and have accepted it with apparent equanimity. Many years earlier Aral Vorkosigan threatens to sacrifice lives, even the life of the hostage Kareen (Emperor Gregor's mother), in order to defeat Vordarian: "She is Vor. She understands" (CH 475).

It is no accident that Bujold leaves it to Elena Bothari, neither male nor of the Vor class, to question one of Barrayar's most respected shibboleths. The professed code of the warrior, "military honor," is "a sham, a hoax, a lie," she discovered: "I've faced fire, and I've killed a man, and it was nothing but butchery. Any robot could have done it" (WA 177).

It is, however, not only the Vor in Bujold's works who value sacrifice. Cazaril seeks ways to sacrifice himself for the sake of the Chalion royal house in *The Curse of Chalion*, and by doing so three times he lifts the curse. Blood sacrifice, of animals and humans, is an integral part of *The Hallowed Hunt*. The sharing knives of the Lakewalkers are produced by self-sacrifice, the giving up of life so that a new knife can be primed. As John Lennard puts it, "Self-sacrifice, donating body and spirit in death, is an ultimate end for individual Lakewalkers, without promise of personal post-mortem survival or divine reward" (there are no gods in the Wide Green World, or, rather, they are seen as absent).[3] It is comparable, Bujold has written, to our real-world practices of the donation of blood or organs.[4]

The world of the Vor is saturated with ideas of sacrifice, but it is not used carelessly, rather with precision to open up different moralities to our gaze. Cordelia refers to troops as "poor lambs . . ." (CH 69), while Miles unconsciously echoes this idea when thinking of the pilot whom Bothari had tortured to death as having died "horribly, like an animal sacrifice" (WA 132). A ritual sacrifice is what Barrayarans offer to the dead, and is one of the few Barrayaran customs that we can be sure are not just Vor customs. The main punishment of the peasant woman who killed a child in "The Mountains of Mourning" is that "she would die without sacrifice. No one [. . .] shall make a burning [of hair] for her when she goes into the ground at last" (BI 95). But sacrifice in the Vorkosigan universe continually refers to the abstract concept of giving life for the sake of another. Generals sacrifice the lives of their followers (though Cetagandan generals generally prefer the lives of their allies:

VG 268–69). Galeni was "big on sacrifices," said his son—the human sacrifices that he had made in order to win freedom for Komarr (BA 157). Aral, with Ezar, sacrifices thousands in order to preserve the good reputation of Prince Serg (while eliminating him at the same time). And Miles is willing not just to sacrifice himself, but others too; Haroche knew that Miles could do this, as he had done it before (Mem 383). Miles himself recognized that: "His first military career had begun with a human sacrifice. Maybe another one was required for its renewal. He'd sacrificed friends enough before, God knew, led them into one bloody good cause or another but not led them back out. And they hadn't all been volunteers" (Mem 382).

It is perhaps ironic, given the connection between honor and belonging to the Vor caste, that it is the outsider Cordelia whom Aral sees as the source of his (and Bothari's) honor. As Sandra Lindow points out, "After the grim necessities of war, Aral finds his personal code of honor broken in shards at his feet."[5] Cordelia helps restore it for him. There is a moving passage at the very end of the main narrative of *Shards of Honor* (the title is, of course, very apposite), where Cordelia and Aral are lying in bed together, in the dark, and she asks him what he and Emperor Ezar had been talking about. It was, apparently, her. Ezar had asked Aral what he saw in her. "I told him [. . .] that you poured out honor like a fountain, all around you." She thinks this is weird, as she does not feel full of honor, just full of confusion; and he replies, "Naturally not. Fountains keep nothing for themselves" (CH 241). This is not easy to interpret. Sandra Lindow comments merely that "both Cordelia and Aral can be considered to be living at the highest level of moral development for their cultures."[6] Even if this is true, I think the significant thing is that Aral feels that he has fallen short of his own standards of honor: not because he could do anything else, given the unpalatable political choices available to him, but because he knows that his own honor has been compromised or destroyed. Cordelia sticks to her principles (even though one of her principles is to put people ahead of principles). Bujold commented to me that "if Cordelia started out with a besetting sin, it was a sort of Betan spiritual pride in her 'superior' Betan principles. She learns better." She acts as Aral's conscience; she is the one against whom he measures himself. He explains this early on in their relationship, after he sees her care for the disabled Dubauer: "You seem able to carry your civilization on the inside" (CH 31). She is always ahead of him in care and concern for others, and she is also more prepared than even Aral himself to put her trust in others, above all in the seriously mad Bothari.

Bothari is certainly one of those benefiting from Cordelia's fountain of honor. She recognizes that he is a psychological mess, that he needs healing: when he is about to rape her, she says to him "I believe [. . .] that the tormented are very close to God. I'm sorry, Sergeant" (CH 114). He refuses to carry out the order to rape her, and, when Vorrutyer takes his place, Bothari kills him. Thereafter, and particularly after Aral orders him to regard her orders as if they were his, he is unfailingly loyal to her, and subsequently to Miles. Again there is a moral problem that is, to some extent, ducked: How far can one use a monster like Bothari and remain morally clean? He is, after all, capable of murder and of torture.

This may be where Bujold is strongest. Torture is not the thing that the enemy does; torture is a thing the best of us are capable of. Torture is not used by Our Heroes by proxy, they do it themselves. When Cordelia needs to evade those who were watching her own home on Beta Colony, she holds Dr. Mehta under the water of her aquarium until she is close to drowning (CH 200)—waterboarding for the purposes of forcing one's will on someone else. She learned it from the Barrayarans who treated Dubauer in this way, comments Bujold. When Miles, just beginning his career of mayhem, needs the codes from the pilot officer of a ship he boards, he orders Bothari to obtain them, which Bothari does by ripping the pilot's implant from his brain (it proves fatal). Miles accepts responsibility for this, as we have seen; but this hardly resolves the ethical problem. Bothari excuses himself in terms of the greater good: one person dies so that many others, both friend and enemy, can live.[7] And the question of how the Vorkosigans can knowingly use a monster like Bothari—"Oh, but he's my monster," Cordelia remarks (CH 532)—is neatly "solved" when Bothari is killed by one of the former victims of his monstrosity. The only time we see Aral confronted with torture, when he sees his men waterboarding Dubauer, he is appalled: not, perhaps, because of the torture itself, however, but because he knows Dubauer to be disabled and, above all, his prisoner (CH 63). This is a matter that touches his honor: "I do not kill prisoners" (CH 14) is one of the first things that illuminates Aral's character, very soon after we meet him. Miles's comment to Bothari, warning him of the future occasion "when I come to explain to my father how it was we happened to torture a prisoner to death" (WA 127), suggests that perhaps killing a prisoner, rather than the use of torture (or certainly as much as the use of torture), might be what will anger Aral the most.

The question of the ethics of torture ties in with the ethics of warfare, which crops up frequently in Bujold's work. Although the Vorkosigan series has been categorized as "military sf," this is not only misleading inasmuch as only a portion of the books deal with warfare at all, but also because (unlike some typical examples of military sf) Bujold's books do not glorify warfare at all. Her attitude is expressed early on in "Aftermaths," the short story appended to *Shards of Honor*. It is an excellent story, though it sits strangely at the end of the novel, containing as it does no characters we have met before. Apart from extending our knowledge of Barrayarans (and their devotion to the ampules containing their mothers' tears that they carry with them into battle), its sole purpose seems to be to remember how the decisions of generals have tragic consequences for those they command and for the relatives of those they command. ("Aftermaths" plays for *Shards of Honor* the precise role played by the chapter on "The Scouring of the Shire" toward the end of *The Lord of the Rings*.) We meet a character who has a position I have never seen elsewhere in space opera: a medtech in the Escobaran office for Personnel Retrieval and Identification. She has the painstaking and stressful task of searching the sites of battles in space, looking for human remains of over one kilogram in weight. Human remains exposed to vacuum would be frozen and brittle: "corpsicles," the rather crass young pilot calls them, but "people," as Tersa, the middle-aged medtech, prefers. Sometimes she finds a Barrayaran. "Throw him back," suggests the pilot, but she explains: "Oh, no. We have identification files for all their missing. Part of the peace settlement, you know, along with prisoner exchange" (CH 248). He finds her kissing the lips of a dead young woman, and he reacts predictably: "You're a damn, damn necrophiliac! A lesbian necrophiliac, at that!" (CH 252). However, when he realizes that the corpse is that of Tersa's daughter, and that Tersa had requested that sector in the hope of finding her daughter's body, he is duly abject. When they find another corpse, he asks if he can help wash it.

"Certainly. [. . .] An honor is not diminished for being shared."
And so he did, as shy as an apprentice saint washing his first leper.

"Don't be afraid," she said. "The dead cannot hurt you. They give you no pain, except that of seeing your own death in their faces. And one can face that, I find."

Yes, he thought, the good face pain. But the great—they embrace it (CH 253).

This is the stunning end to that first Vorkosigan novel. One could think of it as peculiarly American: the recovery of the bodies of the fallen and their careful burial or reburial on American soil has been an obsession that other nations rarely share; it has been regular from the Spanish American War of 1898 onward, and since the Korean War the dead have been flown back to the United States immediately, rather than being buried in temporary battlefield cemeteries.[8] But the idea that the duty of looking after the dead bears honor and carries the connotation of saintliness is a fascinating addition. The final thought, carried by the now-suddenly-more-mature pilot, that the good face pain and the great embrace it, is one that was surely intended as a commentary on the Vorkosigan attitude toward death and war.

Bujold's characters can have a tough-minded attitude toward war. This emerges very early on, in a conversation between Cordelia and Aral. Cordelia thinks of nerve disruptors as uncivilized weapons: they kill. Aral, on the other hand, has an aversion to stunners, precisely because they do not kill. He tells the story of a friend of his who tried to hold up a group of men with a stunner: they rushed him and kicked him to death. If he had been carrying a nerve disruptor, he would have survived and achieved his goal, probably without having to kill anyone. Cordelia admits that she might not be able to pull the trigger of a disruptor, and Aral comments that his dead friend had had the same attitude toward weaponry as Cordelia's: he was soft (CH 46–47).

However, what shows above all throughout Bujold's treatment of warfare is the experience of someone who has worked in a hospital rather than in a military command. There is an innate humanity there that in the earlier novels is primarily put in Cordelia's mouth. Perhaps Aral and Miles learn from her. When Aral offers a rather gloomy thought about the invasion of Komarr, his lieutenant Vorkalloner reminds him that it had been a great victory with very little loss of life; Aral responds, "On our side." "That's the idea, isn't it?" asked the military Vorkalloner (CH 75–76). The more political Aral remarks that if you plan to stay in conquered territory, the dead provide you with a very messy political legacy. Is that a result of his discussions with Cordelia, or is it just that he is an astute politician? Cordelia certainly always thinks of the unnecessary loss of life. When Aral talks of her having the competence to be a mother of warriors, she remarks: "Save me from that! To pour your life into sons for eighteen or twenty years, and then have the government take them away and waste them cleaning up after some failure of politics—no thanks" (CH 40). Aral is able to have a more distanced view of death in battle, in part because he commanded space ships: "At a distance, in space, there's the illusion of a clean and glorious fight. Almost abstract. It might be a simulation, or a game" (CH 44). It is an aspect of war in space, fought at such a distance and a sense of abstraction, that had been examined just a few years earlier than *Shards of Honor* by Orson Scott Card in his hugely successful *Ender's Game* (1985); Card's genocidal hero spends much of the sequel, *Speaker for the Dead* (1986), feeling guilty for it. Aral does at least say that clean fighting in space is an "illusion."

In the Vorkosigan books we see a good deal of the military—but much more of politics. In some cases, as one would expect in a militaristic society, politicians are ex-soldiers like Aral himself. Among the issues Bujold's work explores, in some depth and from different angles, is the nature of power and leadership in both civilian and military contexts. We see people who are portrayed as good leaders—Aral, Cordelia, Miles, Gregor, Cazaril, Dag—and a few people who are patently bad leaders, such as Vorrutyer or Metzov. There is a third category, of course: those who are competent but hardly role models: Ezar Vorbarra might be in that category, and Roya Orico.

When Miles is in Barrayaran military service, he tries to fit into an established institutional structure, in which the habits of deference to the Vor reinforce the tradition of military obedience. His problem in the Barrayaran military, of course, is his urge to lead (as a Vor, or simply as Miles) despite his lowly military rank: there are some amusing encounters with his military superiors in both *The Vor Game* and *Brothers in Arms*. When under the influence of forward momentum Miles comes to create the Dendarii and places himself as Admiral over them, he has to create habits of obedience through sheer force of will. Later, reminiscing with Dr. Riva on Komarr, he talks about the odd illusions people have about power: "Mostly it consists of finding a parade and nipping over to place yourself at the head of the band. Just as eloquence consists of persuading people of things they desperately want to believe" (Kom 257). With sufficient self-confidence (even if it is self-confidence resting, ultimately, on a bedrock of terror) you can convince people that you know what you are doing: and that was the essence of Miles's success. Aral, too, thinks that "leadership is mostly a power over imagination, and never more so than in combat. The bravest man alone," he says, "can only be an armed lunatic. The real strength lies in the ability to get others to do your work" (CH 40). Even Aral, however, has to learn from Cordelia. While on Sergyar, Cordelia takes the time to befriend the military cook, who ends up preparing a very good meal for her, something he had never done for Aral or his fellow officers (CH 68).

Miles has numerous role models. He learns from Aral and from his grandfather Piotr, and no doubt from Cordelia. Out of necessity he realizes that leadership is playing a part, projecting the image of confidence and authority. That is what his masquerade as Admiral Naismith is all about. When, early on in his meteoric career, he needs to project his nonexistent authority in the presence of a female shuttleport administrator, he "plays" his grandfather, glancing up from lowered brows, "shooting her his best imitation General Count Piotr Vorkosigan military glare" (WA 57). Linda Wight argues convincingly that Miles as leader is not only an actor, but also an effective director of his fellow "actors."[9] Indeed, Bothari himself is made to comment on this. When Miles has positioned Bothari, Mayhew, and Jesek in a suitably menacing position around a negotiating table, Bothari comments: "You're not a commander, you're a bloody holovid director" (WA 141). Miles teaches Jesek to imitate a hated but effectively authoritarian engineering officer Miles had once known. Jesek refuses to smoke a cigar as this officer had done, but Miles teaches him how to chew on an unlit cigar in an appropriately intimidating fashion and act as if he is "an airpolluting son-of-a-bitch" (WA 136). Leadership is performance, or even showmanship; but, of course, it also feeds on success, and here Bujold weights the dice, for Miles is shown to be extremely lucky in his military exploits.

Once Miles is removed from the Dendarii, he loses his ability to *perform* leadership. Even as an imperial auditor, he has no function as a leader, instead serving as a glorified policeman. But by the end of the Vorkosigan cycle as it currently exists, the need for leaders has muted. This is no longer a feudal monarchy. Emperor Gregor leads more by patience and intelligence as a constitutional monarch who can sway decisions made in the Council of Counts but cannot dictate how the vote will go. The Council of Counts—we learn, through hints in *Memory* and in *A Civil Campaign*—can no longer command the kind of fealty that underpinned their authority. If at the end of *Civil Campaign* we see Miles mutating into a politician, learning to manipulate and persuade and horse trade, it is because this is the leadership that *his* Barrayar will both need and accept. As the story began as Cordelia's, so, in a sense, it ends that way: Miles, both as person and as representative, is Cordelia's victory over a Barrayar she once entered as a barely tolerated foreigner.

A LOIS McMASTER BUJOLD BIBLIOGRAPHY

FIRST PUBLICATIONS OF FICTION, IN CHRONOLOGICAL ORDER

"Barter." *Twilight Zone*, March / April 1985. Repr. in *Dreamweaver's Dilemma*, 1996, 43–50.

Shards of Honor. Riverdale, N.Y.: Baen, June 1986.

The Warrior's Apprentice. Riverdale, N.Y.: Baen, August 1986.

Ethan of Athos. Riverdale, N.Y.: Baen, December 1986.

"The Hole Truth." *Twilight Zone*, December 1986. Repr. in *Dreamweaver's Dilemma*, 1996, 59–68.

"Aftermaths." In *Far Frontiers V*, ed. Jerry Pournelle and Jim Baen. Riverdale, N.Y.: Baen, 1986. (This short story is appended to the novel *Shards of Honor*.)

"The Borders of Infinity." In *Free Lancers*, ed. Elizabeth Mitchell. Riverdale, N.Y.: Baen, 1987.

"Garage Sale." *American Fantasy*, Spring 1987. Repr. in *Dreamweaver's Dilemma*, 1996, 51–57.

Test of Honor. Omnibus edition of *Shards of Honor* (1986) and *The Warrior's Apprentice* (1986). New York: Doubleday / SFBC, May 1987.

Falling Free. Riverdale, N.Y.: Baen, April 1988. Previously serialized in *Analog*, December 1987, mid-December 1987, January 1988, and February 1988.

Brothers in Arms. Riverdale, N.Y.: Baen, January 1989.

"The Mountains of Mourning." *Analog*, May 1989, 14–74. Repr. in *Dreamweaver's Dilemma*, 1996, 105–63; incorporated into *Borders of Infinity*, 1989.

"Labyrinth." *Analog*, August 1989, 12–84. Repr. in *Intergalactic Mercenaries*, ed. Sheila Williams and Cynthia Manson (New York: Roc, 1996), and incorporated into *Borders of Infinity*, 1989.

Borders of Infinity. Riverdale, N.Y.: Baen, October 1989. Comprises the stories "The Mountains of Mourning," "Labyrinth," and "The Borders of Infinity," with linking material.

"Weatherman." *Analog*, February 1990, 12–75. Incorporated into *The Vor Game*, 1990; repr. in David G. Hartwell and Kathryn Cramer, *The Space Opera Renaissance* (New York: Tor, 1996), 251–96.

The Vor Game. Riverdale, N.Y.: Baen, September 1990. Includes the story "Weatherman."

Vorkosigan's Game. New York: Doubleday / SFBC, September 1990. Omnibus of *The Vor Game* (1990) and *Borders of Infinity* (1989).

Barrayar. Riverdale, N.Y.: Baen, October 1991. Previously published in *Analog*, July, August, September, and October 1991.

The Spirit Ring. Riverdale, N.Y.: Baen, November 1992.

Mirror Dance. Riverdale, N.Y.: Baen, March 1994.

Cetaganda. Riverdale, N.Y.: Baen, January 1996. Previously serialized in *Analog* October, November, December, and mid-December 1995.

Cordelia's Honor. Riverdale, N.Y.: Baen, November 1996. Omnibus of the first two Vorkosigan novels, *Shards of Honor* (1986) and *Barrayar* (1991), with a new afterword by Bujold describing the writing of the novels, pp. 591–96.

Dreamweaver's Dilemma: Short Stories and Essays. Edited by Suford Lewis. Framingham, Mass.: NESFA, March 1996. Collection of four essays and six stories, two original, including the title story, the earliest story in the Vorkosigan universe; introduction by Lillian Stewart Carl, with an interview, timeline, and pronunciation guide by Suford Lewis.

"The Adventure of the Lady on the Embankment." Previously unpublished. In *Dreamweaver's Dilemma*, 1996, 1–42.

"Dreamweaver's Dilemma." In *Dreamweaver's Dilemma*, 1996, 69–103.

Memory. Riverdale, N.Y.: Baen, October 1996.

Young Miles. Riverdale, N.Y.: Baen, June 1997. Omnibus of *The Warrior's Apprentice*, "The Mountains of Mourning," and *The Vor Game*, with a new afterword by Bujold discussing the writing of these pieces.

Komarr. Riverdale, N.Y.: Baen, June 1998.

A Civil Campaign: A Comedy of Biology and Manners. Riverdale, N.Y.: Baen, September 1999.

The Curse of Chalion. New York: HarperCollins/Eos, August 2001.

Miles, Mystery and Mayhem. Riverdale, N.Y.: Baen, December 2001. Omnibus containing *Cetaganda* (1996), *Ethan of Athos* (1986), and "Labyrinth," with a new afterword by Bujold.

Diplomatic Immunity. Riverdale, N.Y.: Baen, May 2002. The unused prologue to this story can be found at http://www.dendarii.com/excerpts/prologue.html.

Miles Errant. Riverdale, N.Y.: Baen, September 2002. Omnibus containing "The Borders of Infinity," *Brothers in Arms* (1989), and *Mirror Dance* (1994).

Paladin of Souls. New York: HarperCollins/Eos, October 2003.

Falling Free. Framingham, Mass.: NESFA, September 2004. Slightly corrected hardcover edition of the 1988 book, with foreword by James A. McMaster; includes Robert I. Jaffee's "A Tribute to Robert Charles McMaster."

"Winterfair Gifts." In *Irresistible Forces*, ed. Catherine Asaro. New York: New American Library, 2004, 1–71.

The Hallowed Hunt. New York: HarperCollins/Eos, June 2005.

The Sharing Knife, Vol. 1: Beguilement. New York: HarperCollins/Eos, October 2006.

Miles, Mutants and Microbes. Riverdale, N.Y.: Baen, August 2007. Omnibus of *Falling Free* (1988), "Labyrinth" (1989), and *Diplomatic Immunity* (2002), with a preface by Bujold.

The Sharing Knife, Vol. 2: Legacy. New York: HarperCollins/Eos6, July 2007.

Miles in Love. Riverdale, N.Y.: Baen, February 2005. Omnibus of *Komarr* (1998), *A Civil Campaign* (1999), and "Winterfair Gifts" (2004), with an afterword by Bujold.

The Sharing Knife, Vol. 3: Passage. New York: HarperCollins/Eos, April 2008.

The Sharing Knife, Vol. 4: Horizon. New York: HarperCollins/Eos, January 2009.

CryoBurn. Riverdale, N.Y.: Baen, November 2010.

Captain Vorpatril's Alliance. Riverdale, N.Y.: Baen, November 2012.

Prota Zoa: Five Early Short Stories. Kindle edition, 2012. Contains "Barter," "Garage Sale," "The Hole Truth," and "Dreamweaver's Dilemma" (all found in *Dreamweaver's Dilemma*) and "Aftermaths" (found appended to *Shards of Honor*).

SELECTED NONFICTION, IN CHRONOLOGICAL ORDER OF FIRST PUBLICATION

"Allegories of Change: The 'New' Biotech in the Eye of Science Fiction." In *New Destinies VIII,* ed. Jim Baen, 181–85. Riverdale, N.Y.: Baen 1989.

"The Unsung Collaborator." *Lan's Lantern* 31 (1989). Repr. in *Dreamweaver's Dilemma,* 175–79.

"Answers." In Bujold, *Dreamweaver's Dilemma,* 197–225.

"Free Associating about *Falling Free.*" In *Nebula Awards 24,* ed. Michael Bishop. New York: Harcourt Brace Jovanovich 1990.

"My First Novel." *Bulletin of the Science Fiction Writers of America* 24.4, no. 110 (Winter 1990): 167–70. Repr. in *Dreamweaver's Dilemma.*

"Getting Started." In *Writers of the Future VIII,* ed. Algis Budrys and Dave Wolverton. Los Angeles: Bridge, 1992. Rev. of "My First Novel."

"Beyond Genre Barriers." *Ohio Writer Magazine* 6, no. 3 (May/June 1992). Repr. in *Dreamweaver's Dilemma,* 171–74

"Introduction." In *Women at War,* ed. Lois McMaster Bujold and Roland J. Green. Riverdale, N.Y.: Baen, 1995.

"Mind Food: Writing Science Fiction." *Journal of Youth Services in Libraries* 10, no. 2 (Winter 1997).

"Letterspace: In the Chinks between Published Fiction and Published Criticism." With Sylvia Kelso. In *Women of Other Worlds: Excursions through Science Fiction and Feminism,* ed. Helen Merrick and Tess Williams, 383–409. Nedlands: University of Western Australia Press, 1999. Repr. in Sylvia Kelso, *Three Observations and a Dialogue: Round and About SF* (Conversation Pieces 24) (Seattle, Wash.: Aqueduct, 2009), 87–122.

"Introduction to 'Barter.'" In *Wondrous Beginnings,* ed. Steven H. Silver and Martin H. Greenberg. New York: DAW 2003.

"Biolog: Lois McMaster Bujold." Updated September 21, 2004. Available at http://www.dendarii.com/biolog.html (accessed October 10, 2014).

"Here's Looking at You, Kid" (on fan fiction, 2005). Available at http://www.dendarii.com/fanfic.html (accessed October 10, 2014).

"Jim Baen Remembered, 1943–2006." June 2006. Available at http://www.dendarii.com/jbaen.html. (accessed October 10, 2014).

"How I Met the Inklings." Speech. Mythcon 37, University of Oklahoma, Norman, August 17, 2006. Available at http://www.dendarii.com/inklings.html (accessed October 10, 2014).

"Writing Sex." December 12, 2006. Available on CD packaged with *CryoBurn.*

"Space Opera, Miles and Me." *Sidelines,* June 2007. Available at http://www.dendarii.com/space_opera.html (accessed October 10, 2014).

"Putting It Together: Life, the Vorkosiverse, and Everything." In Carl and Helfers, *Vorkosigan Companion,* 5–28.

"Publishing, Writing, and Authoring: Three Different Things." In Carl and Helfers, *Vorkosigan Companion,* 63–81.

"Writer Guest of Honor Speech, Denvention 3." August 8, 2008. Available at http://www.
amazon.com/Sidelines-Essays-Lois-McMaster-Bujold-ebook/dp/B00BW5SW66/ref=sr
_1_1?ie=UTF8&qid=1414101253&sr=8-1&keywords=Sidelines%3A+Talks+and+Essays.

Sidelines: Talks and Essays. Kindle edition, 2013. Includes articles; convention speeches;
introductions and afterwords to books; blogs; and travel diaries. Available at http://
www.amazon.com/Sidelines-Essays-Lois-McMaster-Bujold-ebook/dp/B00BW5SW66/
ref=sr_1_1?ie=UTF8&qid=1414101253&sr=8-1&keywords=Sidelines%3A+Talks+and+
Essays.

STORIES IN THE VORKOSIGAN UNIVERSE

In order of internal chronology:

"Dreamweaver's Dilemma" in *Dreamweaver's Dilemma* (1996) [DD]
Falling Free (1988) [FF]
Shards of Honor (1986) [SH; CH]
Barrayar (1991) [Bar; CH]
The Warrior's Apprentice (1986) [TWA]
"The Mountains of Mourning" in *Borders of Infinity* (1989) [MM]
The Vor Game (1990) [TVG]
Cetaganda (1995) [Cet]
Ethan of Athos (1986) [EA]
"Labyrinth" in *Borders of Infinity* (1989) [Lab]
"The Borders of Infinity" in *Borders of Infinity* (1989) [Bord]
Brothers in Arms (1989) [BA]
Linking sections of *Borders of Infinity* (1989) [BI]
Mirror Dance (1994) [MD]
Memory (1996) [Mem]
Komarr (1998) [Kom]
A Civil Campaign (1999) [ACC]
"Winterfair Gifts" (2004) [WG]
Diplomatic Immunity (2002) [DI]
Captain Vorpatril's Alliance (2012) [CVA]
CryoBurn (2010) [Cry]

CHAPTER 1. AN INTRODUCTION TO LOIS MCMASTER BUJOLD

1. Email correspondence with the author, February 17, 2012.

2. See the foreword to the reprint of Bujold's *Falling Free*, ed. Suford Lewis (Framingham, Mass.: NESFA Press, 2004), 13–25.

3. "Biolog" at http://www.dendarii.com/biolog.html.

4. Henceforth I shall use "sf" as my standard abbreviation of "science fiction."

5. Corflu, correcting fluid, was much used in pre-photocopier days by writers of fanzines who used their typewriters to cut stencils for printing multiple copies via a mimeograph machine. Once smelled, never forgotten.

6. Interview with Sandra Lindow, LMB 14.

7. NASFiCs are held in North America when a Worldcon is elsewhere, and in 1985 the Worldcon was Aussiecon Two, in Melbourne.

8. "Biolog," at http://www.dendarii.com/biolog.html.

9. Figures and comment from Bujold, email, February 10, 2012.

10. *Locus* 313 (February 1987), 22.

11. Sales figures published in *Analog*, February 1988, 80.

12. My own review of this started: "If you are someone with a nostalgic yearning for sf which explores the problems of living in space, the consequences of technological developments upon human beings, the possibilities for human evolution, and which ends with the triumph of good old-fashioned virtues like progress, humanity and love, then [. . . this] is for you," and finished with "It's interesting to see a woman writer tackle this kind of sf, and, indeed, for a woman writer to get such prominence in *Analog* at all": *Paperback Inferno: The Review of Paperback SF* 70 (February–March 1988): 13.

13. Bujold, email, February 10, 2012.

14. The goalposts have now been moved, and Heinlein, with one "retro-Hugo" win in 2001 for *Farmer in the Sky* (1951), is currently credited with five. Some might regard that as cheating.

15. See a brief report at http://bujold.lib.ru/vorcon_rep_eng.htm; a transcription of the email conversation between Bujold and the participants is also currently available at http://www.lavkamirov.com/bujold/loischat_19a.htm (both sites accessed October 10, 2014). To the best of my knowledge, the only academic conference on her work took place after this book had been sent to the publishers: it was held at Anglia Ruskin University, in Cambridge, UK, in August 2014, and I had the honor of delivering the keynote address.

16. See http://www.tor.com/blogs/2009/03/weeping-for-her-enemies-lois-mcmaster-bujolds-shards-of-honor (accessed October 10, 2014): Walton and Bujold comments made on April 5, 2009.

17. For a brief and somewhat outdated introduction to Bujold fandom, see Nightingale in VC.

18. Bujold, "Writing Sex."

19. See http://fanlore.org/wiki/Lois_McMaster_Bujold (accessed October 5, 2014).

20. These and other examples of Bujold fanfic can readily be found online with the aid of Google.

21. Bujold, "Here's Looking at You, Kid . . ."

22. See Sturgis in LMB for the only serious examination of Bujold and fanfic that I know of.

CHAPTER 2. THE SCIENCE FICTION

1. See, for example, Pat Harrigan and Noah Wardrip-Fruin, eds., *Third Person: Authoring and Exploring Vast Narratives* (Cambridge, Mass.: MIT Press, 2009).

2. Stableford, in Clute and Nicholls, *Encyclopedia of Science Fiction*, 1138.

3. *Locus* 511, no. 51.2 (August 2003): 43. I have discussed this special "New Space Opera" issue of *Locus* in "The New Space Opera, 1991–2011."

4. Westfahl, "Space Opera," 206.

5. Online 1999; quoted in Nikohl and Lennard, *Reader's Companion*, 57–58.

6. Bujold, afterword to *Cordelia's Honor* (1996), 592.

7. Interview with Mike Levy, 11.

8. Ibid.

9. The term "anti-orphan" is Bujold's: see Lindow in LMB 51.

10. Bujold, "Space Opera, Miles, and Me," available at http://www.dendarii.com/space_opera.html (accessed October 5, 2014).

11. Bujold, afterword to *Miles in Love*, 858.

12. For example, James Blish's *The Triumph of Time* (New York: Avon, 1958), published in the UK as *A Clash of Cymbals* (1959).

13. Letter to Elizabeth Healey, Spring 1896: in D. C. Smith, ed. *The Correspondence of H. G. Wells, Vol. 1: 1880–1903* (London: Pickering and Chatto, 1998), 261.

14. John Lennard in LMB 176.

15. Bujold, afterword to *Cordelia's Honor* (1996), 592.

16. Verlyn Flieger and Douglas A. Anderson, eds., *Tolkien on Fairy-Stories* (London: HarperCollins, 2008), 75.

17. Walton, "Forward Momentum."

18. Bujold, afterword to *Young Miles* (1997; cited from Baen paperback, 2003), 830.

19. Dr. Nile Etland appears in "Trouble Tide," *Analog*, May 1965, and *The Tuvela* (a novel serialized in *Analog*, September and October 1968), later published as *The Demon Breed* (New York: Ace, 1968).

20. Bujold, afterword to *Young Miles* (2003), 831.

21. *Escape from Colditz* was the title given in the United States to the omnibus publication of the former British officer Pat Reid's two books about his experiences in the officer-only

prisoner-of-war camp at Colditz Castle. In the 1970s there was a British TV series about Colditz, featuring David McCallum, whom Bujold had loved as Illya Kuryakin.

22. Bujold, preface to *Miles, Mutants and Microbes* (2007), 4.

23. James McMaster, foreword to the NESFA edition of *Falling Free* (2004), 13–25.

24. Bujold does not very often indulge in Tuckerisms (the insertion of the names of real people, in the manner of sf writer Bob Tucker), although it is worth mentioning Armsman Kelso (ACC 114), clearly named after the Australian critic Sylvia Kelso (see bibliography).

25. Bujold, afterword to *Young Miles* (2003), 835.

26. Ibid., 838.

27. Bujold, afterword to *Cordelia's Honor* (1996), 595.

28. Jo Walton, "One Birth, One Death, and All the Acts of Pain and Will Between."

29. Interview with Mike Levy, 17.

30. Walton, "This Is My Old Identity, Actually."

31. Bujold, afterword to *Miles in Love* (2008), 859.

32. Ibid., 859.

33. Ibid., 860.

34. Kelso, *Three Observations*, 36.

35. Bujold, afterword to *Miles in Love* (2008), 860.

36. Quoted in Nikohl and Lennard, *Reader's Companion*, 26.

37. Walton, "She's Getting Away!"

38. Bujold to the List, September 25, 2010, quoted in Nikohl and Lennard, *Reader's Companion*, 111.

39. Excluding *Falling Free* and *Ethan of Athos*, for obvious reasons, as not being "proper" Vorkosigan books.

40. See http://www.strangehorizons.com/reviews/2011/02/cryoburn_by_loi.shtml (accessed October 5, 2014).

CHAPTER 3. FANTASY WORLDS

1. Fiametta is an early variant of the more normal Fiammetta. Boccaccio wrote a novel called *Elegia di Madonna Fiammetta* in the 1340s, and Fiammetta as a name appears several times in his *Decameron* and elsewhere.

2. See http://www.dendarii.com/map.html (accessed October 10, 2014).

3. The talk—more of a Q&A session—is available as a podcast at http://www.loc.gov/today/cyberlc/feature_wdesc.php?rec=3586 (accessed October 10, 2014).

4. In a letter to Robert Murray, SJ, from 1953: H. Carpenter, ed., *The Letters of J. R. R. Tolkien* (London: Allen and Unwin, 1981), 172. See T. A. Shippey, *J. R. R. Tolkien: Author of the Century* (Boston: Houghton Mifflin, 2000), 176.

5. Bujold pointed out to me that Orico's illness was diabetes; the menagerie was "magical insulin, if you like."

6. Review of *Paladin of Souls*, available at http://www.sfsite.com/11a/psi63.htm (accessed October 10, 2014).

7. See http://www.dendarii.com/bujold_faq.html#chal-provinces (accessed October 10, 2014).

8. See SciFi Wire interview with John Joseph Adams, June 2006, at http://www
.dendarii.com/int-sfw.html (accessed October 10, 2014).

9. Lennard in LMB, 180.

10. John Clute and Peter Nicholls, eds., *The Encyclopedia of Science Fiction* (London: Orbit, 1993), s.v. "Nicholls, Peter," 254–57.

11. For the Sharing Knife as Western, see Jo Walton's review, available at http://www
.tor.com/blogs/2009/01/western-fantasy-lois-mcmaster-bujolds-sharing-knife (accessed October 10, 2014). In the comments below, Bujold notes, "Apparently, the two most dire kiss-of-sales-death themes/tropes for our genre's presumed tastes are romances and Westerns, so naturally I produced an epic that combined both. . . . The HC sales folks explicitly wouldn't let us show Conestoga-style wagons in the background cavalcade on the cover of *Horizon*, even though they are in the book, for this very reason, I was told."

12. See, for example, the comments of "Casey" under http://www.tor.com/blogs/2009/01/western-fantasy-lois-mcmaster-bujolds-sharing-knife.

13. See the discussion of this parallel in Lennard, LMB 182–84.

14. As previous note: comment added January 3, 2009.

15. Lennard, LMB 184.

16. It is worth noting that the Frontier Magic sequence, the young-adult novels that began with *Thirteenth Child* (2009), by Bujold's old friend Patricia Wrede, also deal with the serious scientific study of magic, this time in a clearly alternate-history America. The series occasioned much angry debate online, since it imagined the European colonization of an America without Native Americans, which many readers found offensive.

17. Bujold, email, February 11, 2012.

18. Kate Bonin, "Undermining Cinderella," *New York Review of Science Fiction* 240 (August 2008): 18–19.

19. See comment 25 added to Jo Walton's online review: "Western Fantasy: Lois McMaster Bujold's Sharing Knife Books," http://www.tor.com/blogs/2009/01/western -fantasy-lois-mcmaster-bujolds-sharing-knife.

CHAPTER 4. CULTURAL CRITIQUE

1. Farah Mendlesohn, *Rhetorics of Fantasy* (Middletown, Conn.: Wesleyan University Press, 2008), 1–58.

2. Hallam in LMB 89.

3. See Bujold's comments in DW 212, although her implication that *The Tale of Genji* was written in the ninth century is incorrect.

CHAPTER 5. CHARACTER

1. Bemis in LMB 115.

2. Walton, "Forward Momentum."

3. A list of the chapters with their different focalizations is provided in Nikohl and Lennard, *A Reader's Companion*, 51–52.

4. Compare with Ian Watson, "The Author as Torturer," *Foundation: The Review of Science Fiction* 40 (Summer 1987): 11–25.

5. See her discussion, LMB 145–46.

6. See "Dissociative Identity Disorder," Wikipedia, accessed February 7, 2013.

7. See Regina Yung Lee's discussion in LMB, 34–35.

CHAPTER 6. DISABILITY AND GENETIC MODIFICATION

1. See http://www.sfx.co.uk/2012/09/06/10-inspirational-disabled-characters-from-sci-fi-and-fantasy/1 (accessed October 10, 2014).

2. See http://www.sjgames.com/gurps/books/vorkosigan (accessed October 10, 2014).

3. Interview with Mike Levy, 15.

4. Ibid.

5. Interview with Sandra Lindow in LMB 11.

6. Interview with Mike Levy, 12.

7. Ibid., 9.

8. Ibid., 9.

9. Ibid., 10.

10. Ibid.

11. Ibid.

12. Interview with Ken Lake, 8.

13. Kelso in LMB 153. She is referring to the influential article by Donna Haraway, "A Cyborg Manifesto: Science, Technology and Socialist-Feminism in the Late Twentieth Century," in Haraway's *Simians, Cyborgs and Women* (New York: Routledge, 1991), 149–81.

14. Bujold's afterword to *Cordelia's Honor*, 593.

15. See http://rt.com/usa/us-army-suicide-rate-025 (accessed October 1, 2014).

16. See http://www.independent.co.uk/news/uk/crime/leap-in-disabled-hate-crimes-shows-need-for-paralympics-effect-8135729.html (accessed October 1, 2014).

CHAPTER 7. WOMEN, UTERINE REPLICATORS, AND SEXUALITY

1. Introduction to *Women at War*, 1995, quoted by Bujold in http://www.fantasybookcafe.com/2013/04/women-in-sff-month-lois-mcmaster-bujold (accessed October 10, 2014).

2. Interview with Ken Lake, 8.

3. *Shadowdance* interview (translated from Bulgarian), March 2010: see http://herebeshadows.blogspot.co.uk/2010/03/interview-with-lois-mcmaster-bujold.html.

4. Interview with Mike Levy, 10.

5. Interview with Ken Lake, 8.

6. Kelso, *Three Observations and a Dialogue*, 66.

7. J. R. R. Tolkien, *The Lord of the Rings* (London: HarperCollins, 2001), 1008.

8. Lennard in LMB 179.

9. Lee in LMB 37.

10. Lee in LMB 47.

11. Shulamith Firestone, *The Dialectic of Sex* (New York: Bantam 1971), 238; original italics.

12. Ibid., 239.

13. Bujold tells me (2013) that she has never come across Firestone.

14. CH 238. The point is made by Linda Wight in LMB 127.

15. Note Linda Wight's discussion (LMB 126) of a possible queer reading of the Aral/Bothari and Miles/Bothari relationships.

16. Bujold assures me that By is bi; a backstory showing this did not reach print.

17. Rich, "Compulsory Heterosexuality and Lesbian Existence," *Signs* 5, no. 4 (1980): 631–60.

CHAPTER 8. WAR, LEADERSHIP, AND HONOR

1. From a blog comment, quoted by Lennard in LMB 188.

2. H. Carpenter, *The Letters of J. R. R. Tolkien* (Boston: Houghton Mifflin, 2000), 105, 115.

3. Lennard in LMB 186.

4. LMB 192n23.

5. Lindow in LMB 54.

6. Ibid.

7. Maureen O'Dowd, *New York Times*, March 5, 2013: "Cheney still hearts waterboarding. 'Are you going to trade the lives of a number of people because you want to preserve your honor?' he asked, his voice dripping with contempt."

8. These days, the body of a serviceman or servicewoman can be reunited with relatives stateside within twenty-four hours of his or her death in a place as far away as Afghanistan: Y. J. Dreazen and Gary Fields, "How We Bury the War Dead," *Wall Street Journal* (European edition), May 29, 2010.

9. Wight in LMB 122.

Baker, Lucy. "A Curious Doubled Existence: Birth Here and in Lois McMaster Bujold's Vorkosigan Saga." *Ada: A Journal of Gender, New Media and Technology* 3 (November 2013). Available at http://adanewmedia.org/2013/11/issue3-baker (accessed October 10, 2014).

Bartter, Martha A. "'Who Am I Really?' Myths of Maturation in Lois McMaster Bujold's Vorkosigan Series." *Journal of the Fantastic in the Arts* 10 (1999): 30–42.

Bemis, Virginia. "Chaos and Quest: Miles Vorkosigan's Disability Narrative." In Croft, *Lois McMaster Bujold*, 104–15.

Bonin, Kate. "Undermining Cinderella: Lois McMaster Bujold's *The Sharing Knife* Series, So Far." *New York Review of Science Fiction* 240 (August 2008): 18–19.

Burkhead, Ed. "'What's the Worst Thing I Can Do to This Character?' Technology in the Vorkosiverse." In Carl and Helfers, *Vorkosigan Companion*, 103–17.

Carl, Lillian Stewart. "Through Darkest Adolescence with Lois McMaster Bujold; or, Thank You, but I Already Have a Life." In Carl and Helfers, *Vorkosigan Companion*, 121–28.

Carl, Lillian Stewart, and John Helfers, eds. *The Vorkosigan Companion*. Riverdale, N.Y.: Baen, 2008.

Clute, John, and John Grant, eds. *The Encyclopedia of Fantasy*. London: Orbit, 1997.

Clute, John, and Peter Nicholls, eds. *The Encyclopedia of Science Fiction*. London: Orbit, 1993.

Croft, Janet Brennan. "The Soldier and the Cipher: Miles, Mark, and the Naming Plots of Bujold's Vorkosiverse." In Croft, *Lois McMaster Bujold*, 61–76.

Croft, Janet Brennan, ed. *Lois McMaster Bujold: Essays on a Modern Master of Science Fiction and Fantasy*. Critical Explorations in Science Fiction and Fantasy 37. Jefferson, N.C.: McFarland, 2013.

Haehl, Anne L. "Miles Vorkosigan and the Power of Words: A Study of Lois McMaster Bujold's Unlikely Hero." *Extrapolation* 37 (1986): 224–33.

Hallam, Andrew. "The Emperor's Shoe: Power, Home, and the Other in the Vorkosigan Saga." In Croft, *Lois McMaster Bujold*, 77–103.

Helfers, John. "A Conversation with Toni Weisskopf." In Carl and Helfers, *Vorkosigan Companion*, 77–81.

Jaffee, Robert I. "Robert Charles McMaster, 1913–1986." In *National Academy of Engineering of the United States of America: Memorial Tributes, Vol. 3*, Washington D.C.: National

Academy, 1989, 267–71. Reprinted in Bujold, *Falling Free*, edited by Suford Lewis, 279–82. Framingham Mass.: NESFA Press, 2004.

James, Edward. *Science Fiction in the Twentieth Century*. Oxford: Oxford University Press, 1994.

———. "The New Space Opera, 1991–2011: The European Contribution." In *New Directions in the European Fantastic*, edited by Sabine Coelsch-Foisner and Sarah Herbe, 13–27. Heidelberg: Universitätsverlag Winter, 2012.

Jennings, Kelly. Review of *CryoBurn*. *Strange Horizons*, February 18 2011. Available at http://www.strangehorizons.com/reviews/2011/02/cryoburn_by_loi.shtml (accessed October 10, 2014).

Kelso, Sylvia. "Lois McMaster Bujold: Feminism and 'The Gernsback Continuum' in Recent Women's SF." *Journal of the Fantastic in the Arts* 10 (1998): 17–29.

———. "Loud Achievements: Lois McMaster Bujold's Science Fiction." *New York Review of Science Fiction* 122 (October 1990): 1, 10–16; and 123 (November 1998): 13–15. Reprinted in Kelso, *Three Observations*, 45–86.

———. "Tales of Earth: Terraforming in Recent Women's Science Fiction." *Foundation: International Review of Science Fiction* 78 (Spring 2000): 34–43. Reprinted in Kelso, *Three Observations*, 25–43.

———. *Three Observations and a Dialogue: Round and About SF*. Conversation Pieces 24. Seattle, Wash.: Aqueducts, 2009.

———. "The Decay of the Cyborg Body in Bujold's *Memory*." In Croft, *Lois McMaster Bujold*, 148–58.

Lee, Regina Yung. "Legitimacy and Legibility: Rereading Civil Discourse through Feminist Figurations in *Cordelia's Honor*." In Croft, *Lois McMaster Bujold*, 27–49.

Lennard, John. "(Absent) Gods and Sharing Knives: The Purposes of Lois McMaster Bujold's Fantastic Ir/Religions." In Croft, *Lois McMaster Bujold*, 172–94.

Lewis, Suford, "Appendix III: Some Barrayaran Genealogy." In Carl and Helfers, *Vorkosigan Companion*, 460–69.

Lindow, Sandra J. "The Influence of Family and Moral Development in Lois McMaster Bujold's Vorkosigan Series." *Foundation: International Review of Science Fiction* 83 (Autumn 2001): 25–34. Reprinted in Croft, *Lois McMaster Bujold*, 50–60.

———. "Love and Death in the Vorkosiverse: An Interview with Lois McMaster Bujold." In Croft, *Lois McMaster Bujold*, 9–15.

McMaster, James A. "Foreword." In Bujold, *Falling Free*, edited by Suford Lewis, 13–25. Framingham, Mass.: NESFA Press, 2004. Reprinted in Carl and Helfers, *Vorkosigan Companion*, 129–40.

Mendlesohn, Farah. *Rhetorics of Fantasy*. Middletown, Conn.: Wesleyan University Press, 2008.

Nicholls, Peter. "Conceptual Breakthrough." In Clute and Nicholls, *Encyclopedia of Science Fiction*, 254–57.

Nightingale, Marna. "Come for the Bujold, Stay for the Beer: Science Fiction Writers as Occasions of Fandom." In Carl and Helfers, *Vorkosigan Companion*, 159–66.

Nikohl K. and Lennard, John, eds. *A Reader's Companion to* A Civil Campaign *by Lois McMaster Bujold*. Hassadar (Barrayar): Dendarii Free Mercenary Press, 2011. Available at http://dendarii.com/accc.html (accessed October 10, 2014).

Overhelman, David D. "From Iberian to Ibran and Catholic to Quintarian: Bujold's Alternate History of the Spanish Reconquest in the *Chalion* Series." In Croft, *Lois McMaster Bujold*, 159–71.

Palma, Shannan. "Difference and Ability: Conceptualizing Bodily Variation in the Vorkosigan Series." In Croft, *Lois McMaster Bujold*, 134–47.

Phillips, Julie. *James Tiptree Jr.: The Double Life of Alice B. Sheldon*. New York: St Martin's, 2006.

Putnam, Mary Jo. "Romance in the Vorkosiverse." In Carl and Helfers, *Vorkosigan Companion*, 85–90.

Smulders-Srinivasan, Tora K. "Biology in the Vorkosiverse and Today." In Carl and Helfers, *Vorkosigan Companion*, 91–102.

Stableford, Brian M. "Space Opera." In Clute and Nicholls, *Encyclopedia of Science Fiction*, 1138–40.

Sturgis, Amy H. "From Both Sides Now: Bujold and the Fan Fiction Phenomenon." In Croft, *Lois McMaster Bujold*, 16–26.

Walton, Jo. "All True Wealth Is Biological: Lois McMaster Bujold's *Mirror Dance*." Available at http://www.tor.com/blogs/2009/04/all-true-wealth-is-biological-lois-mcmaster -bujolds-mirror-dance (accessed October 10, 2014).

———. "But I'm Vor: Lois McMaster Bujold's *Komarr*." Available at http://www.tor.com/ blogs/2009/04/but-im-vor-lois-mcmaster-bujolds-komarr (accessed October 10, 2014).

———. "Choose Again, and Change: Lois McMaster Bujold's Vorkosigan Saga." Available at http://www.tor.com/blogs/2009/04/choose-again-and-change-lois-mcmaster-bujolds -vorkosigan-saga (accessed October 10, 2014).

———. "Every Day Is a Gift: Lois McMaster Bujold's *Winterfair Gifts*." Available at http:// www.tor.com/blogs/2009/04/every-day-is-a-gift-lois-mcmaster-bujolds-winterfair-gifts (accessed October 10, 2014).

———. "Forward Momentum: Lois McMaster Bujold's *The Warrior's Apprentice*." Available at http://www.tor.com/blogs/2009/04/forward-momentum-lois-mcmaster- bujolds-the-warriors-apprentice (accessed October 10, 2014).

———. "Hard on His Superiors: Lois McMaster Bujold's *The Vor Game*." Available at http://www.tor.com/blogs/2009/04/hard-on-his-superiors-lois-mcmaster-bujolds-the -vor-game (accessed October 10, 2014).

———. "'He Isn't Like Anything, He's the Original': Some Thoughts on Lois McMaster Bujold's Aral Vorkosigan." Available at http://www.tor.com/blogs/2010/11/he-isnt -like-anything-hes-the-original-some-thoughts-on-lois-mcmaster-bujolds-aral-vorkosiga (accessed October 10, 2014).

———. "'Hyperactive Git': Lois McMaster Bujold's Miles Vorkosigan." Available at http://www.tor.com/blogs/2010/11/qhyperactive-gitq-lois-mcmaster-bujolds-miles -vorkosigan (accessed October 10, 2014).

———. "Innocent Bystander: Some Thoughts on Lois McMaster Bujold's Ivan Vorpatril." Available at http://www.tor.com/blogs/2010/12/innocent-bystander-some-thoughts -on-lois-mcmaster-bujolds-ivan-vorpatril (accessed October 10, 2014).

———. "The Ivan Book: Lois McMaster Bujold's *Captain Vorpatril's Alliance*." Available at http://www.tor.com/blogs/2012/12/book-review-captain-vorpatrils-alliance-lois -mcmaster-bujold (accessed October 10, 2014).

———. "Just My Job: Lois McMaster Bujold's *Diplomatic Immunity*." Available at http://
www.tor.com/blogs/2009/04/just-my-job-lois-mcmaster-bujolds-diplomatic-immunity
(accessed October 10, 2014).

———. "Luck Is Something You Make for Yourself: Lois McMaster Bujold's *Cetaganda*."
Available at http://www.tor.com/blogs/2009/04/luck-is-something-you-make-for
-yourself-lois-mcmaster-bujolds-cetaganda (accessed October 10, 2014).

———. "The Most Expensive Plumbers in the Galaxy: Lois McMaster Bujold's *Falling
Free*." Available at http://www.tor.com/blogs/2009/08/the-most-expensive-plumbers
-in-the-galaxy-lois-mcmaster-bujolds-falling-free (accessed October 10, 2014).

———. "One Birth, One Death, and All the Acts of Pain and Will Between: Lois McMaster
Bujold's *Barrayar*." Available at http://www.tor.com/blogs/2009/04/one-birth
-one-death-and-all-the-acts-of-pain-and-will-between-lois-mcmaster-bujolds-barrayar
(accessed October 10, 2014).

———. "Quest for Ovaries: Lois McMaster Bujold's *Ethan of Athos*." Available at http://
www.tor.com/blogs/2009/04/quest-for-ovaries-lois-mcmaster-bujolds-ethan-of-athos
(accessed October 10, 2014).

———. "She's Getting Away! Lois McMaster Bujold's *A Civil Campaign*." Available at
http://www.tor.com/blogs/2009/04/shes-getting-away-lois-mcmaster-bujolds-a-civil
-campaign (accessed October 10, 2014).

———. "A Soldier Like My Mother. Lois McMaster Bujold's Vorkosigan Saga." Available
at http://www.tor.com/blogs/2012/01/a-soldier-like-my-mother-lois-mcmaster-bujolds
-vorkosigan-saga (accessed October 10, 2014).

———. "Something Else Like . . . Lois McMaster Bujold's Vorkosigan Saga." Available at
http://www.tor.com/blogs/2012/11/something-else-like-lois-mcmaster-bujolds
-vorkosigan-saga (accessed October 10, 2014).

———. "This Is My Old Identity, Actually: Lois McMaster Bujold's *Memory*." Available at
http://www.tor.com/blogs/2009/04/this-is-my-old-identity-actually-lois-mcmaster
-bujolds-memory (accessed October 10, 2014).

———. "Those Two Imposters: How Aral and Miles Vorkosigan Deal with Triumph and
Disaster." Available at http://www.tor.com/blogs/2012/12/those-two-imposters-how
-aral-and-miles-vorkosigan-deal-with-triumph-and-disaster (accessed October 10, 2014).

———. "Tussling with Tolkien: Lois McMaster Bujold's *The Sharing Knife: Horizon*."
Available at http://www.tor.com/blogs/2009/02/lois-bujolds-the-sharing-knife-horizon
(accessed October 10, 2014).

———. "Weeping for Her Enemies: Lois McMaster Bujold's *Shards of Honor*." Available at
http://www.tor.com/blogs/2009/03/weeping-for-her-enemies-lois-mcmaster-bujolds
-shards-of-honor (accessed October 10, 2014).

———. "Western Fantasy: Lois McMaster Bujold's Sharing Knife Books." Available at
http://www.tor.com/blogs/2009/01/western-fantasy-lois-mcmaster-bujolds-sharing-
knife (accessed October 10, 2014).

———. "What Have You Done with Your Baby Brother? Lois McMaster Bujold's *Brothers in
Arms*." Available at http://www.tor.com/blogs/2009/04/what-have-you-done-with
-your-baby-brotherq-lois-mcmaster-bujolds-brothers-in-arms (accessed October 10, 2014).

———. *What Makes This Book So Great*. New York: Tor, 2014.

———. "Why He Must Not Fail: Lois McMaster Bujold's *The Borders of Infinity*." Available

at http://www.tor.com/blogs/2009/04/why-he-must-not-fail-lois-mcmaster-bujolds-the
-borders-of-infinity (accessed October 10, 2014).

Westfahl, Gary. "Space Opera." In E. James and F. Mendlesohn, eds., *The Cambridge Companion to Science Fiction* (Cambridge: Cambridge University Press, 2003), 197–208.

Wight, Linda. "Broken Brothers in Arms: Acting the Man in *The Warrior's Apprentice*." In Croft, *Lois McMaster Bujold*, 116–33.

Wollheim, Donald A. *The Universe Makers: Science Fiction Today*. Gollancz: London, 1972.

SELECTED INTERVIEWS WITH LOIS McMASTER BUJOLD

Charles Brown, "Lois McMaster Bujold: Coming Full Circle," *Locus* 343 (August 1989): 4, 69–70.

Ken Lake, "Interview with Lois McMaster Bujold," *Vector* (February/March 1993): 7–11.

Charles Brown, "Lois McMaster Bujold: No Fault Series," *Locus* 415 (August 1995): 4–5, 70–71.

Elizabeth Counihan, "The Worst Possible Thing," *Interzone* 101 (November 1995): 20–23.

Michael M. Levy. "An Interview with Lois McMaster Bujold," *Kaleidoscope* 34 (1997): 6–19.

Charles Brown. "Lois McMaster Bujold: On the Cusp," *Locus* 481 (February 2001): 4, 84–85.

Mike Hodel, *Mike Hodel's Hour 25*, July 17, 2001, MP3 files available at http://www.hour25 online.com/Hour25_Previous_Shows_2001-7.html#lois-mcmaster-bujold_2001-07-17 (accessed October 10, 2014).

Sara, *Writerspace.com*, July 31, 2001, available at http://www.writerspace.com/chat/ chat073101.html (accessed October 10, 2014).

Susan Profit, *Washington Talking Book and Braille Library's Evergreen Radio Reading Service Science Fiction Hour*, August 4, 2001, available at http://www.dendarii.com/wtbbl.html (accessed October 10, 2014).

Corrina Allen, *Explorations* (Barnes and Noble F&SF newsletter), August/September 2001, available at http://www.dendarii.com/explorations.html (accessed October 10, 2014).

Tina Morgan, *Fiction Factor*, August 11, 2001, available at http://www.fictionfactor.com/ interviews/loisbujold.html (accessed October 10, 2014).

Lali Rico, *Portada*, translated from Spanish and available at http://www.cyberdark.net/ portada.php?edi=3&cod=2 (accessed October 10, 2014).

Mike Houlahan, New Zealand Press Association, April 1, 2003, available at http://www .dendarii.com/int-nz.html (accessed October 10, 2014).

Mike Hodel, on *Mike Hodel's Hour 25*, May 17, 2004, MP3 files at http://www.hour25online .com/Hour25_Previous_Shows_2004-05.html#lois-mcmaster-bujold_2004-05-17 (accessed October 10, 2014).

Adrienne Martini, *Bookslut*, May 2005, available at http://www.bookslut.com/ features/2005_05_005637.php (accessed October 10, 2014).

Charles Brown. "Lois McMaster Bujold: It's All in the Footnotes," *Locus* 534 (July 2005): 5–7.

John Joseph Adams, *Sci Fi Wire Interview*, June 2006, available at http://www.dendarii.com/ int-sfw.html (accessed October 10, 2014).

Carlos Aranaga, *SciFiDimensions*, October 2006, available at http://www.scifidimensions .com/Oct06/loismcmasterbujold.htm (accessed October 10, 2014).

Karen Miller, *LiveJournal* (blog), August 5, 2007, http://karenmiller.livejournal.com/52391 .html (accessed October 10, 2014).

Jim Minz, for Baen, August 2007, available at http://www.baen.com/Interviews/ intBujold.htm (accessed October 10, 2014).

Jenny Boa, for Bujold's Chinese publishers, May 2008, available at http://www.dendarii .com/int-china.html (accessed October 10, 2014).

Michael Lohr, *Internet Review of Science Fiction*, June 2008, http://www.dendarii.com/ int-mlohr.html (accessed October 10, 2014).

Lillian Stewart Carl, "A Conversation with Lois McMaster Bujold," in Carl and Helfers, *The Vorkosigan Companion*, 29–62.

Simeon Tsanev, *ShadowDance* (Bulgarian online magazine), February 2009, available at http://www.dendarii.com/int-bulgarian.html (accessed October 10, 2014).

Dmitry, *Mir Fantastiki* (Russian magazine), February 2009, http://www.dendarii.com/ int-russian.html (accessed October 10, 2014).

Jo Walton, "Interview with Lois McMaster Bujold about Writing the Vorkosigan Saga," available at http://www.tor.com/blogs/2009/04/interview-with-lois-mcmaster-bujold -about-writing-the-vorkosigan-saga (accessed October 10, 2014).

Shadowdance interview (translated from Bulgarian), March 2010, available at http:// heretherebeshadows.blogspot.co.uk/2010/03/interview-with-lois-mcmaster-bujold.html (accessed October 10, 2014).

Online Writing Workshop Newsletter, May 2010, http://sff.onlinewritingworkshop.com/ newsletter/2010_05.shtml#interview (accessed October 10, 2014).

Liza Groen Trombi. "Lois McMaster Bujold: Topias," *Locus* 612 (January 2012): 6–7, 54.

Beta Colony, 27, 92, 131; attitudes toward Barrayarans, 79–80; attitudes toward women on, 137; Beta Colony compared to Barrayar, 141; culture on, 75–81; deference on, 77; egalitarianism on, 75–76, 77; founding of, 26; science on, 77; sexual customs, 78–79; uterine replicators on, 147; as utopia, 80; women's position on, 80, 141

Betriz di Ferrej, 56, 58, 71, 137

bioengineering, 25, 31, 34, 86. *See also* genetic manipulation

Boni, Tersa, 165–66

Bonin, Kate, 71

Borders of Infinity, 33–34

"Borders of Infinity, The," 31, 32, 33, 88

Bothari, Elena, 71, 109, 132, 137, 138; on Beta Colony, 78, 80; birth of, 30, 37, 132; career choices of, 80, 141–42; criticism of honor, 162; on father's death, 134; fear of genetic determinism, 94–95, 132; fear of insanity, 132; on Ivan, 113, 114; and Miles, 83, 100, 101, 134, 138; on Miles, 97. *See also* Visconti, Elena

Bothari, Sergeant Konstantin, 11, 112, 125, 127, 140; and Cordelia, 36, 163, 164; death of, 18, 29–30, 94, 103; and Elena Bothari, 37, 139; ethics of, 164; and Ivan, 112; kills Vordarian, 78, 133; kills Vorrutyer, 28, 147, 164; looked after by Vorkosigans, 135; and Miles, 134, 168; on Miles's leadership, 167; psychological problems of, 122, 132–33; rapes Elena Visconti, 133; tortures jump pilot, 135, 162; on women soldiers, 141

Brin, David, 20

Brontë, Charlotte, 42, 43

Brothers in Arms, 32–33, 40, 88, 167

Bujold, Anne, 7

Bujold, John, 7, 13

Bujold, Lois McMaster: on abortion, 140; and awards, 12; birth of, 1; on book covers, 14; on characterization, 121; on characters, 18, 95, 107; on children, 139; as convention guest of honor, 13; on Cordelia, 163; on death, 91; on disability, 120–21, 138, 124; on environment, 85; and family, 124; and fanfic, 150; and fans, 14–15; fantasy novels compared to sf, 71, 72; and fantasy novels, 50; her female characters, 71; and feminism, 136–37, 144; and focalization, 101; on haut women, 147; on healthcare, 92; on hermaphrodites, 155; and homosexuality, 154–55; and Hugo Awards, 14, 20, 35, 37; humor in, 17, 44, 58, 73; and leadership, 157; on Miles, 29, 100, 138; on narrative mode, 104; on quaddies, 121–22; on reader feedback, 121; and readership, 11, 14; on sacrifice, 162; satire in, 73, 85–86; and sex scenes, 14; on Sharing Knife sequence, 157; and space opera, 23–24; on trans people, 153; and Vorkosigan books, 26; and war, 156; on writing, 20, 24, 27; on writing about sex, 14, 15, 154–55; on writing the Vorkosigan books, 22

Bujold, Paul, 7

butter bugs, 43–44

Byerly. *See* Vorrutyer, Byerly

Campbell, John W., 2, 68

capitalism, 34, 85, 87

Captain Vorpatril's Alliance, 14, 22, 48–49, 96, 112; Byerly in, 150; focalization in, 106; Ivan in, 115–18

Card, Orson Scott, 50, 67, 166

Carl, Lillian Stewart, 3, 9, 31; childhood friend of Lois, 4, 5, 6; in writing group, 7–8

Cattilara, 53, 59–60

Cazaril, Lord Lupe de, 56–58, 62, 70; his disability, 121; as leader, 167; as peacemaker, 157; self-sacrifice in, 162

Cecil, Major, 97

Cee, Janine, 130

Mississippi River, 66
Mitchell, Betsy, 8
Moon, Elizabeth, 43
Mother, the, 54, 55
motherhood, 138. *See also* parenting
"Mountains of Mourning, The," 10, 18;
  awards, 12; in *Borders of Infinity*, 33–34;
  Miles in, 39, 124, 127–28, 141, 162
MPD. *See* DID
Murasaki Shikibu, 90
mutants, prejudice against, 33, 95, 123, 127,
  131
mutations, 67, 95, 124
mystery plot, 24, 45 62

Naismith, Admiral Miles. *See* Vorkosigan,
  Miles
Naismith, Cordelia, 27, 41, 119, 122; and
  abortion, 140; and Admiral Vorrutyer,
  148, 160; and Aral, 27, 47, 78, 116, 148,
  160–61; and Aral's honor, 158, 163; in
  artwork, 11; on assumptions, 82; and
  Barrayar, 74, 76, 79–80, 103; in *Barrayar*,
  36–37; and Barrayaran custom, 79–80;
  as a Betan, 128, 137; bodyguard, 142; and
  Bothari, 132–34, 164; and Butcher of
  Komarr, 158; as Captain, 159; careers of,
  80, 141–42; comparing Mark and Miles,
  108; and Dubauer, 125–26, 135; and feminism, 137; as feminist heroine, 141; as
  focalizer, 104, 107; and hermaphrodites,
  131; and homosexuality, 148; and Ista,
  60; and Ivan, 113, 115–16; and killing of
  Vordarian, 18, 36–37; and languages, 81;
  as leader, 167; and Mark, 38, 108; and
  Miles, 34, 96, 97, 101, 143; origin of character, 8; and other female characters, 71;
  and Piotr, 76; principles of, 163–64; and
  rape, 28; and reform, 83, 84; and sanity,
  96; and torture, 164; and uterine replicators, 139–40, 144, 147; victory over Bar-

rayar, 168; and violence, 36–37; and Vor
  aristocracy, 96; and war, 156, 162, 166,
  167; and weapons, 166
Narayan, R. K., 101
nature vs. nurture, 9, 95, 108, 119
Nebula Award, 11–12, 32, 33
Negri, Captain, 160, 161
Nicholls, Peter, 65
Nicol, 11, 34, 45–46, 129
Nijenhuis, Ellert, 111
Nikki. *See* Vorsoisson, Nikki
Niven, Larry, 68
Norton, Andre, 50

Ochs, Thur and Uri, 51–52
Ohio River, 66
Ohio State University, 2, 4, 6, 7, 122
Oklahoma, 66
Orico, Roya, 56–58; illness of, 179

pairs of protagonists, 96
Paladin of Souls, 4, 53, 56, 58–60, 153; awards,
  12; and religion, 54
Palma, Shannon, 110
parenting, 28, 33, 36–37, 135; in *Cordelia's
  Honor*, 139
Parker, K. J., 52, 55
Passage, 64
peacemakers, characters as, 23, 157
penis symbolism, 44
Piercy, Marge, 137
Piper, H. Beam, 21
planned evolution, 145
poverty, 46–47, 76, 92
Pratchett, Sir Terry, 15, 54
prejudice, 33, 34, 69. *See also* mutants, prejudice against
prisoners of war, 126, 158, 164–65
psionic powers, 67
punishment, 79
Pym, Armsman, 127–28, 149

quaddies, 11, 34, 107; as disabled, 121–22, 123–24; in *Diplomatic Immunity*, 18, 45–46; in *Falling Free*, 31–32, 74

Quinn, Elli, 30–31, 71, 87, 93, 130, 137; and Barrayarans, 79–80; on Cetaganda, 88; and childrearing, 145; as a freak, 113–14, 131–32; Ethan proposes to, 18; Ivan on, 113–14; on Miles, 100, 103; Miles proposes to, 39, 75, 109

racial classification, 118

Raina. *See* Czurik, Raina

rape, 28, 132, 140, 151, 153; and Elena Bothari, 29–30, 95, 133; Mark and rape, 109; Vorrutyer and rape, 132, 147, 164

recovery of battle dead, 166

Regency romances, 42

religion, 31, 54

Renaissance Italy as setting for fantasy, 52–53

Reynolds, Alastair, 20

Reynolds, Mack, 3

Rhine, J. B., 68

Rich, Adrienne, 153–54

Rish Arqua, 48, 150

Riva, Dr., 42, 167

Roddenberry, Gene, 73

Roessner, Michaela, 52

Roic, Armsman, 44–45, 46, 96; as focalizer, 106

romances, 65

Rowling, J.K., 15

Russ, Joanna, 137

Russell, Eric Frank, 3, 21

Russian culture on Barrayar, 5, 13, 26, 75, 81–82

Ryoval, House, 36, 86, 110, 131

sacrifice in Barrayaran culture, 162–63

Sargent, Pamela, 137

Sato, Jin, 46, 93; as focalizer, 106; and Mina, 139

Sayers, Dorothy, 42, 43

Scalzi, John, 14

Schmidt, Stanley, 10

Schmitz, James H., 3, 21, 30

Schroeder, Karl, 20

self-sacrifice, 161, 162

Serg, Prince (Serg Vorbarra), 132, 139, 141, 142, 159–60; death of, 159, 160, 161, 163; madness of, 149

Sergyar, 26, 93, 157, 168; Aral and Cordelia on, 48, 80

SF writers writing fantasy, 50

SFWA, 12

SFX, 120

Shakespeare, William, 4, 43, 51

Shards of Honor, 8, 9, 17, 47, 96; Aral in, 157, 163; and *Barrayar*, 36; Cordelia in, 74, 77, 80, 93, 163; Cetagandans in, 87; earnings from, 10; honor in, 163; Illyan in, 111; review of, 14; as *Star Trek* novel, 7; war in, 156, 167; writing of, 27–28, 29–30, 37. *See also* "Aftermaths"

Sharing Knife books, 46; as science fiction, 67; sex-scenes in, 14; and Tolkien, 71–72. *See also* Wide Green World

sharing knives, 162

Shiras, Wilmar H., 67

Simmons, Dan, 20

slash fiction, 15

slavery, 56–57, 86, 136, 144; in Chalion, 57, 153; quaddies as, 31, 32

Smith, Cordwainer, 3, 21

Smith, E. E. "Doc," 156

Smith, Sherwood, 60

Snyder, Midori, 52

Solian, Lieutenant, 44

Son, the, 54, 55, 62

"Sorcerer's Apprentice, The," 30, 99

space opera, 19–21, 34, 137, 139, 165; Bujold and, 16–17, 22, 23–24, 28, 42; New Space Opera, 20, 23; traditional space opera, 3, 11, 91, 123, 156

EDWARD JAMES is Emeritus Professor of Medieval History at University College Dublin. He co-edited the Hugo Award-winning *Cambridge Companion to Science Fiction* and is the author of *Science Fiction in the Twentieth Century*.

MODERN MASTERS OF SCIENCE FICTION

THE UNIVERSITY OF ILLINOIS PRESS

is a founding member of the

Association of American University Presses.

Designed by Kelly Gray

Composed in 10.75/14.5 Dante

with Univers display

by Lisa Connery

at the University of Illinois Press

Manufactured by Cushing-Malloy, Inc.

University of Illinois Press

1325 South Oak Street

Champaign, IL 61820-6903

www.press.uillinois.edu